D1106190

LIFE'S COLOR CODE

McGraw-Hill Series in Population Biology

Consulting Editors
Paul R. Ehrlich, Stanford University
Richard W. Holm, Stanford University

LIFE'S COLOR CODE

William J. Hamilton III

Professor of Ethology
Division of Environmental Studies
University of California
at Davis

McGraw-Hill Book Company

New York   St. Louis   San Francisco   Düsseldorf   Johannesburg
Kuala Lumpur   London   Mexico   Montreal   New Delhi   Panama
Rio de Janeiro   Singapore   Sydney   Toronto

Library of Congress Cataloging in Publication Data

Hamilton, William John, 1931–
    Life's color code.

    (Population biology)
        1.   Color of animals.   2.   Color of man.
3.   Animals, Habits and behavior of.   4.   Animal
populations.   I.   Title.
QL767.H34   591.5   78-38582
ISBN 0-07-025740-X
ISBN 0-07-025741-8 (pbk.)

LIFE'S COLOR CODE

1234567890KPKP798765432

This book was set in Helvetica by Black Dot, Inc., and
printed and bound by Kingsport Press, Inc. The designer
was John Horton; the drawings were done by Danmark & Michaels,
Inc. The editors were James R. Young, Jr., and Phyllis T. Dulan.
Matt Martino supervised production.

TO MY PARENTS

CONTENTS

PREFACE

In the century following the discovery of the principle of natural selection there has been a continuing development of concepts and evidence dealing with the significance of the coloration of animals. Much of the evidence that led Charles Darwin and Albert Russell Wallace to their monumental discovery was based upon consideration of the colors of birds, butterflies, and other animals. As the field of biological evolution has flourished, the evaluation of the significance of the colors of man has not kept pace. Most of the evidence that deals with the coloration of men has been supplied by physiologists, whose special concern is the defense of the functional systems of man against disease and environmentally induced trauma. It should come as no surprise, therefore, that the standing explanations of the adaptiveness of human skin coloration suggest that pigmentation and the lack of it are related to defenses of the body against the environment.

The approach to the evaluation of the coloration of man offered here is broadly comparative, with man considered in the context of the spectrum of living animal species. For this reason there is much emphasis on the adaptive significance of animal coloration. This evidence is fundamental to the conclusions reached here concerning man and his coloration.

Comparative biologists are now in a strong position to make comparative studies. A massive body of information is available, more than any one individual can possibly assimilate. In documenting the theory of natural selection, Darwin sometimes found it necessary to consult laymen and correspondents for even the most rudimentary information. Today there are extensive investigations of many animal and human populations, data that have taken tens of thousands of man-years of painstaking investigation to secure. Some animal species have been the subject of detailed biological studies, and the habits of thousands of species of animals occurring throughout the world have been subjected to at least cursory examination. Physiological studies of diverse functional systems in many species are available, and species comparisons are being extended to the physiological level. With expansion of our knowledge, the potential horizons of comparative biologists also expand. Most terrestrial environments have been examined, and we know some life history details of most large living animals. Yet comparative biology remains in its infancy. Natural animal populations are only beginning to be studied by biologists, and no animal species has been studied where it lives with the tools, physical and intellectual, that are now available. But perhaps most important of all, there is a real scarcity of trained individuals willing to undertake long-term comparative studies of wild animals or to work with teams that are dedicated to such long-term studies.

In the meantime, new facts continue to be discovered at an increasing rate. Consider tool use by vertebrates, for example. In 1963 the second nonhuman mammal and the first ape, the chimpanzee, was found to be using tools to obtain food in nature. In 1967 the number of birds known to use tools to obtain food was extended from one, the Galapagos finch, to two, when the Van Lawicks discovered a vulture using stones to break ostrich eggs. In 1968 another tool-using bird was discovered, this time a nuthatch living in North America. Also in 1968 came the report that a South American primate, the cebus monkey, uses peeled twigs to secure bark insects. It seems probable that additional examples of tool use by animals will be discovered at an increasing rate as studies of animal behavior in nature multiply. Today, comparisons attempting broad phyletic comparisons are inevitably restricted by the inadequacy of available information. This is one more reason to regret the diminishing faunal diversity of our planet. Some of the most interesting species have vanished, and others will disappear before we have had a chance to do much more than give them a name. The characteristics of earth's animals have in part been shaped by interaction and association with other animal species. Loss or decline in numbers of the larger predators that play a particularly important role is especially regrettable.

Jim Wittenberger and George V. N. Powell have been constant critics of and contributors to this book, and I owe them an immeasurable debt. The subject matter of the book has been the content of courses at the University of California at Davis. Discussion with the students in these courses has always been refreshing, and I am indebted to them for original ideas and for assistance in the refinement of concepts.

Other colleagues who have been particularly stimulating and helpful include William Buskirk, William Gilbert, Frank Heppner, William Adams, and Jon Planck. Patricia Warner played a major role in the resolution of bibliographic problems, as did Cathy Wallace in the editing of the manuscript. It is a particular pleasure to acknowledge the stimulation and continual inspiration of my colleague, Kenneth E. F. Watt.

In comparative studies one must draw freely upon data from the studies of others, and any credits would be incomplete without acknowledging my indebtedness to the authors cited in the bibliography and in turn to the authors cited by them.

William J. Hamilton III

LIFE'S COLOR CODE

PART 1   MAXITHERMY

The purpose of this book is to present the results of my own personal investigation into man's place in nature from the perspective of the colors of the animals of the world and what I and other biologists think they mean.

Every animal must be some color. The color of a particular animal therefore provides only relative information about the value of that animal's coloration to it. Thus the coloration of each species represents the evolutionary force most significant to that animal's survival. There are three main functions of animal colors and patterns: (1) They may optimize heat-exchange and radiation relationships. (2) They may camouflage an animal, thereby minimizing communications with predators. (3) They may be positive adaptations to communication. Radiation colors, which generally are black or white, may optimize radiative heat exchange, particularly relative to sunlight or, according to an alternative interpretation, may protect the animal from excessive radiation. The function of camouflage is obvious. Visual communication may involve social intimidation, species recognition, courtship, synchronization of group activities, or parental behavior. Visual communication may also involve warning colors adapted so as to warn predators that the owner is somehow able to defend itself. A fourth, less important category is coloration which is incidental, superficially revealing underlying physical or physiological characteristics.

This book is not a review of animal coloration concepts or discussions per se. It deals with the information that animal coloration provides concerning the relative significance of certain biological relationships to various animal species. These relationships vary, depending upon the species, its environment, its sensory systems and those of its predators and prey, its social organization, and its evolutionary history. The relative importance of these variables determines which coloration category each animal species has adopted.

The more detailed the color patterning of each animal, the more evidence it provides. At the same time more complex interpretations may be necessary, and conclusions concerning the significance of the color and pattern may be less convincing. There are, in fact, so many hypotheses available that some researchers have been inclined to lump all explanations into the category of arbitrary decisions and to conclude that meaningful choices between alternatives are impossible. The opposite attitude is reflected in this book. Given sufficient comparative information, many hypotheses can be as effectively tested as by the most rigorous laboratory experiments. Evolution has been an enormous experiment, the replicates have been numerous, and the number of completely different experiments —the individual species—is enormous. What is necessary is for the biologist to determine what the experiment has been, what conditions have prevailed, what the controls were, and the relevance of these results to other findings. The colors of animals are one product of these experiments, and they are often a special lever in the analysis of environmental relationships.

The significance of the analysis of coloration in understanding animal habits has been underestimated. Many animal colors, even of animals as conspicuous as elephants and crows, have received little or no attention. This seems remarkable considering the overwhelming respectability of the evolution theory and the general recognition that evolution has shaped even the minutest details of animal structure. Color is, after all, an additional structure of life, and one which almost inevitably interacts with the environment. It is thus surprising to find many instances where the standing explanation of animal surface coloration is that it is neutral—a mere genetic by-product, or a deposit of waste materials. A major contention of this book is that coloration characteristics usually are explainable on the basis of interactions with the physical and biological environment.

More hypotheses are presented here than problems solved. Questions cannot be answered until they are posed, and in my opinion some of the most significant questions concerning the origin and evolution of life and its function are not presently a focus of research.

EVOLUTION OF HOMEOTHERMY

Homeothermy—the continuous maintenance of a relatively constant body temperature well above ambient temperature levels—provides one key to an understanding of the strategies of energy transfer by animal life. Since the rate of energy utilization by an animal increases with its body temperature, and since homeotherms are operating near the maximum possible body temperatures, it follows that homeothermic animals are not adapted to minimizing energy expenditure. For homeotherms, and for a wide variety of ecologically important animals, the advantages of high body temperatures must be so great that they more than balance the disadvantages of the inefficiency of excessive energy expenditure.

The hypothesis presented here is that homeothermy is a by-product of the advantages to be gained by maintaining *maximum* body temperatures. It is further concluded that for many animals the *ecologically adaptive* limit for body temperatures has not been evolutionarily achieved. These animals are prevented from attaining this potentially adaptive state by some physiological barrier to further thermal adaptation, a barrier common to all multicellular animals. Homeothermy has resulted from the elevation of body temperatures to this unpenetrated barrier, and thermal constancy has been an incidental by-product.

Hypotheses concerned with the evolution of homeothermy must deal with two distinct phenomena: (1) body temperature constancy and (2) the actual level of the thermostatic setting. Some hypotheses and discussions of the process fail to make the distinction. Any hypothesis considering only one part of the problem encounters serious logical difficulties, as a review of existing hypotheses demonstrates.

According to the maximum-tolerable-level hypothesis suggested above, the actual level of the thermostatic setting of most homeotherms is imposed by the failure of all multicellular animals to adapt in such a manner as to persistently withstand body temperature levels much above 37 to 40°C. Constancy is an incidental result of raising the body temperature to this maximum level and maintaining it there as long as possible.

LETHAL LIMITS AND HOMEOTHERMY: LETHAL MAXIMA

Lethal temperatures, extremes beyond which animals no longer are able to sustain life, are a species-specific characteristic. These temperatures are determined by three conditions:

1 The environmental temperatures which poikilothermic animals generally encounter in their natural environment. Thus in aquatic environments lethal tolerances are closely correlated with normal ambient conditions. For many poikilotherms, particularly aquatic animals, upper lethal temperatures are not much higher than normally encountered environmental temperatures. Thus the upper lethal temperature of certain Antarctic fishes (*Trematomas bernacchii, T. hansoni, T. borchgrevinki*) is 6°C. Normally these fish live in −1.9°C waters (Somero and DeVries, 1967). Other poikilotherms are adapted to intermediate temperature ranges which adjust them to their natural thermal environment. The temperature tolerance of Australian mayfly larvae inhabiting slow, warm streams is higher than that of inhabitants of swift, cool streams (Harker, 1950). The North American Sierra toad *Bufo cognatus* survives laboratory temperatures 2 or 3°C higher than *B. hemiophrys*, which lives in the same mountains at higher altitudes and in colder waters (Schmid, 1965). It is not difficult to understand the basis of these differences. Thus adaptation to upper thermal extremes is correlated with and depends upon

encounters with higher ambient temperatures, with genetic in-
corporation of responsiveness to conditions encountered by
preceding generations.

2   The ambient conditions recently encountered by each individual.
All animals normally encountering variable ambient conditions
are able to physiologically adapt to them to some degree. Often
the extent of this physiological adaptation is extensive (Figure
1–1). A part of this physiological adaptation includes a shift in
the upper limit of thermal tolerance.

3   The absolute temperature level of conditions 1 and 2. When
conditions 1 and 2 reach critical levels so that body temperatures
reach the 37 to 40°C level, the influence of condition 2 is reduced.
The evidence supporting this conclusion is presented later in
this chapter.

Because many of the lethal temperatures reported in this chapter
are based upon experiments with recently captured wild animals,
the acclimatization temperatures to which the test subjects have

Figure 1–1.   Upper and lower lethal temperatures
of the golden shiner, *Notemigonus crysoleucas,*
acclimated to various temperatures. (After Hart,
1952.)

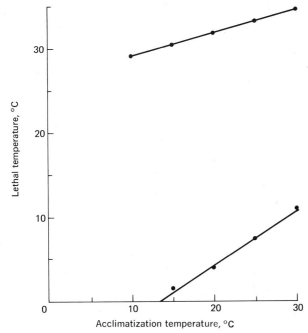

been subjected have seldom been identified. Casual measurement of environmental temperatures is insufficient. A precise knowledge of the temperature at the occupied niche is necessary, and in the case of poikilotherms and even some homeotherms, actual body temperatures are necessary. The assumption that body temperatures decline to ambient levels may be justified in the case of many small animals, but until methods for determining actual body temperatures become available, the actual thermal tolerances of small terrestrial animals are approximations. Body-temperature data seldom are available, except in the case of small aquatic animals whose body temperatures seldom rise much above water temperatures.

GENETIC DEATH VERSUS PHYSIOLOGICAL DEATH

Precise definition of lethal thermal maxima is difficult. The criteria for establishing heat death are often arbitrary and may vary according to the interests and expectations of the experimenter. To be most useful, heat-tolerance determinations should include delayed mortality, reduced longevity, and infertility effects (Cowles, 1965). Simple survival of a particular thermal condition is not necessarily meaningful. Consider, for example, experiments with the larvae of the fruit fly, *Anastrepha ludens* (Darby and Kapp, 1933). When these grubs are heated they can withstand brief exposure to temperatures above 46°C, but they lose the ability to complete their development (Figure 1–2). Pupation success drops sharply following exposure to temperatures above 40°C. This experiment provides no clue to the actual cause of physiological heat death, but it does establish that, for the larval form of this species, selection is inoperative above 42°C. Heat tolerance of the larvae above this level is evolutionarily meaningless.

In spite of the difficulties in defining lethal limits, some conclusions can be drawn from a critical evaluation of existing temperature tolerance data. One conclusion is that many animals often or normally live just below the upper lethal limit. Even more interesting is the fact that in several phyla and classes within these phyla, including animals representing hundreds of millions of years of independent evolution, the upper extreme for the most heat-tolerant member of the group is near 47°C. The uniformity of this upper limit for lethal maxima cannot be explained in terms of correlation with normally encountered ambient thermal conditions. An adaptive barrier is implied, a barrier to life which tens of billions of years of independent evolution have not succeeded in penetrating.

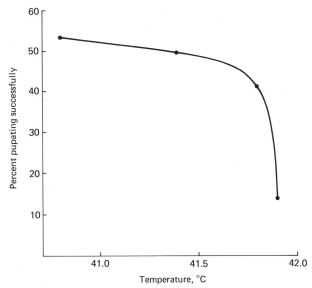

Figure 1-2. Pupation success of larval fruit flies, *Anastrepha ludens,* following exposure to high temperatures during larval development. (After Darby and Kapp, 1933.)

Temperature Preferences

Preferred temperatures provide a different measure of the thermal tolerance of animals. Numerous measurements of thermal preferences have been made in thermal gradients. A comparison of these measurements for a diversity of poikilotherms shows that the most heat-tolerant representatives of several diverse animal groups lie in the range from near 37 to not much above 40°C. The behavior of lizards provides a fine example of the voluntary limits of thermal tolerance. In thermal gradients offering a cafeteria of potential thermal conditions and possible body temperatures, the most heat-tolerant species of a number of families opt for body temperatures in the range from 37 to 42°C (Table 1-1). Under these conditions body temperatures above 40°C are a rarity.

Maximum Voluntarily Tolerated Body Temperature

Many animals are occasionally or regularly observed to develop body temperatures above the level that they would normally choose in a laboratory gradient (Tables 1-2 and 1-3). This may be true in spite of the fact that cooler temperatures are available to them if they burrow into the sand (Chapter 5) or retreat to crevices, shade, etc. A spectrum of these behavioral thermoregulation mechanisms is

Table 1–1. Preferred body temperatures of the most heat-seeking lizard species when they are held in thermal gradients.

Species	Temperature, °C	Latitude	Environment	Source
Iguanidae (*Dipsosaurus dorsalis*)	41.0	35°	Desert (United States)	Cowles and Bogert, 1944
Iguanidae (*Sauromalus obesus*)	42.0	35°	Desert rock outcrops (United States)	Cowles and Bogert, 1944
Agamidae (*Amphibolurus caudicinctus*)	40.3	25°	Desert (Australia)	Licht et al., 1966
Agamidae (*Amphibolurus scutatus*)	40.7	25°	Desert (Australia)	Licht et al., 1966
Gekkonidae (*Gehyra variegata*)	40.3	30°	Dry forests (Australia)	Licht et al., 1966

reviewed in Chapter 4. Here I wish only to note that there is often a significant difference between maximum preferred body temperatures and those voluntarily tolerated in nature (DeWitt, 1967).

These measurements show that the maximum voluntarily tolerated body temperatures are often remarkably close to lethal levels. For example, the fiddler crab, *Uca annulipes*, has been observed in nature with a measured body temperature of 42.0°C, whereas at this temperature mortality can result in laboratory experiments following 15 minutes of submersion under water (Edney, 1961). These comparisons show that many animals crowd lethal limits in spite of the availability of more moderate temperatures.

Maximum Observed Natural Body Temperature
Some animals have no opportunity to retreat from environmental extremes. A camel on the desert has no place to hide from the noon-day sun, and there are a few large native desert mammals such as the oryx that may live in environments providing little or no opportunity for extensive behavioral thermoregulation. These animals may show behavioral signs of heat stress, but they regularly tolerate body temperatures higher than the levels of animals which can retreat when they want to.

Lethal Limits
The compilation of upper lethal limits (Table 1–4) for the most heat-tolerant representative of a diversity of animal groups shows less agreement than the other measures of thermal tolerance. This may in part be due to the diverse criteria for heat death that have been employed. It may also reflect the relatively meaningless nature of this value even when it is precisely determined. What is needed for an evolutionarily meaningful comparison is the level at which fecundity is impaired, and this measurement is not available for many animals. Nevertheless, even these crude data show a remarkable sameness at the upper limits of multicellular life (Figure 1–3).

Adaptive Limit Hypothesis
The uniformity of the maximum preferred body temperature for the most temperature-tolerant representatives of several animal groups throughout a wide spectrum of life suggests an explanation of this relationship. Many species, homeotherms and poikilotherms, are killed by temperatures near 50°C (Table 1–4), but there are none that extend much higher. In nature few animals voluntarily tolerate body temperatures much above 42°C (Tables 1–2 and 1–3), but many animals survive at least temporary exposure to temperatures at or

Table 1–2.   Maximum body temperatures observed under natural conditions for a spectrum of animal species and groups. Some are experimental measurements of animals in thermal gradients. Others are temperatures of animals in nature, some of which were surely under heat stress. These records are the extreme values reported for the groups they represent. The figure for man is rectal temperature following long-distance running or fever temperatures.

Species	Color	Temperature, °C	Latitude	Environment	Source
Homeotherms					
Mammals					
Camel	Brown	40.7		Desert	Schmidt-Nielsen, 1964
Steinbok	Cryptic	40.3	0°	Semiarid bush (east Africa)	Author's observation
Man		41.1	Pandemic	Diverse	DuBois, 1949; Buskirk and Bass, 1960; Robinson, 1963; Pugh et al., 1967
Birds					
Towhee (*Pipilo aberti*)	Cryptic	42.0	35°	Desert (Arizona)	Dawson, 1954
Dove (*Zenaidura macroura*)	Cryptic	42.5	35°	Desert (Arizona)	Bartholomew and Dawson, 1954
Dove (*Streptopelia senegalensis*)	Cryptic	44.0	25°	Desert (south-west Africa)	Brain and Prozesky, 1962
Dove (*Oena capensis*)	Cryptic	43.8	25°	Desert (south-west Africa)	Brain and Prozesky, 1962
Hawk (*Falco sparverius*)	Cryptic	40.5	40°	Savannah and forest edge (North America)	Bartholomew and Cade, 1957
Guinea Fowl	Black and white	41.8	0°	Arid (East Africa)	Author's observation
Vulture (*Cathartes aura*)	Black	41.0	0–40°	Temperate and tropical, diverse	Enger, 1957

Poikilotherms

Fish					
Carp (*Cyprinus caupio*)	Background	40.0		Warm temperate water	Hart, 1952
Desert pupfish (*Cyprinodon macularius*)	Background	40.0	35°	Desert (Arizona)	Miller, 1949
Brown bullhead (*Ictalurus nebulosus*)	Brown-black	39.0	35°	Warm fresh water	Hart, 1952
Amphibians					
Frog (*Pseudacris triseriata*)	Background	40.0	37°	Fresh water swamps (United States)	Clarke, 1958
Frog (*Acris crepitans*)	Background	40.0	37°	Fresh water swamps (United States)	Clarke, 1958
Arthropoda					
Crustacean (*Uca*)	Variable	43.3		Mud flats (South Africa)	Edney, 1961
Grasshopper (*Chortoicetes terminifera*)	Background	42.0		Arid grassland (Australia)	Clark, 1947
Beetle (*Onymacris rugatipennis*)	Black	43.8	20°	Desert (Namib, southwest Africa)	Author's observation
Mollusca					
Snail (*Tegula rugosa*)	Background	41.0	30°	Intertidal (Mexico)	Author's observation

Table 1–3.   Maximum voluntarily tolerated body temperatures of lizards captured in the field.   The first seven examples were selected because they are the most heat-seeking lizards known in terms of *voluntarily* tolerated body temperatures.

Species	Maximum voluntary temperature, °C	Lethal temperature, °C	Locality	Latitude	Source
Iguanidae (*Iguana iguana*)	44.0	46.5	Tropical lowland (Mexico)	21°	McGinnis and Brown, 1966
Gerrhosauridae (*Gerrhosaurus flavigularis*)	41.0		Arid grassland (South Africa)	25°	Stebbins, 1961
Lacertidae (*Scaptira suborbitalis*)	41.5	46.0	Desert (Kalahari, South Africa)	25°	Stebbins, 1961
Lacertidae (*Eremias lineo-ocellata*)	41.5	45.6	Desert (Kalahari, South Africa)	25°	Stebbins, 1961
Iguanidae (*Dipsosaurus dorsalis*)	46.4 41.0		Desert (United States)	39°	Norris, 1953; Dewitt, 1963
Iguanidae (*Uma notata*)	40.5		Desert (United States)	35°	Licht et al., 1966
Agamidae (*Amphibolurus inermis*)	43.0		Desert (Australia)	25°	Licht et al., 1966
(*Aporosaura anchietae*)		45.1	Desert (Namibia)	24°	Brain, 1962
gekkonidae (*meroles cuneirostris*)	39.1	45.4	Desert (Namibia)	24°	Brain, 1962
gekkonidae (*ptenopus garrulus*)	20.0	44.2	Desert (Namibia)	24°	Brain, 1962
gekkonidae (*rhoptropus afer*)	36.5	43.9	Desert (Namibia)	24°	Brain, 1962

Table 1-4. Upper lethal body temperatures of a spectrum of life forms. Death points were determined by various procedures and the values reported here are thus not strictly comparable. A comparison of these temperatures with those of Tables 1–2 and 1–3, however, emphasizes how closely voluntarily tolerated temperatures approximate lethal levels. The latitude is for the species as a whole, not necessarily for the population from which these experimental animals were obtained.

Group	Species	Temperature, °C	Latitude	Environment	Source
		Homeotherms			
Mammals	"Rabbit"	44.8		Domestic	Marsh, 1954
	Man	45.0		Diverse	DuBois, 1949
					Edwards, 1824
Birds	Chicken (*Gallus domesticus*)	44.4	20°	Domestic	Robinson and Lee, 1946
		Poikilotherms			
Fish	Killifish (*Fundulus heteroclitus*)	42.0	30°	Estuaries	Huntsman and Sparks, 1924
	Gambusia affinis	41.5	40°	Stagnant fresh water (California)	Original data
Mollusca					
Snail	*Littorina*	52.5	30°	High intertidal (Mexico)	Original data
Snail	*Littorina knysnaensis*	48.6	30°	Coast, upper intertidal (South Africa)	Broekhuysen, 1940
Snail	*L. neritoides*	46.3		Coast, upper intertidal	Evans, 1948;
		46.5			Fraenkel, 1961
Snail	*Tegula funebralis*	41.0	30°	Coast, upper intertidal (California)	Original data
Bivalve	*Venus mercenaria*	54.2		Coast, sublittoral	Henderson, 1929

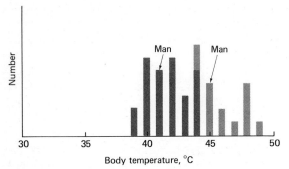

Figure 1-3. Distribution of upper lethal (lighter) and highest voluntarily tolerated (darker) body temperatures of the most heat tolerant multicellular animal species. The data include the three most heat-tolerant species of molluscs, insects, fish, amphibians, reptiles, birds, and mammals, including man. These data are derived from Tables 1-1, 1-2, and 1-3.

above this level. This suggests that some impenetrable barrier has been reached. There must be unstable materials or processes which fail at about the same level, regardless of the phyletic affinities. Identification of the biological basis of this barrier is not simple. Numerous investigators have considered the question of the biological basis of heat death. Two general categories of conclusions have been drawn. One is that heat death is based upon the failure of several systems. This interpretation is based on the observation that several physiological processes fail at approximately the same level. The alternative conclusion is that one system is responsible for the failure, and since an organism depends upon the continual function of all systems, the failure of the other systems is inevitable. For animals living at the upper limits of life, I favor the latter conclusion. This conclusion is based upon the widespread agreement in level of maximum thermal tolerance. It is implausible that several processes and materials should fail at the same level, given the millenia that have passed and the advantages that could accrue to any organism able to penetrate the barrier.

Animals which crowd life's thermal limits I have termed "maxitherms." The term is meant to include the multicellular animals, homeothermic and poikilothermic, which have maximum preferred body temperatures above 36°C. Since the concept of maxithermy has not previously been available, previous workers have not distinguished between maxitherms and other less heat-tolerant organisms.   However, numerous investigators have considered the phenomena of heat death in organisms that are defined here as maxitherms.   Failure of each of a number of specific biological systems has been implicated as the cause of heat death.   A review of the extensive evidence leaves us with no obvious candidate for the critical system.   We are faced with a logical and heretofore unrecognized problem: that when any part of a biological system fails due to heat stress, selection will no longer be operative and selection for greater thermal tolerance at higher levels of all systems will be inoperative. Thus, the failure of any one system is likely to result in the failure of all of them.   For this reason an investigator considering his own particular speciality, whether the circulatory system, lipids, specific enzymes, or something else, is likely to discover that *his* system fails at the thermal limits of life.   This in no way establishes that failure of this system is the evolutionary basis of the failure of that animal species to adapt to still higher temperatures.   Resolution of this logical difficulty in the interpretation of data dealing with the upper thermal limits of maxitherms will tax the ingenuity of future investigators.   Many investigators have concluded that they have identified *the* barrier to upper thermal adaptation.   It is possible that a tightly reasoned logical argument, based upon a comparison with unicellular and dehydrated multicellular organisms which do tolerate higher thermal levels, and a broad comparative analysis may be extended much further than the kind of quantitative evidence that has so far been supplied.   Identification of the basis of this barrier will be of no further concern to us here.   Subsequent conclusions depend only upon the validity of the premises that there is a limit, and that this limit is shared by a diversity of multicellular organisms.

This analysis is directly applicable to man. Mean human deep body temperatures fluctuate about 37°C. During uncontrolled fever, i.e., without the intervention of antibiotics and other fever-blunting medicines, deep body (rectal) temperatures rise to about 40°C. There are several significant features of these feverish individuals: (1) the distribution of rectal temperatures shows a maximum between 40 and 41°C (Figure 1–4), (2) few individuals develop temperatures above 41°C, and (3) the probability of eventual recovery from the illness declines sharply if the fever rises much above 41°C (106°F). Nevertheless, some individuals have survived temperatures as high as 45°C (113°F) (DuBois, 1949). The maximum at 40.5°C (Figure 1–4) seems to implicate a regulatory capacity, adaptively placed to prevent heat death,

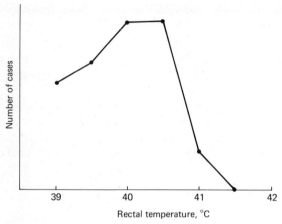

Rectal temperature, °C

Figure 1-4. Distribution of rectal temperatures of 275 patients suffering from lobar pneu-
monia, relapsing fever, and malaria in a New
York City hospital prior to 1932. (Compiled
from DuBois, 1949.)

near 41°C. This is precisely the level at which most organisms, from
beetles to lizards, are no longer willing voluntarily to tolerate higher
levels (Tables 1-2, 1-3).

A Hypothesis: Homeothermy Is a By-product
The maximum temperatures some animals can attain is limited by
their ability to produce and absorb heat. Others, particularly species
living in exposed environments such as deserts or at low latitudes
could, during at least part of the day, attain temperatures well above
those which they actually develop. Since the advantages of a high
body temperature include increased metabolic and growth rates
(Chapter 2), both of which have time-dependent factors, habits resulting in a maximum time spent at the highest possible body temperatures would be expected, at least in some species. Such situations, where a higher body temperature can be maintained than that
which is attained, are readily identified. They are the situations in
which energy must be expended or behavioral adjustments made so
as to lower body temperatures (Chapter 4) or to keep them from rising
futher. The maximum body temperature attainable in these cases is
not limited by an ability to produce or absorb heat.
    Selection for maximum body temperatures and the presence of an
impenetrable barrier to further heat tolerance could result in homeothermy. The evolution of thermal constancy (i.e., homeothermy) is
thus likely when there are adaptations to make it an economical

process. The evolution of insulation was probably such an adaptation. Considerable evidence supports this conclusion:

1 Wherever maxithermy has evolved, whether essentially complete, as in the case of homeothermic birds and mammals, or incomplete, as in the case of insects and reptiles, the constant temperature is just below the lethal temperatures of the group (compare Tables 1–1 to 1–4). No alternative hypothesis can account for the remarkably uniform limit, which does not follow phyletic lineages, body characteristics, or environmental relationships. These data are fully compatible with the conclusion that there is some uniform impenetrable barrier preventing adaptation to higher body temperatures.

2 Observation of active poikilotherms in nature establishes that high temperatures which might be achieved are avoided when the thermal limits are approached. That no multicellular poikilotherm has adapted to higher thermal levels, regardless of the environment in which it lives, is further evidence of the existence of this barrier.

3 In most environments homeothermy would demand considerably less energy if the thermostat had been set at a lower level. That is, most homeotherms spend more energy keeping warm than staying cool, and total thermoregulatory energy would be lessened if a lower thermostatic setting were maintained.

If the first consideration in the adaptive process in homeotherms is directed primarily toward economy and efficiency in energy expenditure, the process must be most concerned with the competitive advantage of increased reproductive and growth rates. If this is true, a fundamental premise of the concept of homeothermy becomes vulnerable. Energy is being used to maintain a *maximum* body temperature rather than a *constant* body temperature. Furthermore, energy expenditure to reduce body temperature is not an adaptation to secure constancy but to avoid inevitable heat damage and death.

The consequences of an unpenetrated upper limit for the evolution of life are extensive. For homeotherms it establishes a constant against which other adaptable variables such as insulation thickness, circulatory adaptations, and body size must be adjusted. The consequences are equally extensive in the case of poikilotherms. For them this relationship has dictated when and where life and environment are compatible. Thus it has been particularly significant to animals living in deserts and other highly exposed environments. A more subtle consequence of this limit is that, in many animal groups and many environments, it is also the operating level of the most successful animal species and groups.[1]   A majority of the macroscopic animal energy on this planet is transferred at this level.

Environmental Efficiency Hypothesis

An alternative explanation of the uniform level of homeothermic constancy is that homeothermy and the maxithermic constant evolved in some region where and at some time when this level was the most economically defended level. According to this hypothesis subsequent evolution of homeotherms has involved adjustment of insulation rather than the thermostat. A tropic origin of homeothermy is suggested. Only in a relatively warm climate would the relatively high temperatures of modern homeotherms be the most economical levels to maintain.

Subsequently, perhaps due to the evolution of an efficient biochemical system at this temperature, speciation and penetration of different environments carried this set level as an immutable legacy. To compensate for the inappropriateness of this level in new environments, other adaptations such as changes in insulation, circulatory systems, and behavior accounted for the time adjustment of the organism to the new climate. If, for example, homeothermy evolved in the tropics, then a descendent penetrating a more temperate region would develop heavier insulation, larger body size, behavior patterns which conserve or generate heat, etc. This hypothesis can also account for the fact that the homeothermic thermostat is set at the same level as the maximum voluntarily tolerated level for poikilotherms, regardless of environment.

The reasons I prefer the maxithermy hypothesis to this legacy hypothesis are:

1   The upper lethal level is not limited to one phyletic group but includes a group of basically different animal phyla. If adaptation to higher levels had been advantageous and possible, the physiological systems of these groups would have done so. Yet they have gone through billions of years of independent evolution without differentiating to any significant degree in this regard.
2   The same limit is shared by poikilotherms. Their thermal adaptation cannot be buffered by insulation. Hence, once they were separated from the hypothetical benign ancestral environment,

---

[1]Preliminary measurements suggest that this generalization can also be applied to multicellular plant life. The leaves of vascular plants are among the most extraordinary thermoregulatory products of evolution. Given the limitation of relatively sedentary location, a flat surface capable of extensive evaporative cooling allows for great flexibility in thermoregulation. Comparisons of leaf temperatures with the temperatures in Tables 1–1 to 1–4 suggest that the thermal limits of multicellular animal life described here may be equally applicable to plant life.

there would be no compensatory adaptation to prevent adjustment of the chemical factory to new levels.

HOMOGENIZING SELECTION—A CONSTRAINT UPON THERMAL ADAPTATION

The tolerable body temperatures of poikilotherms often span a considerable range, but this range has limitations and seldom exceeds thirty degrees. The upper and lower lethal limits are generally much closer together, and sometimes they are separated by only a few degrees. These animals of limited tolerance generally are found only in species living in relatively homogeneous environments—seas, tropical forests, burrows, and caves. For most species the upper temperature tolerance is closely correlated with the lower temperature level; the higher the upper lethal limit, the higher the lower lethal limit. Since animals with high upper lethal levels generally are species living in the warmest environments, this rule may be related to the environmental temperatures normally encountered by each species. But this is probably not the whole story. Many animals are restricted to certain environments by their temperature tolerances. Most primates, for example, have been unsuccessful in ranging far from the tropics, and few primate species thrive where ambient temperatures consistently drop below 10°C. The world was unpopulated by primates until human populations reached them. Failure to penetrate these regions may be explained by limits imposed by genetic interchange with populations adapted to warmer environments. To adapt to cooler climates, it is necessary to reduce genetic interchange with neighboring populations in less rigorous environments, permitting special adaptation to local conditions, as in the theoretical situations described in Figure 1–5(c) and 1–5(d). Therefore one would anticipate primate populations in northerly climates only where gene flow has been reduced owing to effective geographic barriers, as on the islands of Japan where primates that are well adapted to cold do indeed exist.

These observations illustrate a more general rule that has seldom been applied to the explanation of natural biological phenomena. This is that the adaptation of each species must serve all members of the population and adjacent populations with which there is genetic exchange. A population can adapt to the environmental mosaic by (1) increasing its variability, (2) adjusting to a limited part of the environmental mosaic, or (3) compromising and adapting to the average condition within its occupied environment. This homogenizing action of selection may result in adaptive compromises which

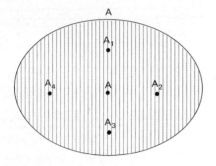

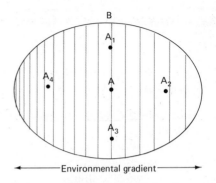

No gradient, no limitation on gene flow.
Entire population adapts to condition
at any point in occupied space,
A, A^1, no isolating mechanism.
Morphology and behavior: $A = A^1 = A^2 = A^3 = A^4$
Fitness and abundance: $A = A^1 = A^2 = A^3 = A^4$

Environmental gradient, no limitation of
gene flow. Population adapts as
in case 1, no isolating mechanism.
Morphology and behavior: $A = A^1 = A^2 = A^3 = A^4$
Fitness and abundance: $A = A^1 = A^2 = A^3 = A^4$

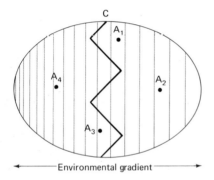

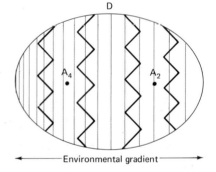

Gradient, isolating mechanism, no
limitation on gene flow.
Morphology and behavior: $A^3 = A^4 \neq A^1 = A^2$
Fitness and abundance: $A^2 = A^4 > A^1 = A^3$

Same as C but additional isolating
barriers.
Fitness and abundance: A^2 and A^4,
this figure $> A^2$, A^4, Figure C.

Figure 1–5. Homogenizing selection: The degree of adaptation at each locality depends upon the occurrence and steepness of environmental gradients, the presence or absence of barriers to gene flow (jagged lines), and the position of these barriers. Environmental gradients are indicated by shading.

cause localized populations to be less than optimally adapted to their environment. What results is an adaptation fitting each population to the conditions encountered by an average member of the population. The nature of this adaptation will depend upon the action of selection throughout the range of each species. The number of individuals, their location, and the rate of gene flow between different segments of the population are thus critical to the evaluation of animal adaptation. When such a compromise is the basis of adaptation, there may be definite limits placed upon the fitness of peripheral populations, especially when they freely interbreed with large central populations [Figure 1–5(b)]. When a species has free genetic exchange with several populations over broad geographic ranges, some peripheral populations may be genetically better adapted to a region other than the one in which they live. Because they are still genetically in touch with this region, their capacity to adapt to local conditions may be severely limited.

In Chapter 5, additional examples of homogenizing selection are considered with respect to desert background-matching coloration, and the principle is probably broadly applicable to the evolution of camouflage. With respect to thermal adaptations, homogenizing selection may explain why certain marine organisms have failed to expand their temperature tolerance to any considerable degree. Reef-building corals are limited to the tropical waters of the ocean and cannot survive temperatures below 20°C. If each species is evolving independently and is always pressed by population densities to expand home ranges, why have none of these species adapted to colder waters? One possibility is that lower temperature tolerance limits are in fact determined by upper tolerance limits. If adaptation to a high temperature tolerance precludes adaptation to extremely low temperatures, species adapted to high temperature tolerances might be geographically trapped in warm regions. Corals, for example, with their enormous populations in tropical seas and their adaptations to withstanding high water temperatures, may be unable to penetrate northern waters because of the sizeable gene pools in warm seas, precluding adaptation to lower temperatures. Ocean waters provide fewer geographic barriers to gene flow than do most terrestrial environments, limiting the opportunity for the extension of adaptations.

LETHAL MARGIN

The margin between lethal temperatures and voluntarily tolerated temperatures may be even narrower than Tables 1–1 to 1–4 suggest. The upper body temperature normally tolerated may be exceeded, especially during violent exercise. There are few studies of the temperature rise of animals during exercise. The body temperature of man may rise above 41°C during persistent strenuous exercise, only a degree or two from heat death. Other animals may also press the narrow edge of heat death during violent exercise. But there is so little information on the normal range of extremes for natural animal populations that it is impossible to say how often animals in nature approximate their lethal limits during normal behavior. With the development of radio telemetry techniques which permit long-term monitoring of body temperatures, at least in large animals, study of extreme normal body temperatures under natural conditions promises to become a fascinating investigation.

ALTERNATIVE HOMEOTHERMY HYPOTHESES

There are several alternative hypothetical interpretations of the evolution of homeothermy:

Optimum CNS Function Hypothesis

> The maintenance of a constant body temperature has advantages for those animals whose survival depends to a considerable extent on the function of a central nervous system, especially a cerebrum. The rate of nervous processes depends on the temperature. Our reaction to environmental influences, promising or threatening, is attuned to a certain velocity of nervous processes. Without a constant body temperature, we probably could not develop in our mind a coherent picture of the world in which we function (Kleiber, 1961, p. 146).

When I first considered this explanation of homeothermy, it seemed to me that it failed to distinguish between the consequences of evolution—in this case a prolonged period of evolution at a body temperature near 37°C—and its causes. It is the matter of causation —of the evolutionary bases of homeothermy—that is the central concern of this chapter. The physiological-failure hypothesis, stated by Kleiber in the above quotation, deals with consequences. While it is certainly true that the central nervous system (CNS) of man and most homeotherms is, at best, inefficient when chilled much below 37°C, failure of nervous function at these lower levels is not a general characteristic of life. Low and changeable ambient and body temperatures are compatible with all life processes, including rapid reaction times and effective and efficient CNS function. Octopuses, living in cold waters and active at temperatures little above ambient ocean temperatures, are able to learn rapidly (Boycott, 1954) and to move quickly. Their compound eyes, independently derived but quite similar to vertebrate eyes in general appearance, are capable of complex visual discrimination (Young, 1961). Antarctic fishes swim rapidly and otherwise perform the normal functions of fishes at −2.5°C (Somero and DeVries, 1967). There is thus no reason to conclude that low temperatures are incompatible with effective CNS function. However, Kleiber's statement is concerned with changeable body temperatures, and change may indeed place limits on the effective function of the system. Most physiological processes are temperature dependent, with the remarkable exception of biological "clocks."

However, my own recent observations of insect behavior in the field have convinced me that thermal vagility does play a significant role in reducing the effectiveness of responses to the environment. The locomotion rate of the black African desert beetle, *Onymacris rugatipennis*, is closely correlated with its body temperature. This beetle is highly responsive to prospective predators and man. In the middle of the day, with body temperatures near 40°C, it responds quickly to the approach of a predator and runs off faster than a man can walk. But in the morning, when its body temperature is nearer 20°C and it moves much more slowly, it is much less responsive to potential predators. Often I could be within a meter or two of these beetles before they took alarm. This is exactly wrong for the most highly adaptive response, which would couple a rapid response and broad perceptive field with the limited locomotion capacity at low temperatures. So thermal variability does seem to place some limits on optimum function of animal response systems, as Kleiber suggests.

Nevertheless the optimum CNS function hypothesis cannot provide an adequate explanation of the actual setting of homeothermic levels. In the process of the evolution of homeothermy, thermal adaptability, including that of the CNS, has been reduced. Like other temperature tolerance phenomena, lack of selection pressures from the environment may result in low thermal adaptability. The physiological temperature tolerance of animals is correlated with the range of environmental temperatures normally encountered (page 6). This in turn results in functional failures when natural or, as is more commonly observed, experimental conditions exceed species-specific temperature tolerances.

Heat-stress Hypothesis

"In a hot environment a hot body temperature is advantageous because it diminishes the heat load and thus the use of water in heat dissipation" (Schmidt-Nielsen, 1964, p. 206).

This statement, in various forms, can be found in any one of a number of recent publications. This conclusion is based on the correlation between physiological heat stress and behavioral responses to it. The higher the body temperature, the higher the temperature at which heat stress appears. Thus we are reminded of the problems animals have keeping cool. In response to these problems, animals have evolved a variety of devices, physiological and behavioral. These include phenomena such as sweating, increased respiration, panting, bathing, postural changes, and sheltering (Chapter 4). Observation of such activities and the experimental occurrence of heat-induced mortality has often led to the conclusion that a basic and primary function of homeothermy is to maintain viable body temperatures in the face of extreme heat. A *regulatory* ability, it is argued, is valuable in the maintenance of a sublethal temperature, since heat stress must be avoided.

The heat-regulation argument is weakened by examination of its premises. That the emergence of heat-dissipating behavioral and physiological responses to heat establishes an unfavorable thermal relationship of animals to their environment is a questionable assumption. If these actions occur regularly they demonstrate the significance of heat stress on life, but the relative significance of heat stress in comparison with cold stress has generally not been measured. Heat stress is related to the extent to which heat can be tolerated and excessive heat dissipated. The low body temperatures of poikilotherms may actually place them in a favorable position to tolerate heat, because the body mass can be used as a heat sink, postponing activation of physiological and behavioral thermoregulatory mechanisms. When cooling is necessary, poikilotherms have available to them most of the same kinds of cooling mechanisms used by homeotherms. In addition the body can be used as a potential heat sink.

In order to maintain thermal constancy (or homeothermy), some insulation and the higher metabolic heat production of homeotherms result in thermal equilibrium (i.e., "thermoneutrality") at temperatures no higher than 35°C and usually considerably lower. Tucker (1966) provides an example of the comparative performance of a poikilotherm and a homeotherm. If one places a maxithermic lizard and a mouse (*Mus*) in a 37°C box, the lizard will survive indefinitely, but the mouse will perish.

In general support of this argument, Norris (1953) supports the argument that the evolution of homeothermy is an adaptation to the penetration of extremely warm environments by maintaining body temperature at sublethal levels. He points out that no poikilotherm has succeeded by physiological means in penetrating environments where daily temperatures exceed 50°C. But the same seems also to be true of homeotherms. Indeed, it seems possible that poikilotherms are at a considerable advantage in the warmest environments since they need not utilize energy to maintain high body temperatures during much of the day. Arid-region homeotherms have taken advantage of this circumstance by allowing body temperatures to fall somewhat overnight, and partial poikilothermy characterizes many tropical and desert homeotherms (Chapter 5). The relatively greater role of lizards and other poikilotherms in the hot ecosystems suggests that poikilothermy has been a particularly advantageous adaptation there. The metabolic rate of poikilotherms is lower than that of homeotherms of comparable size and with the same body temperatures by a factor of three to eight (Benedict, 1932). Thus poikilotherms may have a positive competitive advantage over homeotherms where reliable environmental heat sources are available to develop comparable body temperatures.

Metabolic Efficiency Hypothesis

It has been suggested (Burton and Edholm, 1954) that optimum metabolic efficiency can be achieved at about 37°C. If true, this observation might suggest a hypothesis that could easily explain both the level and the fact of homeothermy. There appear, however, to be no data upon which to base such a conclusion other than the very fact of homeothermy. The explanation seems to be ad hoc and circular, although this does not necessarily mean it is also invalid. That certain homeotherm enzyme systems are most effective today at this level is irrelevant to a discussion of the evolution of that temperature. Any biological system tends to become increasingly efficient within the limits of other selective pressures and limitations. If evolution is taking place at 37°C, the enzyme systems will adapt to that level. But this hypothesis provides no clue to why this level was adopted in the first place, and the interpretation seems to mistake an effect for a cause.

Climatic Change Hypothesis

Another hypothesis is that homeothermy was a response to unfavorable climatic changes during the Mesozoic era (Cowles, 1946). According to this hypothesis, poikilothermic ancestors of homeotherms responded to geological cooling trends by adapting to climates not previously tolerable. If the Mesozoic climate changes took place slowly enough to permit changes in this basic characteristic of life, this suggestion might be plausible. But an alternative explanation seems more likely. As cooling took place, geographic displacement of existing populations to regions where existing tolerances had already adapted the established fauna to its environment was probable. Therefore, climatic changes need not necessarily have involved changes in the temperature tolerance of the species. During any period of climatic change a range of thermal environments will be available. As the change takes place, each species may shift to adjacent environments, carrying with it the physiological adaptations it already had at the time it was challenged by the climatic change. The potential for such adjustments exists today, for example, in the latitudinal and altitudinal climatic gradients of the earth. These same gradients, although less extreme, also occurred in Mesozoic times.

In some cases the temperature tolerance and other adaptations of a species include a potentially broad response to environmental conditions. In other cases the thermal responsiveness may be narrower and the adaptiveness of the organism more limited. One would not expect in any geologic age or under any set of environmental circumstances to find a much different situation. Each species will be adapted to limited ranges of ambient temperatures and exposure. The advantage to be gained by penetrating colder climates is always present as long as these environments are contiguous with more temperate regions. The advantages that Cowles (1946) proposes for homeothermy, therefore, are present today and would have been present regardless of the earth's overall climatic condition. Past climatic changes probably had little effect upon the balance of selective pressures influencing the general characteristics of life on this planet, and of homeothermy in particular. Modern environments undergo climatic changes that are relatively rapid. But this process creates no spatial hiatus. Gaps provided by the elimination or, more often, the shift in the distribution of one species, are occupied by other species already well adapted to the newly habitable space.

Coincidence of the development of homeothermy with past climatic changes is likely to be brought about by the advantage of homeothermy which is derivable under any circumstance, given the development of a reasonably effective insulative layer.

CONCLUSIONS

1 The upper lethal body temperatures of the most heat-tolerant multicellular animals, both poikilotherms and homeotherms, are about the same, between 47 and 50°C.
2 The maximum preferred body temperature of these same animals is also about the same, 37 to 40°C.
3 This combination of circumstances can be explained by assuming that these most heat-tolerant animals are attempting to maintain the highest possible body temperature and are limited by some barrier to further thermal tolerance common to all these groups.
4 Crowding of this barrier to thermal tolerance has resulted incidentally in the development of homeothermy among birds and mammals.

HEAT AND BLACKNESS

Men have always been fascinated by black and white animals. Such animals as whales, ravens, black leopards, and white foxes dominate folklore and are set apart from the rest of the animal world in the minds of men. Superstitions about them have a firm and fundamental biological basis, the exploration of which is the subject of much of the rest of this book. One of the special features of black and white animals is that they have special defenses enabling them to minimize the probability that they will be preyed upon. These defenses often include protection against disturbance by man. Black and white nonpolar animals often are neither predator nor prey. Yet in in terms of mass and numbers they dominate some of the animal faunas of our planet.

The remainder of Part 1 is concerned with some of the selective forces which have favored these colors. There are three major bases for animal coloration: enhancement of communication, minimization of communication, and the role of black and white coloration in heat-exchange and radiation protection. The third basis is emphasized here. The term "energy colors" refers to black and white animal coloration adapted to optimizing the radiation relationship of animals to their environment. It cannot be concluded that these pigments serve in all cases for either heat exchange or radiation protection, but their basic function in many cases is to optimize biological relationships with environmental radiation. When this can be demonstrated, the term "energy colors" is employed.

ADVANTAGES OF HEAT TO ANIMALS

Raising body temperatures above ambient levels (1) increases metabolic rates and (2) increases maintenance costs. Many dominant animals have evolved adaptations which result in the development of body temperatures well above ambient levels (Chapters 4 and 5). Life is energy-limited, and development of tissue temperature levels higher than necessary costs energy. To offset the cost of elevated body temperatures there must be a combination of advantages that more than compensate for the disadvantage. The problem can be resolved by separating the adaptive significance of metabolism from the mechanism of its maintenance. If energy conservation alone were the determining factor, elevated temperatures would indeed be disadvantageous, and animals would evolve adaptations allowing them to live at or below ambient temperature levels whenever possible, i.e., to be maximally efficient. The less energy an animal uses, the less it needs, and the less it will be affected by competition and food scarcity. Thus efficiency is evolutionarily advantageous to animals. In addition to increasing energy requirements, elevated body temperatures increase growth and reproduction rates. They also increase the potential rate of food storage, measured either in terms of fat deposition or in terms of additional tissue grown, both potentially advantageous processes. Thus, balanced against the cost of increased energy demands, elevated body temperatures may secure several potential advantages. In many cases the results of evolution establish that advantages have prevailed, and that efficiency has been a secondary consideration to energy throughput, the maximization of the rate of energy processing. Thus, increases in energy expenditure will be accepted as long as increases in yield result, *regardless of the absolute cost per unit of productivity.*

There are ways to sacrifice efficiency for throughput other than by manipulating body temperature. Examination of the cases where throughput prevails, some examples of which will be considered in greater detail in subsequent chapters, suggests that there is a tendency to emphasize throughput in new and successful adaptive strategies, while efficiency has greater significance to evolutionary hasbeens.

The cultural adaptations of man range to both ends of the efficiency-throughput spectrum. At one end of the spectrum there are individuals living at bare subsistence levels—processing considerably less than 2,000 calories a day—while practicing all the tactics of efficiency. At the other extreme there are individuals whose total energy consumption numbers in the tens of thousands of calories per day—calories which have been commandeered from agriculture, from domination of other human beings, and from fossil fuels. The hypothesis presented above concerning evolutionary success of

Figure 2-1. Throughput versus efficiency. Productivity (in this case, growth and capacity) may increase with increased energy expenditure (curves *A* and *B*). It may also decline as the rate of energy expenditure is increased (curve *D*). The arrows indicate the optimum strategy for each curve, which is to maintain maximum useful productivity at the minimum energy expenditure rate. Curve *C* suggests the situation in which maintenance is possible, the animal is an adult, and no useful productivity above the maintenance level results until the reproductive threshold is reached. There will be continual selection for efficiency as long as it is compatible with maximum useful productivity. This will result in a tendency to push the maxima for all these curves to the left as, for example, curve *A* to *A'*.

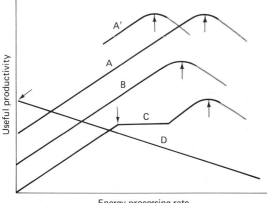

Energy-processing rate

animal populations suggests that throughput is likely to be the tactic of evolutionary success. Yet we are all familiar with the multiple problems that throughput economies produce. This is the current problem of mankind—how to achieve the seemingly antievolutionary goals of efficiency in a system that seems to reward only throughput.

Increased Metabolic Rates

Metabolic rates of homeotherms and poikilotherms increase with tissue temperature within the temperature tolerance limits of each species. This metabolic rate is, within limits, correlated with the growth rate of poikilotherms. The relationship is much the same for the growth phases of most poikilotherms. For some animals, such as the migratory locust (Figure 2-2), developmental rates increase until lethal limits are approached. For other species the development curve may drop sharply, well below the lethal maximum.

Why are high developmental rates advantageous? This question has several answers. Every individual of each population is, to a greater or lesser extent, in competition with every other individual in that population. This is not necessarily competition for resources such as food, but competition for evolutionary success. Relative growth rate is a trait often involved in this kind of evolutionary competition. High growth rates are advantageous when they lead to higher reproductive rates or earlier reproduction. In a reproductive contest, time is a valuable resource. To be advantageous, increased reproduction must lead to the production of offspring which themselves produce living offspring. Selection will favor increased reproductive rates as long as the advantage is not dissipated by, for example, increased mortality or reduced reproductive efficiency. The limit may be set by a reduced ability to care for each offspring, reduced probability that the parent will live to continue reproductive episodes, and many other causes. Nevertheless, given equal assets, the individual developing most rapidly will be represented most frequently in subsequent generations.

There is another advantage to rapid development beyond enhanced reproductive rates. Predation rates are related to the size of predator and prey. As an animal becomes larger, fewer predators are, on the average, hunting it, and predatory strikes become less frequent. Thus, the life expectancy of most animals increases with size during development, and it becomes advantageous to increase body size as rapidly as possible. High body temperatures sometimes make this possible by increasing growth rates.

Reproductive rates of many poikilotherms also increase with temperature. Some insects reach their maximum reproductive rate at temperatures as high as 42°C. Given temperature-dependent fecun-

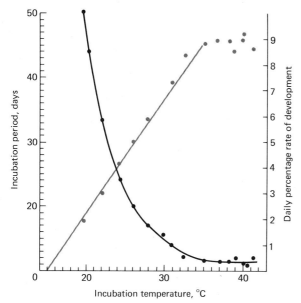

Figure 2-2. Rate of development of eggs of the migratory locust at increasing temperatures. (After Hunter-Jones, 1968.)

dity, that part of the population which can most closely approximate the temperature at which maximum reproduction rates are possible will probably come to dominate a population.

If some individuals of an animal population have genetically determined characteristics enabling them to reproduce more rapidly than other less fecund members of the population, other factors being equal, the numbers of the more prolific kind will increase relative to the less fecund. Over a number of generations the abundance of most animal species fluctuates over approximately the same range. Thus, if one genetically determined kind of individual within a population is more productive than another kind, and both die at the same rate, the proportion of the more fecund will increase in abundance at the expense of the less fecund and eventually will eliminate it. Such differences in fecundity can be related to body temperatures.

Slight differences in reproductive rate may be amplified by evolutionary time. For example, if two alternative genetic types in a population operate, on the average, at a temperature difference of just 0.10 degrees, and this temperature differential increases the generation time to the extent that other metabolic processes do (i.e., with a Q_{10} of about 2.0), if body types are present in equal numbers in the population, if the total population density remains constant, if the mortality rate of adults and young of both genetic types is the same, and if the reproductive rate is directly proportional to the metabolic rate, then starting with the same initial number of the two genetic types in the population, the type living at the higher body temperature will increase relative to the cooler type by 0.01 percent during the first generation. The rate of change in relative representation of the two types will increase in succeeding generations as compound interest does, and it will take only a relatively small number of generations for the cooler (less fecund) type to be eliminated from the population. Thus adaptations providing thermal economy need not provide great temperature differences to be evolutionarily meaningful.

Are Food Supplies Generally Limiting?
High metabolic rates can be sustained only if there is an adequate supply of fuel. If an elevated body temperature secures for animals the advantages of higher developmental and reproductive rates, the implication is that there is no insurmountable problem in securing enough food to attain and maintain these rates. Yet many ecologists have emphasized the role of food supplies in limiting the abundance and reproductive rates of animals. Furthermore, this emphasis is well substantiated by experimental and observational analyses of natural populations of birds (Lack, 1954, 1968). Since the advantages of high body temperatures include increased reproductive and growth rates, there appears to be a paradox, because limitation of animal abundance by food implies food scarcity, which would be aggravated by increasing the metabolic rates.

There are a number of possible solutions to this paradox. It may be (1) that the role of heat has been misinterpreted, and that it is in fact not advantageous to maintain a high body temperature, or (2) that the role of food in limiting animal populations has been overemphasized. It is also possible (3) that if food is limiting it is not the absolute amount of food which establishes the limit but the rate at which food can be processed by an animal's digestive machinery. Finally, it is possible (4) that food scarcity is seasonal and that in times of food shortage animals retreat from high body temperatures by diapause (Tucker, 1966) or inactivity, emphasizing throughput only when necessary.

There is evidence supporting each of solutions 2 to 4, but it is impractical to review the evidence here. The evidence for the first alternative is that the digestive tracts of many herbivores, both homeotherms and poikilotherms, are constantly crammed with undigested vegetation. For these animals processing rates must be critical. Since digestive rates are temperature-dependent, the raised body temperatures within the digestive tract may accelerate the rate of food processing.

Carnivores process food more rapidly and are less limited by food conversion rates than herbivores. The morphological adaptation of the digestive tract, which is longer in herbivores than in carnivores, is correlated with this basic difference between herbivory and carnivory. Nevertheless, many predaceous animals, especially stalking and sentinel hunters (Chapter 6) that exploit relatively large prey items pause for considerable intervals following feeding while digestion takes place. Some of the largest poikilothermic carnivores spend several days digesting each captured prey item. Thus, to a lesser degree than herbivores, carnivores may also be limited by processing rates.

ENERGY-COLOR HYPOTHESIS

Photosynthesis is not the only biological mechanism for converting solar energy to a form usable for growth and reproduction by life. The heat of solar radiation may be absorbed and directly converted to heat by both poikilotherms and homeotherms. One hypothesis considered here is that black and white animal colorations maximize the development and maintenance of body temperatures above ambient levels. Because the advantage of these colors may be concerned with optimizing the cost of maintaining the optimum body temperature of homeotherms and because it substitutes directly for this energy in poikilotherms, the term "energy colors" is used here to refer to them. Since this is an evolutionarily advantageous characteristic, all diurnal animals should profit from being black (or white —Chapter 3). Obviously, animal coloration secures advantages other than regulation of heat exchange. Nor is the coloration of all black animals necessarily a primary adaption to heat exchange. Certain animals, for various reasons, are not attempting to maintain maximum body temperatures (consider Figure 2-1), and many black animals are rarely exposed to solar radiation.

Black Homeotherms

Birds and mammals maintain relatively constant body temperatures. Since these temperatures are often maintained in the face of drastic ambient temperature fluctuations, environmental heat might seem unimportant to homeotherms except as an overheating hazard. There is some justification for this attitude because the major climatic adjustment of homeotherms is in terms of their insulation (Chapter 4), and insulation thickness is adapted to provide comfort under normal resting conditions. When animals become active, generation of muscular energy and increased metabolic heat may cause over-heating. However, like man, many terrestrial animal species spend the majority of their time inactive or indulging in activities that expend little energy above the minimum level. If the initial assumptions concerning efficiency and throughput are correct, these animals have open to them the options of curves *A* and *B* of Figure 2–1. This implies that additional energy expenditure will push the system past the point of maximum productivity. Relatively inactive animals, such as the leaf-eating monkeys, certain grazing mammals, and herbivorous intertidal snails, are often black, and their special tendency to sun-bathe emphasizes their positive adaptation to environmental heat gain. Some of these species may orient limited black surfaces to the sun, and others are completely black.

The relationship of coloration to homeotherm energy expenditure has been investigated experimentally (Hamilton and Heppner, 1967). If radiant energy is profitable to homeotherms, it must operate by conserving energy, since no animal on this planet is known to have a mechanism for converting thermal energy into work. To test the energy-conservation hypothesis, a white domestic strain of the Australian zebra finch, *Poephila castanotis*, was selected. These white birds could be dyed black and washed white again, and so it was possible to evaluate the significance of visible radiant energy. The effect of the light upon energy expenditure was measured in terms of oxygen consumption. In these experiments it was not practical to use natural sunlight because identical radiant conditions do not persist long enough to complete a critical experiment and its controls. For this reason a small 600-watt quartz lamp was substituted for the sun (Figure 2–3). Measurements of net radiant energy levels near the bird confirmed that energy levels were approximately equal to full sunlight.

The result of these experiments was that, at 10°C, energy utilization averaged 23 percent less by black birds than by white ones (Table 2–1). The role of black coloration in reducing energy expenditure was confirmed. The advantage of solar radiation and therefore of dark coloration will, of course, not be as great at higher ambient temperature levels, and black coloration will be a legacy as temperatures rise to the point where overheating becomes a problem, especially if shelter is unavailable.

These experiments were extended by Ohmart and Lasiewski (1970) working with roadrunners (*Geococcyx californianus*) confined in an

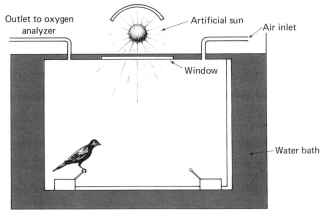

Figure 2-3. Experimental apparatus used to determine the efficiency that a homeotherm is able to effect by being black and exposed to sunlight. The bird is in a submerged constant temperature bath. Its oxygen consumption is monitored when the artificial sun is on and off and before and after these white birds are dyed black. (After Hamilton and Heppner, 1967.)

apparatus similar to that in Figure 2-3. Roadrunners spend considerable time in the morning and early afternoon in a peculiar posture (Figure 2-4) with the dorsal surface oriented directly toward the sun. At these times the wings, which normally cover the dorsal surface, are deflected to the side, and the body feathers are held erect, exposing a black skin surface directly perpendicular to solar radiation.

Under experimental conditions, roadrunners allow their body temperatures to drop if ambient temperatures drop below 10°C from a mean value of 38.4 to 34.4°C. Within the geographic range of the roadrunner, ambient temperatures commonly fall to 0°C and below during winter months. Hence, there is every reason to believe that

Table 2-1. Mean O_2 consumption of white zebra finches and the same finches dyed black, in milliliters of oxygen per gram of body weight per hour. From Hamilton and Heppner, 1967, p. 197.

White		Black	
Sun on (Number of trials)	Sun off (Number of trials)	Sun on (Number of trials)	Sun off (Number of trials)
9.30 (38)	9.90 (34)	7.17 (22)	9.87 (22)

Figure 2–4. Normal (*a*) and sunbathing (*b*) posture of the roadrunner, *Geococcyx californianus.* The sunbathing posture exposed the black skin (*c*), which is normally covered by feathers.

the results obtained by Ohmart and Lasiewski are fully applicable to this species under natural conditions. The energy consumption of these chilled birds also falls by an average of 41 percent. Thus, a distinctive behavioral response, an unusual distribution of pigmentation, and critical physiological measurements under simulated environmental conditions demonstrate the significance of dark coloration in optimizing energy exchange with the environment.

Radiant Solar Energy

So far the assumption has been that black coloration absorbs more radiant solar energy than other colors. While this is true, many biologists continue to assume that the heat energy of the sun is confined to the invisible infrared part of the spectrum. Is there heat energy in the visible end of the spectrum? In the eighteenth century Benjamin

Franklin performed a series of experiments to determine the role of fabric coloration in the absorption of solar radiation by placing pieces of colored cloth on ice. In the sun the black bits of cloth melted deep impressions in the ice below them. The next most effective color was dark blue, followed by paler colors. A white swatch had no effect upon the surface. Franklin logically concluded that light colors absorb less heat than darker ones.

Subsequently, Franklin's conclusions were challenged by Tyndall (1897), who believed that the thermal energy of solar radiation was invisible. Tyndall seemed to establish experimentally that colors were irrelevant to radiant heat exchange by experiments in which invisible infrared radiation was directed toward vessels containing alum and iodine. The visible dark iodine heated less rapidly than the white alum. Since the infrared radiation that he provided was the equivalent of solar radiation, Tyndall concluded that Franklin's "hastily done" experiments were invalid. Since Tyndall was a highly regarded physicist who lived at a time when neither scientific nor political authority was freely challenged, his conclusions had a profound effect upon the field, and the role of coloration in animal heat exchange was not considered again during the nineteenth century. Actually, Tyndall's conclusion was in error. He was basing his argument on the fallacious premise that most solar radiation is invisible. His misinterpretation was based upon an unfortunate choice of reagents.

About half of all radiant solar energy is seen by man as visible light (Figure 2–5). The caloric value of daily radiation includes 655 cal/cm^2 of energy visible to man and 691 cal/cm^2 of invisible energy. For this reason the colors of animals can be effectively interpreted by our eyes relative to incident radiant energy. It is remarkable that the thoroughly documented nature of radiant solar energy is still so widely misinterpreted. Respected authorities continue to agree with Tyndall that there is no "thermal" energy in the visible portion of the spectrum (e.g., Bates, 1968).

We now know a great deal about the composition of radiant energy when it reaches the planet earth. In 1967 this energy was measured directly at an altitude of 82 km by an X-15 rocket. The new measurement, 1.95 cal/cm^2/min (Laue and Drummond, 1968), replaced the widely used and still frequently quoted figure of 2.00 cal/cm^2/min. As radiant energy penetrates the atmosphere it is selectively filtered, and nearly half of it is gone by the time it reaches sea level (Table 2–2). This means that an animal species with a center of distribution at relatively high altitudes in relatively clear regions will be particu-

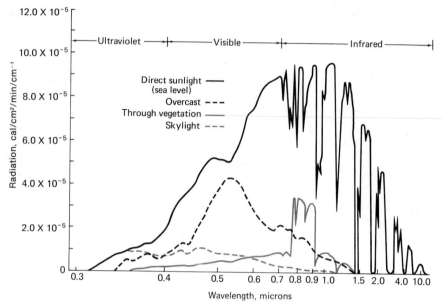

Figure 2–5. The frequency distribution of solar energy reaching planet earth. Approximately half the total energy is visible to man. (After Gates, 1965.)

larly subject to selection for behavioral and morphological adaptations that put this energy source to use. It is quite possible that these conditions were fully applicable to preman.

Black Coloration and Animal Heat Gain

Is there evidence that black coloration enhances animal heat-gain rates? Recent reviews of the role of coloration to heat exchange of animals have either minimized (Digby, 1955; Edney, 1967) or questioned (Schmidt-Nielsen, 1964) the relevance of coloration to animal heat exchange. Buxton (1924) established the role of dark animal coloration in exaggerating heat gain by a simple experiment. He tethered two differently colored morphs of the desert grasshopper, *Calliptamus coelesyriensis*. In sunlight the dark morph, nearly black, reached a temperature of 4.5 degrees warmer than the "desert colored" pale morph. Under artificial sunlight, Hill and Taylor (1933) found that the dark morph of migratory locusts (probably *Schistocerca gregaria*) had a 3.5 degrees higher body temperature than the green one.

Other closely related animal species which differ in coloration exhibit differences in heat-gain rates in sunlight. Two species of the turban snail, Tegula, live along the central California coast. *Tegula brunnea* is brown and lives deeper than *T. funebralis*, at subtidal levels and in tide pools. When I placed specimens of the two species in sunlight, the black *T. funebralis* heated more rapidly than the brown *T. brunnea* (Figure 2-6). Additional evidence of this sort comes from comparisons of black and white desert beetles belonging to the same genus (Hamilton, personal data). Experiments with these insects, reviewed in Chapter 5, provide additional confirmation of the significance of natural animal coloration to heat absorption. These experiments do not by themselves support the hypothesis that black coloration is in any instance an adaptation to thermoregulation. However, the behavior of these black species gives substance to the thermoregulatory argument.

Comparisons of the heat-exchange rates of dimorphic insects such as grasshoppers or other closely related species which differ in color may be deceptive because of the tacit assumption that, except for color, the morphs are alike. This assumption is surely untrue. The dark morph of the migratory locust, *Schistocerca gregaria*, for example, differs from the light phase with respect to external (Dudley, 1964) and internal (Ellis and Carlisle, 1961) structural characteristics and growth rates (Norris, 1964). The behavioral attributes of the two color varieties differ strikingly (Ellis, 1963a, b). All these differences must inevitably affect heat exchange to a greater or lesser extent. It is true that the experimental conditions have restrained these insects, and this would tend to minimize the effect of these differences. Nevertheless, such comparisons cannot be entirely unequivocal.

RADIATION-PROTECTION HYPOTHESIS

Most evidence supporting the energy-color hypothesis for black coloration may also be used to support another quite different hypothesis: that black coloration is advantageous to diurnal animals because it intercepts radiant energy that otherwise would penetrate in harmful amounts, inducing mutations and damaging tissues. These

Table 2-2. Comparative energy available per square centimeter per minute at various elevations above sea level on the planet earth.

Elevation	Energy, calories
Sea level	1.07
1,000 meters	1.28
2,000 meters	1.38
3,000 meters	1.45
Extraterrestrial	1.95

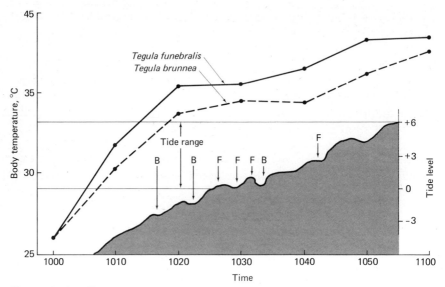

Figure 2-6. Temperature rise of the black turban snail, *Tegula funebralis* (*F*), and the brown turban snail, *T. brunnea* (*B*), exposed to sunlight (upper curves). These snails were taken from the same tide pool near Cambria, California, and exposed to direct sunlight. However, the vertical distribution of the black turban in the intertidal is on the average higher and more exposed than that of the brown turban. It is thus more able to take advantage of solar heating.

effects of ultraviolet and near ultraviolet radiation are well documented (reviewed by Porter, 1967). Most ultraviolet radiation is reflected or absorbed by the skin of larger animals. However, some of this energy does penetrate to deeper tissues. The radiation-protection hypothesis for black animal coloration suggests that heavy pigmentation is an adaptation to increasing the effectiveness of radiation absorption at the surface, reducing its harmful effect upon more sensitive deep body tissues.

Life's Limits

Before the radiation-protection hypothesis is evaluated, a more general problem needs to be considered. Because of the fantastic adaptations to special life conditions on planet earth, it is easy to forget that there are some specific limits to adaptation. Often the same limit may be confronted by a broad phyletic spectrum of life forms, implicating the presence of a basic barrier to adaptation. The adaptation of an animal may be limited at any point in time for one or several reasons:

1   An animal may only recently have experienced certain conditions, due to a changing environment. It may be in the process of adapting, but be incompletely adapted. In this case, actual observation of generation-to-generation change in nature may be possible. It is more likely, however, that change will be taking place so slowly as to be unmeasurable. Rigorous laboratory selection may establish in this case that further selection is possible, but it is difficult to demonstrate that the resulting adaptation is potentially advantageous under natural conditions. The most obvious examples of this limit come from observations of man, whose social structures have generally been unable to keep pace with his rapidly changing demography.

2   The animal may never have experienced the conditions at sufficiently high dosage levels to induce selection, either because of its chosen environment or because it is otherwise buffered from the effect of this condition by other factors of its biology and the biology of its competitors.

In this case more extensive adaptation by closely related species establishes the potential for further evolution. Yet laboratory experiments or observations of physiological failure in nature when the environmental stress is increased beyond the normally encountered environmental dosage establish the limits of adaptation.

3   Further adaptation may be prevented by some other characteristic of the species which would be adversely affected by further adaptation. In this case the adaptive compromise may be obvious, but subtle interaction effects are likely to be difficult to identify.

4   The animal may be at the absolute limits of potential adaptation.

In considering the limits of life it is necessary to evaluate each of these categories. Critical experiments and analysis logic differ according to the case. Animals with similar systems share similar limits. The absolute limit to adaptation can be distinguished by a lack of response to selection experiments, or, by comparative evidence, it may be established that the extreme tolerance of a certain variable is essentially the same within a group of species occupying broadly differing habitats.

Comparative Evidence Favoring the Radiation-protection Hypothesis

The radiation-protection hypothesis has no lack of supporting evidence, both comparative and experimental. The validity of this evidence will now be considered. The comparative evidence has been effectively summarized by Cole (1943), who points out certain highly suggestive correlations:

1   Among vertebrates there is an inverse relationship between the degree of pigmentation of internal organs and the extent of surface shields such as hair and feathers.
2   Transparent animals such as certain fishes tend to have highly pigmented internal organs.
3   Internal pigmentation is generally correlated with diurnal habits.

These correlations are the soundest substantive evidence that pigmentation is an evolutionary adaptation to ultraviolet radiation protection. There is no viable current alternative hypothesis to explain the presence of internal pigmentation. The same arguments have been applied to the interpretation of the black peritoneal lining of many diurnal desert reptiles (Porter, 1967). Hunsaker and Johnson (1959) have suggested that internal pigmentation may be a heat-exchange adaptation. This seems unlikely because all the incident energy is absorbed by the tissues of animals as large as the reptiles they considered, and in terms of heat exchange it makes virtually no difference whether the last few quanta of unreflected energy are absorbed by the peritoneal lining, the viscera, or the ventral body wall.

Other comparative evidence seems to support the conclusion that peritoneal pigments are adapted to radiation protection. On the basis of behavioral and environmental observations of six sympatric lizards of the genus *Anolis* living near Havana, Collette (1961) concluded that the degree of peritoneal pigmentation is closely correlated with exposure to sunlight. Two woodland species, *A. alutaceus* and *A. angusticeps*, have little peritoneal pigmentation, and *A. sangrei*, a lizard of open fields, is most heavily pigmented.

Acceptance of the hypothesis that black peritoneal pigmentation is an adaptation to radiation protection establishes two tentative additional conclusions:

1   There is a limit to the extent to which animals can adapt their tolerance to ultraviolet (UV) radiation.
2   If subsurface (peritoneal) pigmentation protects animals from excessive radiation, the same kind of protection could be provided by surface pigmentation. Radiation protection may, therefore, be an adaptive basis of surface pigmentation as well. The obvious reasons for not placing the radiation shield on the surface is that heavy pigmentation may be incompatible with the signal enhancing or muting functions of surface coloration.

Quantitative Evidence: Is it Relevant?

Many discussions have dealt with the quantitative relationships of ultraviolet radiation to mutation, tissue damage, and death. All this evidence seems irrelevant, because all of it deals with radiation levels far in excess of radiation intensities encountered by animals in their natural environments. Consider, for example, Porter's (1967) calculations, based upon Kubitschek's (1967) experiments on the effect of near UV light upon *Escherichia coli* mutation rates. Based upon this evidence Porter concluded that for the stated wavelengths, ". . . twice the minimum energy needed to increase mutations by an order of magnitude in *E. coli* would reach the internal organs of a desert iguana without its black peritoneum" (Porter, 1967, p. 294).

This statement may be true as it stands, but it is probably not evolutionarily meaningful to a lizard for the following reasons:

1 *Escherichia coli* is an internal parasite of mammals, normally living in environments almost completely lacking ultraviolet energy. Comparisons with a sun-dwelling lizard are irrelevant. The experiments by Kubitschek (1967), showing a doubling of mutations, were performed at light intensities of 4,000 erg/cm^2/sec, 50 times Porter's calculated value for noontime sunlight. There is no environment on earth where these radiation intensities are even approximated.

2 Porter's measurements of lizard radiation dosage levels are based upon the entire dorsal surface of the animal. Kubitschek's measurements are based upon radiant flux per arbitrary unit surface area. For the comparison to be valid, it is necessary to compare radiation flux levels per unit tissue area.

3 There is no evidence that radiation-induced mutation rates are the same for all animal species and tissues. Mutation rates within a species are subject to selection (Mayr, 1963) as is the ability to repair radiation damage (Rupert and Harm, 1966). Therefore it seems reasonable to conclude that there can be evolutionary responses to adapt the UV tolerance of organisms to ambient UV conditions in their natural environments.

How can a quantitative test of the radiation-protection hypothesis be made? Stress to animal species by particular environmental conditions may be assumed to be inversely related to frequency and duration of occurrence of those conditions in nature. This general principle comes from the specific observation of thermal tolerance levels at intermediate levels (Chapter 1) and is applicable to numerous other processes such as tolerance of water loss, salinity, etc. In general, experimental data supposedly confirming the radiation protection hypothesis do not deal with the effects of normally encountered UV dosage levels. The first requirement for an adequate test of the hypothesis, therefore, would be to determine these levels *in nature*, recording the amount of UV radiation which reaches an animal in the course of its *normal* daily and seasonal activities. This might be accomplished by attaching ultraviolet recorders to and within an animal's body. With such measurements from free-ranging animals one might then determine mutation rates, carcinoma frequency, and longevity at the high and low ends of the natural sample. Or, one could subject experimental samples *of the same species* to the ends of the natural range of radiation. If there are differences, a possible role of UV radiation in shaping animal adaptation would be implicated. Until such contextually appropriate experiments are performed, I maintain that the relevant evidence is entirely comparative. This conclusion, if valid, has considerable significance to us in the interpretation of the significance of human skin coloration (Chapter 10).

Black Surfaces and Radiation Protection
The acceptable comparative evidence supporting the radiation-protection hypothesis deals directly only with deep body pigmentation and says nothing about the adaptive significance of black *surfaces*. Nevertheless, the radiation-protection hypothesis often has been invoked to explain black animal coloration, including the coloration of black man (Chapter 10). Evidence supporting this hypothesis is unsubstantial. Often it has been stated that comparative evidence supports this hypothesis. For example, it can be pointed out that black coloration is largely restricted to diurnal animals, especially those living in exposed environments. This evidence is particularly unconvincing because the same arguments support the alternative thermoregulation hypothesis already presented.

   A statement frequently accompanying the radiation-protection hypothesis is that the additional heating resulting from the black coloration is disadvantageous, but must be endured to provide the necessary protection (Porter, 1967). Observations of the behavior of mammals and birds orienting these black surfaces to the sun (Figure 2–5) strongly favor the energy-color hypothesis. But the tables can be turned and the point made that, given such behavior patterns, the protection afforded by pigmentation is necessary to prevent excessive radiation exposure. However, this argument leaves unanswered the question of why these animals are seeking sunlight in the first place.

If the radiation-protection hypothesis is to be further considered, one must also ask why these animals have not adopted the alternative of reflecting the hazardous energy rather than absorbing it. This they could do by being white. Such a strategy would both prevent excessive radiation penetration and avoid the heat gain. For this reason it is at the very least necessary to conclude that black pigmentation is *also* an adaptation to heat exchange.

Only animal species relatively immune to predation (Chapter 6) have adopted energy coloration and social coloration (Chapter 8). Many animals are neither white nor black, and it is clear that these colors are not absolutely necessary to protect animal tissues from excessive radiation. But this argument also has a logical counter: all species might be able to use such protection, thereby extending their time afield, reducing deleterious mutation rates, and extending longevity. Only a few of them can afford to do so. Other species must compromise with selective pressures from other sources. For them the threat from predation and the value of coloration and pattern in communication may be more important.

Another finding—the relatively greater longevity of black animals than their relatives (Chapter 7)—may also be used to support the radiation-protection hypothesis. Only because of the radiation protection afforded by dark coloration, one may argue, are these species able to sustain their longevity.

CHOOSING BETWEEN ALTERNATIVE HYPOTHESES

Thus, the alternatives of the energy-color and radiation-protection hypotheses, as different as they are, are surprisingly difficult to separate. Such problems are of interest with respect to the interpretation of biological evidence in general. A biological hypothesis is generally considered to be supported if separate lines of evidence independently support it. Some would contend that the "ultimate test of a mathematical model is how well it describes a situation in nature" (Ehrlich and Holm, 1962, p. 652).

Nevertheless, in the case of black coloration a model (or hypothesis) accurately predicting and describing well the situation in nature was of little value in suggesting or separating alternative hypotheses dealing with adaptive significance. If the alternative hypothesis of a thermoregulatory role had never been proposed, the original hypothesis of radiation protection would seem to be an overwhelming choice, as indeed it has to many investigators. The surprising result in the case of the two obvious alternatives presented here is that, while they are obviously difficult alternatives to separate, they are opposites. In one case it is suggested that sunlight is hazardous, in the other that it is positively advantageous. The crux of the matter is that mathematical models may have high predictive value and even suggest new hypotheses; but comparative investigations, quantitative or not, are more valuable in choosing between or assigning relative value to alternatives. To me, at least, the logical and comparative difficulties with the radiation-protection hypothesis as it applies to surface coloration have more significance than the result of any experiment I can conceive of. Platt (1966) puts it well:

> Many, perhaps most, of the great issues of science are qualitative, not quantitative, even in physics and chemistry. Equations and measurements are useful only when they are related to proof; but proof or disproof comes first, and is in fact, strongest when it is absolutely convincing without any quantitative measurement (pp. 33–34).

This book attempts a synthesis of qualitative and quantitative evidence; but where a choice must be made, I have taken a thoroughly cautious look at the quantitative evidence before reversing a qualitative judgment.

CONCLUSIONS

1 Black coloration may enable diurnal poikilothermic animals to maintain higher body temperatures than would otherwise be possible and homeothermic animals to maintain elevated body temperatures more economically.
2 Black internal coloration may also enable diurnal animals to protect themselves from excessive UV radiation. This conclusion is based solely upon comparative evidence.
3 The radiation-protection and heat-exchange functions of black pigmentation are difficult to separate, but the behavior of animals in seeking radiation exposure suggests that heat exchange is the leading variable and that radiation protection is an incidental and possibly dispensable result of the pigmentation.
4 The role of black pigmentation in increasing poikilotherm body temperatures above ambient levels suggests that developmental rates and reproductive rates (throughput) are more important to these black species than conservation of energy (efficiency).

WHY WHITE?

White animals often have close relatives that are black. Most swans are white, but one, the Australian swan, is black. White is found on multicolored animals most commonly in company with black. For this reason it seems reasonable to assume that an understanding of the adaptive significance of one will help in developing understanding of the other, and that there may be some relationship between the two. A relationship of black coloration to solar radiation is discussed in Chapter 2, and white coloration might also have some thermal significance. One obvious suggestion is that if black coloration serves to absorb radiation, white is an adaptation to reflecting it. If so, basically different physical requirements or different environmental relationships of black and white species are implied.

If white coloration provided protection from extreme radiation hazard, either overheating or radiation damage, a predominance of white coloration among desert animals and other animals exposed to intensive solar radiation would be anticipated. Not only is there no increase in the number of kinds of white animals found in deserts, but a significant increase in the number of black species occurs there (page 85). The obvious explanation of white coloration as a simple adaptation to maximizing reflectance therefore does not seem to suffice. Thus, we will consider alternative hypotheses for white coloration, as well as more obvious hypotheses related to heat exchange. The following discussion concentrates on birds because in broad comparisons such as the one below, behavior patterns may provide valuable clues, and birds are the animal group with which I am most familiar.

WHITE AND BLACK BIRDS

What is the adaptive significance of black and white coloration to homeotherms? The analysis presented here is concerned with a limited group of bird species, the all-black and all-white birds of western North America. Polar species are excluded because of the probable alternative explanations of white coloration in the Arctic (page 61). While the following discussion is based upon a geographically limited group of birds, I am familiar with the habits of the birds of the world, and the generalizations derived from the quantitative data for western North America are in agreement with more casual observations of the living birds of the rest of the world. Furthermore, the conclusions derived from this analysis may be applicable to mammals as well.

Environmental Camouflage Hypothesis
Comparison of the general environmental relationships of black and white birds shows that none of the white birds of western North America forage exclusively in terrestrial environments, while nearly two-thirds of the black species do so. The correlation between white coloration and life at sea cannot escape the notice of even the most casual observer. This relationship suggested an explanation of the white coloration of sea birds to Tinbergen (1967). His interpretation of this circumstance is that from below, white surface coloration provides effective camouflage against the sky, permitting these birds to be effective predators by preventing subsurface prey from noticing them. This idea seems reasonable enough, but close inspection reveals difficulties. Among black birds, 13 species—most of them predators—also forage exclusively at sea. If camouflage is significant to sea birds and if white coloration secures this advantage, these black birds have complicated their existence by being black. Since this hypothesis accounts for only 45 percent of

the difference between black and white birds [Table 3–1(E)], additional hypotheses providing better explanations of the situation need to be considered.

Social Mimicry Hypothesis

Moynihan (1960, 1962, 1968) has suggested that the colors of black and white birds are not adapted to a common feature of the environment but rather are part of a mimicry ring. According to this hypothesis, coloration convergence among black birds facilitates interspecific encounters by establishing the same basic signal for several species:

> Many of the more gregarious species of birds have evolved particularly conspicuous plumage colors and patterns, in either one or (more frequently) both sexes.
>
> A very large proportion of such species, for example, are predominantly black (e.g., many corvines, many icterids and sturnids, anis, cormorants, cathartid vulture, etc.), or predominantly white (e.g., many herons, spoonbills, swans and some geese, some cotingas, etc.), or pied (e.g., magpies, many gulls, terns, and shorebirds, etc.).
>
> The adaptive value of such coloration seems fairly clear. It will be generally advantageous for *any* species to be as conspicuous as possible, insofar as conspicuousness will make it easier for individuals to locate and recognize one another. It is also possible that conspicuousness may actually make a bird more "attractive" to its fellows; or even enable it to convey stronger and more effective sign stimuli for all sorts of social reactions (Moynihan, 1960, p. 525).

The evidence supporting this hypothesis (Moynihan, 1960, 1968) is that:

1 Birds belonging to these coloration categories tend to form mixed-species flocks. Thus, several species of gulls and terns or of blackbirds may move and function as integrated groups.
2 The joining and following actions of these birds do not involve obvious hostile reactions.
3 Many of the species forming these aggregations and sharing the same color are not closely related to one another, implying convergence.
4 There are other species living in the same regions which do not share these colors. In the case of black birds, close relatives of these species are colored differently.
5 The background is much the same for all species in a local area, and the black and white species do not match this background.
6 There is no indication that these species are particularly distaste-

ful. Hence Batesian and Mullerian mimicry (see Wickler, 1968, for a review of these terms) can be eliminated as possible explanations.

From this evidence Moynihan concludes that these colors are a form of mimicry facilitating social interactions, i.e., each species is a social mimic of its coloration counterpart.

The ensuing discussion leads eventually to the conclusion that the observed phenomena can be quantitatively assigned and logically explained by an environmental effect. Like the radiation-protection argument for black coloration, coloration may serve a secondary or even primary role in communication as suggested by Moynihan, but it is not likely to be the basis of the adaptation. In any event, the comparative approach presented by Moynihan suffers badly from a failure to consider alternative hypotheses. The more versed an individual is in the characteristics of diverse animal species, the more likely he is to be able to develop evidence for a favorite hypothesis. All the evidence Moynihan presents supports his hypothesis because it is the only hypothesis he considers.

Social Organization of White Birds

Another possible explanation of the difference between black and white birds is that the social organization of one group differs from that of the other. Examination of this possibility reveals that most of the black and white birds are refuging [Table 3-1(B)], i.e., they live in groups at dispersal centers from which they regularly radiate to the surrounding terrain to obtain food (Hamilton et al., 1967; Hamilton and Watt, 1970). That most black and white species share this relatively uncommon avian socioeconomic system suggests that there may be evidence relevant to the question: What distinguishes both black and white birds as a group from other coloration categories of birds? But social organization offers no help for distinguishing between them [Table 3-1(C)].

Size Relationships of Black and White Birds

White birds are on the average significantly larger species than black birds [Table 3-1(D)]. Since avian predators are, on the average, larger than avian omnivores and herbivores, the observed size correlation might be explainable by some secondary relationship of coloration to food habits. For example, if white birds were primarily carnivorous and black species were not, then a role of white coloration as camouflage (page 61) would seem plausible. However, the diets of black and white birds do not differ significantly [Table 3-1(A)], and another promising line of reasoning must be abandoned.

Table 3-1. Some characteristics of the all-black and all-white birds of western North America. The probabilities that each characteristic is the same for black and white species of birds as a group are given in the last column. Intermediates, the second column for each characteristic, are assigned half value to each of the extremes.

		Food Habits				
		Predators	Scavengers, Omnivores	Herbivores	X^2	Probability, Percent
A	Black	22	17	0		
	White	14	9	4	0.7	40
			Flocking			
		Flocking	Sometimes Flocking	Never Flocking		
B	Black	29	3	7		
	White	27	0	0	5.8	2
		Refuging Social Organization				
		Refuging	Sometimes Refuging	Not Refuging		
C	Black	20	12	7		
	White	23	3	1	6.8	1
			Size			
		Large (50+ cm)	Medium (25-50 cm)	Small (12-25 cm)		
D	Black	7	15	17		
	White	17	9	1	11.9	0.1
		Feeding Environment				
		Aquatic	Both	Terrestrial		
E	Black	13	1	25		
	White	16	11	0	13.4	0.01
			Night Cover			
		Exposed	Sometimes Exposed	Covered		
F	Black	3	3	33		
	White	27	0	0	48.5	0.01

A second possible explanation related to body size deals with heat-exchange relationships. Could the difference in size between black and white birds be an adaptation to heat exchange? Animal heat-loss rates are related to body size (page 69). The rate of heat exchange of large organisms with their environment is lower than that of smaller ones. Is coloration related to this correlation? Is there a causal link, not with environment, but with dimension? Or is this another secondary relationship to the environment, particularly the feeding environment? A logical case can be made for this explanation. White birds do tend to feed in or on the water [Table 3-1(E)].

Their *potential* heat-loss rates might therefore be more severe. The high conductance of water and the exposed nature of their environment contribute to their potential heat-loss problems. Thus, large body size could be more advantageous than it would be in more protected situations.

Thermal-protection Hypothesis

The most striking and significant difference between black and white birds is their relationship to the environment at night [Table 3-1(F)]. With six exceptions the black birds take shelter at night—in rock crevices, burrows, or under a vegetative canopy. None of the white birds included in this analysis does so. This relationship of nocturnal habits to coloration provides the best fit of coloration to environment. A relationship to heat exchange is implicated. Explanation of this relationship requires a more extensive consideration of heat-exchange phenomena and of insulation in particular.

Heat retention is facilitated by increasing insulation thickness. Details of the insulation process have been examined by Scholander et al. (1950a, b, c). Insulation can be thickened until it retains most of the body heat produced. Thus, terrestrial animals living in extremely cold environments do not necessarily have more serious heat-loss problems than related species living in temperate regions. In fact, heavily insulated arctic mammals change their metabolic rate less per unit temperature change than do tropical mammals, and the retention of body heat may even be too effective under some circumstances. As insulation is increased, the value of radiant environmental energy declines because the portion of thermoregulatory energy contributed by metabolism increases. These insulation relationships explain the significance of white coloration to insulated animals. White birds are on the average more heavily insulated than black species of similar size. The same is true of adjacent black and white surfaces on the same individual (Table 3-2).

If the advantage of heat is essentially the same for all animals (Chapter 2), why do some species increase their insulation and become white and others reduce their insulation and become black? The explanation offered here is that this difference is related to the observed difference in the nocturnal relationships of these coloration groups. White birds, because of their inability or unwillingness to secure shelter at night, are subject to more potential heat stress than black birds inhabiting protected night places. Thus, they require and have developed heavier insulation than black birds, which allows them to achieve the same degree of nocturnal thermal protection. During the day the heavier insulation of the white birds may become

Table 3-2. A comparison of the relative thickness of the black and white feather insulation of various species of birds.

Species	Surface Black	Surface White	Black as a Percentage of White	Habitat
Bonaparte's Gull (*Larus philadelphia*)	Head	Breast	60	Marine
Horned Puffin (*Fratercula corniculata*)	Back	Breast	56	Marine
Magpie (*Pica pica*)	Anterior Breast	Posterior Breast	71	Woodland
Toucan (*Ramphastos tucanus*)	Posterior Breast	Anterior Breast	51	Tropical forests
Turnstone (*Arenaria interpres*)	Anterior Breast	Posterior Breast	79	Coastal
Silver pheasant (*Gennaeus nycthemerus*)	Breast	Back	67	Tropical forests
Merganser (*Mergus serrator*)	Back	Breast	53	Streams

a legacy rather than an asset. These white birds are diurnal. When they are active, solar radiation is adding to the increased metabolic load, and ambient temperatures are rising. The part of the extra heat load induced by sunlight can be minimized by white coloration. According to this hypothesis white coloration enables insulated animals to increase their thermal protection against nocturnal heat loss. By my calculation this hypothesis is in closest agreement with the comparative evidence (Table 2-1), and white coloration is what the eye suggests it might be, an adaptation to reflecting heat.

This hypothesis also helps explain the mean size difference between black and white birds [Table 3-1(D)]. Since white birds are restricted to open roosting sites [Table 3-1(F)], they live under conditions of greater thermal stress and have more to gain from a relatively low surface-to-mass ratio. This hypothesis also provides an explanation of the significant but incomplete correlation between coloration and feeding environment [Table 3-1(E)]. In terrestrial environments almost all birds can find cover at night regardless of their body size. In aquatic locations, night cover is less available, for islands and bare rocky cliffs that border the sea are often the only available roosts. Representatives of the same groups as the white species which are able to secure nocturnal protection in burrows or vegetation are black.

Thus it appears that, of the alternative hypotheses to explain the

difference between the coloration of black and white birds summarized in Table 3-1, all but the heat-loss problems of birds at night
are based upon secondary relationships to the critical problem of
nocturnal thermal protection.

HEAT-LOSS DIFFERENCES CORRELATED WITH COLORATION

Do black and white dissipate heat energy at different rates? If it were
established that they did, heat-loss differences would be a logical
alternative or additional hypothetical explanation of the correlation
between night cover and coloration. Since birds that are exposed
at night require more heat conservation, adaptation of white coloration would best serve them.

The popular misconception concerning the relationship of coloration to heat loss has been ably summarized by Norris (1967) for lizards, and the same evidence is equally applicable to other animals,
insulated or not:

> The prevalent error in understanding centers around the characteris-
> tics of black body radiators. It has sometimes been assumed that be-
> cause a reptile is visibly black it reradiates at a greater rate than a white
> lizard (Parker, 1935; Klauber, 1939; Cole, 1943). In actuality the visible
> color is not relevant to a lizard's capacities as a black body radiator, and
> both the light and the dark lizard may emit long-wave radiation at the
> same rate per unit area. Bodies, animate and inanimate, radiate long-
> wave infrared energy at wavelengths which are determined by their
> absolute temperature (the Wien Displacement Law). The thermal zone
> within which living processes occur is centered around 290°K (17°C),
> and this results in a radiation peak centered at about 8 to 10 microns.
> The Kirchhoff Law (see Hess, 1959, p. 3) relates the intensity of emission
> by a body to its *fractional absorption* of incident radiation *at the same
> wavelength*. This indicates that the better a substance absorbs radiation,
> the better it emits, at the same wavelength. The error seems to have
> come from the mistaken idea that good absorption of visible light (a
> visibly black lizard, for instance) is therefore a good emitter (a black
> body), and that a poor absorber of visible light (a white lizard) is there-
> fore a poor emitter.
>
> A reptile can be a black body radiator approaching perfection if it
> absorbs nearly all energy impinging upon it in the long-wave infrared
> centering around 8 to 10 microns, while it may also be visibly white and
> hence a very reflective object in the visible spectrum. The input of heat
> derived from absorbed visible sunlight raises the absolute temperature
> of the lizard, causing a slight shift in the emissivity wavelength peak
> toward shorter wavelengths (still in the far infrared, however) and causes
> a somewhat greater amount of long-wave radiation to be emitted (Figure
> 3-1) (Norris, 1967, p. 198).

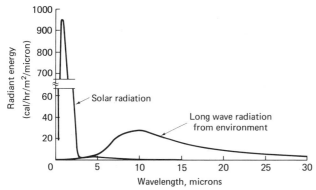

Figure 3-1. Solar radiation is concentrated at relatively short wave lengths compared with the radiation energy emitted from a black body at 27°C, which approximates the radiation characteristics of a living animal. This relationship explains why the visible coloration of an animal provides little information about its heat loss characteristics. (After Norris, 1967.)

Color Correlations with Heat-loss Differences

In spite of the fact that there is no obvious physical basis for believing that there are differences in heat-loss rates between animal surfaces which differ only in coloration, the hypothesis that black and white colors differ in their heat-loss characteristics, with darker colors losing more heat than lighter ones, is well entrenched in the biological literature. According to this hypothesis, white animal coloration serves a thermostatic function, enabling animals to expend less energy in maintaining an elevated body temperature than would otherwise be necessary (Hesse et al., 1937; Stullken and Heistand, 1953).

White Coloration and Heat-loss Rates

Since there is conflicting experimental evidence concerning the heat-loss hypothesis, it is of some interest to consider the experiments and comparisons that have been applied to the problem. There are several ways that possible heat-loss differences between two animals which differ in coloration can be measured. The actual radiant energy from two objects of different colors, but otherwise identical, can be measured. Also, either the temperature change of objects over a period of time can be monitored or the use of food as metabolic energy can be used as an indirect index of heat expenditure. Emphasis here, of course, is upon experiments in which animals or parts of animals are the subjects. Probably the most meticulous, careful, and yet confusing study of the heat-loss characteristics of animal colors was made by Stullken and Heistand (1953). They measured the oxygen consumption of white house mice, then dyed the same mice black and again measured their resting use of energy. As an additional control, they compared the results with the performance of a naturally black strain of the laboratory mouse. The results of these experiments (Figure 3-2) seemed to identify a relationship of pelage coloration to heat loss. The blackened and the naturally black mice used more energy than the white mice. It is of special interest to note that the difference in metabolism between the black and white strains increased at lower temperatures. This result seems to imply that color differences play a role in the regulation of body temperature, since greater amounts of energy must be used to maintain a constant body temperature as the ambient temperature drops further below the constant level.

There are, however, objections to interpreting these data as establishing that coloration accounts for the observed experimental difference. The use of artificial coloring to create black mice may have damaged the heat-retaining characteristics of the pelage. If so, the same results would have developed. The experiments with naturally pigmented mice can be questioned on the basis of strain differences, which may have introduced variables other than coat color. It is possible that these unidentified variables account for

Figure 3-2. Oxygen consumption of white laboratory mice and white laboratory mice dyed black. The energy expenditure of the darkened mice was significantly greater at all temperatures except 30-32°C. (After Stullken and Heistand, 1953.)

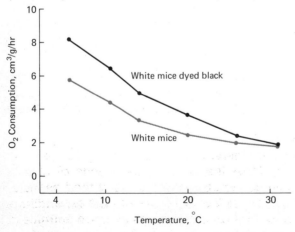

Table 3-3. Heat loss and food consumption of white rats and of white rats dyed black. The sample size in each case was 10 rats, and no rat was used twice in any experiment. From Svihla, 1956.

Energy use, calories per hour		Food, grams per day	
		5°C	25°C
White			
2.80 (2.57–3.82)		29.7	18.2
Black			
2.81 (2.18–3.52)		29.4	17.3

the experimental result, and that coat color is not the critical variable.

Subsequently, a mammalogist, Arthur Svihla (1956) was prompted by Stullken and Heistand's results to perform a similar experiment using white laboratory rats. Svihla also dyed his subjects black and measured both metabolic rate and food consumption. His experiments showed no difference between the black and the white rats. Average heat-loss rate and food consumption of experimentals and controls was essentially the same (Table 3–3), even at low temperatures (5°C). However, the small sample size and the wide variability within the results make his data less useful than those developed by Stullken and Heistand.

ALTERNATIVE EXPLANATIONS OF WHITE COLORATION

Radiation Protection
It is not necessary for an animal to be heavily insulated to be disadvantaged by too much heat. Some uninsulated white animals have adopted white coloration to avoid excessive thermal radiation. This is particularly true of sessile and slow-moving animals such as barnacles and snails that live in warm environments (Chapter 5).

Metabolic Efficiency and Infection Reduction: Depigmentation
A traditional explanation of the pale colors of cave animals is that in this lightless environment color has no adaptive value, and it is more efficient to avoid the unnecessary energy expenditure of pigment production. Cave animals have lost other tissues and organs—eyes in particular—the adaptive basis of which has been interpreted in the same way. An alternate interpretation of the eyelessness of cave-dwelling animals is that the eyes are a common source of infection, and their absence is positively advantageous. The infection-reduc-

tion and metabolic-efficiency hypotheses have been freely debated for some time, but there is little evidence upon which to base an evaluation of them. To my knowledge, no measurement of the energy cost of pigment production has ever been made. Real data would be of great interest because evolutionary explanations of diverse phenomena depend on them. The energetic cost of developmental sequences and alternatives promises to be an interesting focus for future research and for communication between ecologists and developmental biologists. But to date the first experiment has not been done.

Hypotheses dealing with explanations of depigmentation have particular relevance to the interpretation of coloration for most of the readers of this book (see page 183). They are also generally applicable to the insulated portions of the skin of most homeotherms.

COUNTERSHADING

The pale ventral surface of many insects, birds, fish, and mammals has been interpreted as an adaptation to camouflage. The hypothesis that these pale underparts, when naturally illuminated, enable animals to match their backgrounds more accurately (Thayer, 1918; Cott, 1940) is supported by the observation that these animals are more conspicuous when they are inverted under natural lighting conditions. Pale underparts contribute to the effectiveness of camouflage in avoiding predation.

Acceptance of the countershading hypothesis does not mean that all interpretations of pale animal underparts as countershading are acceptable and supportable. Several other potential explanations of pale ventral surfaces are available.

One possible alternative is that dark dorsal surfaces are adaptations to heat gain. Since the dorsal surface will inevitably moderate most of the visible radiant energy, it may be advantageous to optimize heat-exchange relationships with the environment by heavy dorsal pigmentation.

Even if the role of countershading in heat exchange can be eliminated as, for example, in certain midwater fishes, the function of camouflage as predation protection is not necessarily proved. The tacit assumption that countershading establishes the functional role of an animal's color pattern as an adaptation to predation protection led Longley (1917) and others to conclude that the coloration of reef fish is basically an adaptation to predation protection. This conclusion follows from the fact that nearly all reef fish species, regardless of how highly colored they are, are darker above than below (Hamilton, personal data). Another possibility, however, is that the countershading, coupled with a rapid color change, may actually facilitate communication. The butterfly fish, *Chaetodon lunula*, eliminates a part of its camouflage during aggressive encounters (Figure 3-3). The sudden elimination of the camouflage reveals bright lemon-yellow areas, making the fish highly conspicuous. Thus the countershading may conceal a signal from counterspecifics rather than the animal from predators, thus providing the fish with a dynamic signaling system. It is, of course, possible that both explanations are valid, i.e., that the countershading provides camouflage except when it is necessary to communicate. However, in the case of the butterfly fish, other features of the basic color pattern (Hamilton and Peterman, 1971) and the overall conditions of the life of this and other highly colored reef fish in natural environments make this interpretation seem implausible.

ARCTIC WHITENESS

In polar and alpine regions the pervasive whiteness of snow and ice suggests the possible explanation of white animal coloration as camouflage. This explanation agrees with the dramatic increase in the proportion of white species and individuals in the Far North, particularly among mammals. Polar and alpine whiteness is a phenomenon restricted to birds and mammals. The relatively few large arctic and alpine poikilotherms lack white representatives.

Camouflage
Discussion of the significance of polar whiteness may seem academic. Isn't it obvious that this whiteness is camouflage? There is certainly considerable evidence to support this conclusion:

Figure 3-3. The coral reef fish *Chaetodon lunula* blanches the dark countershading pigment on the dorsal surface of the flattened body during social encounters. Thus the countershading may be an adaptation to the enhancement of communication rather than to camouflage.

A   B

1   Under most conditions, white arctic animals closely resemble the coloration of their backgrounds.

2   Several northern animals—for example, the lemming, *Dicrostonyx groenlandicus*; the varying hare, *Lepus americanus*; the stoat, *Mustela erminea*; and the ptarmigans, *Lagopus lagopus, L. mutus*, and *L. leucurus*—change to brown plumage or pelage in the summer. These darker colors presumably provide more effective camouflage in the snowless arctic or alpine summer.

3   Closely related species or races of arctic mammals living in adjacent snowless or less snowy regions have not adopted white coloration. For example, the Washington hare, *Lepus washingtoni*, a close relative and probably a conspecific of the varying hare, *L. americanus*, does not undergo a seasonal change in color. The varying hare is restricted to northern and montane environments, while the Washington hare lives in the snowless districts of Washington and British Columbia.

4   The behavior of some white arctic animals supports the camouflage hypothesis. For example, snowshoe hares often remain motionless in place when they sense danger, or slowly retreat until they are safe (Grange, 1932). In the arctic spring, when the environment is a mosaic of snow-free bare ground and patches of snow, ptarmigan keep to backgrounds which match their coloration, whether they have adopted the summer brown phase, are in a mottled intermediate plumage, or have become winter white. Enhancement of the effectiveness of camouflage by behavior emphasizes its role as camouflage.

5   White coloration in the arctic is largely restricted to species with the greatest need for camouflage in predator-prey relationships. This significance of coloration in predation-prey interactions is considered in Chapter 6, where differences in the relative significance of camouflage according to hunting methods and relevance to predation are emphasized. In the arctic, active predators and heavily preyed-upon species tend to be white, while the few arctic nonwhite homeotherms tend generally to fall outside predator-prey cycles. Large northern grazing animals such as the musk-ox and the caribou are gregarious animals, unable to take advantage of camouflage because of the inevitable conspicuousness of their herds. Camouflage would be of little advantage to them. The arctic raven and wolverine are scavengers or scavenge hunters (Chapter 6) and most of their attacks do not depend upon stealth or camouflage. They are relatively predator-free, the wolverine because of its aggressive nature and size and the raven due to its cunning, flight ability, size, and gregariousness. None of these

animals are camouflaged. On the basis of a broader phyletic comparison (Chapter 6) my conclusion is that once predation upon or by a species is relaxed, the animal is able to adopt other adaptive bases of coloration.

Protection from Excessive Heat

Is it possible that there are overheating problems in the arctic, so that white coloration might actually be an adaptation to prevention of overheating? The basic thermoregulatory adaptation of birds and mammals to arctic environment is to increase insulation thickness (Scholander et al., 1950a). This insulation must protect them from excessive cold even when they are at rest. Thus, while some tropical and some temperate region mammals are at thermal equilibrium at $+30°C$, arctic foxes attain the same balance at $-30°C$. In the course of the arctic year the temperature range may be more than 80 degrees, and a daily cycle may include half that range. If insulation is an adaptation to maintenance of thermal equilibrium at the low end of the thermal range, the heavy insulation may be positively disadvantageous at other times of day or at other seasons. Arctic and mountain explorers have problems with excessive heat during activity and especially during heavy exercise. During winter sports competition, the main thermal problem is not to stay warm but to avoid overheating (Buskirk and Bass, 1960).

As in the case of white birds in temperate regions, which are apparently adapted to avoiding overheating by being white (page 000), reflectance of sunlight by the white coat of arctic animals minimizes this problem and should enable arctic animals to increase their insulation. That this is a real possibility is emphasized by Pedersen's observation of the heat gain of the dark hide of a musk-ox. When a furred hide was hung out in the weak arctic sun at $-27°C$, a thermometer at the surface of the skin under the fur read $+2°C$ after only 10 minutes in the sun. The possibility for substantial (and possibly deleterious) solar radiative heat loads in the arctic at certain seasons cannot be ignored. The physical basis of the problem is exaggerated by the broad amplitude in daily and seasonal availability of radiant energy in the arctic as compared with more tropical latitudes. There is actually more incident radiation per unit horizontal surface per day on a June day at 80°N than there is at the equator on any day of the year (Figure 3–4).

Certain comparative evidence also lends support to the hypothesis that white arctic coloration may play a significant role in reducing radiation absorption. Not all arctic birds and mammals change to dark colors in the summer when white coloration would play its most

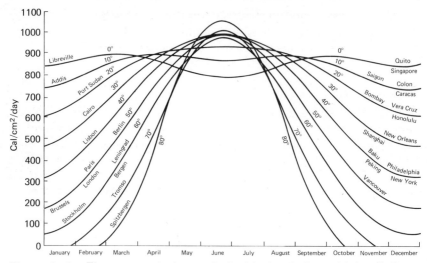

Figure 3-4. The seasonal change in incident extraterrestrial radiation per unit surface area at different latitudes. (After Gates, 1962.)

significant role in minimizing heat gain. For example, the arctic hare, the male ptarmigan in Greenland (Pedersen, 1966), and most arctic birds that are white at any season remain white during the summer (Table 3-4). The same is true of the mountain goat, *Oreamnos americanus*. At this season white pelage and plumage are highly conspicuous. Do these animals retain white insulation because it is uneconomical to molt during the short arctic summer, i.e., the short season of nonwhite backgrounds? This is certainly a possibility. But the cost of a molt would seem to be relatively cheap predation protection, and it is possible that some other more significant selection pressure, possibly thermal protection, has more significance than camouflage to white arctic animals.

Some of the permanently white arctic birds—gulls, swans, and geese—are particularly interesting because they belong to the same groups of birds as the temperate region species included in analysis of the white coloration of birds (see Tables 3-1, 3-4). In the analysis of white coloration on pages 50 to 56, comparative evidence supports the conclusion that white coloration is basically an adaptation to preventing excessive heat gain during the day. According to this line of reasoning the adaptation depends upon the significance of the sun as much as it does upon heat-loss problems during the arctic summer night. In the winter, several of the animals included in Table 3-4—the polar bear, the arctic hare, and the ptarmigan—protect themselves from the extreme arctic cold by burrowing into the snow.

In the summer, this convenient shelter is less available or lacking. In fact, most or all of the animals of Table 3-4 spend their nights exposed, a trait also shared with temperate-region white birds (page 54). These observations and comparisons suggest an alternative, but not necessarily a mutually exclusive one, to the camouflage hypothesis as an explanation of the white coloration of polar animals.

Heat-loss Differences

If there are coloration correlations between coloration and heat loss (page 56), this hypothesis will have obvious relevance to the interpretation of polar whiteness. The coloration of white arctic mammals has in fact been interpreted on this basis (Hesse et al., 1937; Hamilton, 1939). This argument rises or falls with the inconclusive evidence concerning the relationship of white coloration to heat loss provided on pages 56 to 59.

Black Tails and Ears

In the snow, the black ear tips of arctic hares; the black tail tips of ermine; the black facial markings of male ptarmigans, *Lagopus mutus*; the black tails of all the ptarmigan species; and the black horns and nose of the mountain goat are often the only features that can be distinguished by a human observer. If we assume that the white pelage of these animals is camouflage, what accounts for these flaws? The most reasonable explanation is that they are visual social signals. These markings share many of the characteristics of visual signals (Chapter 8). Contrasting colors are placed next to one an-

Table 3-4. Some arctic birds and mammals that retain white plumage and pelage in the arctic summer.

Species	Sexes White in Summer	Food Habits	Background Coloration
Polar bear	Both	Diverse	Various
Arctic fox (white morph)	Both	Scavenger, scavenger-hunter	Various
Arctic hare	Both	Herbivorous	Not snow or ice
Ptarmigan	♂ only	Herbivorous	Dark
Gulls (ivory gull resident)	Both	Scavenger	Various
Geese (snow, ross, both migratory)	Both	Herbivorous	Green or brown
Swans	Both	Herbivorous	Dark

other, the change from one color to another is sharply defined, and the markings are located on the head where these signals will be particularly prominent during frontal encounters. The ears of hares are moved forward during agonistic sequences and tail movements by weasels are common during social interactions. Hence, these markings may be visual signals enhancing the effectiveness of threats (Hingston, 1933). They may also serve to coordinate activities such as the massed movements of arctic hares or the group hunting activities of weasels.

CONCLUSIONS

From this review of the adaptive significance of white coloration to homeotherms, it follows that:

1 The most extensive differences in thermal conditions encountered by homeotherms are those between night and day rather than those following latitudinal gradients. It is for this reason that energy colors are largely confined to diurnal animals that can or must take the brunt of solar radiation. Animals are better able to adapt to local geographic conditions than they are to the dramatic differences between night and day, because the latter are more extensive and take place over short time intervals, thereby effectively preventing physiological adaptation to both ends of the normally encountered environmental range.

2 The coloration of animals probably plays no significant role in the loss of heat, only in the relative rate of heat gain.

3 Unlike poikilotherms, homeotherms have little opportunity to adapt their coloration to both ends of the daily environmental temperature cycle because the coloration of their insulation cannot be readily manipulated.

4 Tolerance at the extreme low end of the daily cycle of thermal conditions experienced by homeotherms is accomplished by increasing the thickness of insulation.

5 The insulation thickness required to maintain thermal equilibrium at night depends more than any other factor upon the opportunity to obtain nocturnal protection against wind, unfavorable radiation conditions, and other conditions exaggerating heat loss.

6 Homeotherms able to secure cover at night or during the inactive phase of their daily activity cycle tend to do so.

7 The thick insulation required to withstand nocturnal conditions when no cover is available may induce potential overheating

problems at the warmer end of the daily thermal cycle during the day.

8   White homeotherm coloration is in many and perhaps the majority of instances an adaptation to minimizing overheating during the day. This is accomplished by maximizing the reflection of radiant energy.

9   In the arctic, camouflage may be an overriding basis of white coloration, but it is also possible that it is an adaptation to preventing overheating.

10 White homeotherm coloration is part of a series of adaptations to minimizing heat exchange with the environment. By comparison, black homeotherms emphasize heat exchange during the day and minimize it at night. Loss of heat is minimized at night by black animals by establishing favorable thermal relationships to the environment.

BEHAVIORAL THERMOREGULATION

In a real sense all animal traits, behavioral and structural, are thermoregulatory, because each structure and every action influences the heat-exchange relationship of an animal with its environment and thus its thermal relationship with the physical and social environment. In this chapter, however, only characteristics that specially adapt animals to heat exchange are considered.

Thermoregulatory mechanisms may be broadly classified as structural, physiological, and behavioral. Structural temperature-regulation mechanisms involve permanent modification of the body surface—coloration, insulation, and body proportions. Behavioral thermoregulation includes choice of environment and manipulation of environmental conditions in various ways. Physiological thermoregulatory mechanisms include circulatory adjustments, respiration, and metabolic heat production. Behavioral thermoregulation in homeotherms in particular operates to make physiological thermoregulation more efficient. A consideration of some thermoregulatory processes demonstrates the close relationship among behavioral, morphological, and physiological thermoregulatory mechanisms.

All terrestrial animals and a great many aquatic species utilize a combination of processes to optimize thermoregulation within the constraints of the basic body plan of the group to which they belong. Other processes and adaptations may be more important and take precedence. The evolutionary direction for thermoregulatory adaptation frequently has been established on the basis of economy, the less energy-demanding alternative being adopted. This economy often has been achieved by modifying some routine activity so that it becomes a thermoregulatory mechanism.

HOMEOTHERM THERMOREGULATION

The phenomena of body size, surface area, and metabolic rate must be considered together because of their interdependence. An understanding of their relevance to animal thermoregulation is possible only in terms of interrelationships. To discuss one aspect without the others would be like trying to understand a symbiosis by studying only one member of the association. One way to manipulate body temperature and heat balance would be to manipulate metabolic rates and thus metabolic heat production. However, metabolic rates are essentially fixed for each animal group. This does not mean that each species in that group has the same metabolic rate, because metabolic rates per unit of body mass decrease with increasing body size. But most animal species lie on or near a fixed linear relationship of body size to metabolic rate, regardless of the environment in which they live. This is true for nearly all animal groups—birds, mammals, and invertebrates—and for poikilotherms as well. Thus, variation of metabolic rates within each animal group is apparently a nonadaptive feature of each animal group and the species which compose it. Other adaptations seem to be structured around it.

Manipulation of body temperature is another way of adjusting thermoregulation in diverse environments, either by adjusting the thermostat or by allowing the body temperature to fluctuate. However, in the case of homeotherms, the actual thermostatic setting varies little if at all, and relatively minor species-specific differences in body temperature are related to body size rather than to environment. Some homeotherms do undergo a considerable daily cycle in body temperature, but body-temperature fluctuations in homeotherms are generally not extensive and cannot account for their basic thermal adaptations to diverse environments. Body temperature is another constant in the complex of thermoregulatory variables.

The most manipulable variable in the thermoregulatory complex of homeotherms is insulation—hair and feathers. Hair and, to a lesser extent, feathers (Irving, 1964) may be manipulated externally with environment and with species and upon different surfaces of the same individual. By seasonally adding or subtracting insulation through selective molts, birds and mammals can optimize their thermal relationships. Insulation manipulation seems to be the most important climatic thermoregulatory adaptation of homeotherms (Scholander et al., 1950a, b, c).

Foils

The size of an animal's surface area can be modified without changing its basic body size. The role of expanded flat surfaces in dissipating heat is a familiar adaptation to engineers concerned with practical mechanical problems of heat dissipation. Appendages can be extended or otherwise manipulated to alter and optimize heat exchange relationships.

In animals, such structures may secure or dissipate heat, depending upon environmental conditions. The African desert tenebrionid beetles *Onymacris multistriata* and *O. bicolor* extrude their genitalia when their body temperature reaches about 40°C, exposing a moist surface and increasing the evaporative surface area (Bolwig, 1957). Elephant ears are the largest foils of any living animal. These structures, liberally supplied with blood vessels, probably play a major thermoregulatory role when they are flapped back and forth in the characteristic manner.

When foils function to absorb heat, their role in this capacity is sometimes confirmed by their black coloration. For example, in the morning and late afternoon, the white whistling swan, *Olor columbianus*, often holds one of its black feet above its back. The feet of other swans are also black and may be used in a similar manner. There have been no quantitative studies of the countercurrent heat exchange nor any aspect of heat exchange by the feet of swans, but coloration and behavior suggest that the possibility is worth investigating. Turtles that sunbathe on banks often extend black feet, thus increasing the rate of heat gain. These surfaces seem small, but may secure a significant amount of thermal energy. Assuming a minimum value of 1.0 cal/cm^2/min from sunlight, 10 cm^2 of surface on the four feet of a turtle could absorb enough heat in an hour to raise the temperature of a 1-liter turtle 2.4 degrees (1 cal/cm^2/min $\times$ 60 min $\times$ 40 cm^2 of feet $= \dfrac{2{,}400 \text{ cal}}{1{,}000 \text{ cm}^3}$ of turtle $= 2.4$ degrees heat gain per hour).

The familiar Allen's rule, that the tails, ears, bills, and other extremities of animals are smaller or shorter in the cooler districts occupied by particular races of species, is a variation of the use of foils as heat-exchange surfaces.   The increased surface area in warmer regions increases heat loss, and may also permit more rapid heat gain.   The circulatory constriction and dilation response to heat and cold is a built-in physiological mechanism to maximize the effectiveness of these morphological adaptations.

Convection

Convection plays a prominent role in animal heat transfer, but ambient air flow is seldom measured or manipulated in the study of animal metabolism.   Experimental arrangements in that most unique of all environments, the laboratory, usually minimize air flow.   There the wind never blows and the sun never shines, but in nature, sun and wind are unavoidable characteristics of most terrestrial environments.   Wind can be most easily manipulated by animals by moving to an environment with different convection characteristics.

Evaporative Cooling

Evaporative cooling is not restricted to respiration and perspiration. When a beehive becomes overheated, the workers gather water, return to the hive, and fan in place inside the hive.   The coordinated actions of hundreds of individual bees creates a draft which cools the hive.   These actions are enhanced by the extension of the moist proboscis (Lindauer, 1955).   Certain butterflies extrude water droplets onto the coiled proboscis and then return them to the digestive tract.   This action, described by Adams and Heath (1964) in the sphinx moth, *Pholus achemon*, is adopted only at very high body temperatures, and results in immediate cooling.   A variation on this theme is extrusion of fluid from the penis of butterflies and the return of this fluid to the body via the proboscis (Clench, 1966).   Presumably, this action involves the evaporative cooling of the droplet which is then returned to the body after the heat has been dissipated.   During periods of heat duress, many Australian marsupials lick their paws, the bare surfaces of the tail, and the ears.   Domestic cats lick their paws and chest fur under similar circumstances (Robinson and Lee, 1946).   Some lizards lick their lips when they are overheated (Brain, 1962).   All these behavioral methods of evaporative cooling appear to be limited to periods of extreme heat stress.

Color Change

Color change is considered here in the broad sense of any change in surface coloration during life.   In this sense most animals change color during their lifetime. Color changes are accomplished in many ways and on various schedules, some aperiodic, others cycling seasonally, daily, or over even shorter intervals. Certain color changes appear to be directly concerned with thermoregulation; others serve a background-matching function or enhance communication. Some color changes shift the coloration from one adaptive basis to another, as from camouflage to warning or intraspecific communication. Thus the color changes may demonstrate a passing change in the relative value of various selective pressures.

Regulation of Color Change

The mechanisms of color change have received much more attention than their adaptive significance. This emphasis upon the physiological processes of color change has persisted since the field came under intensive investigation in the nineteenth century. The literature dealing with color change frequently confuses the relationship of adaptive significance with the mechanism of its maintenance. This confusion is illustrated, for example, by Dingle and Haskell's observation (1967) of the role of humidity in influencing color change in the polymorphic grasshopper, *Melanoplus differentialis*. Young hoppers raised at low humidity levels are pale brown, but when they are raised at high humidity levels they are green. The process of coloration differentiation is based upon the water vapor in the hopper's environment or some correlate of it. Dingle and Haskell concluded that the adaptive significance of the color change is directly concerned with humidity, but the adaptive significance of this change is most probably not concerned with the effect of humidity per se, but rather with the fact that at high humidities the environment is likely to have had recent rainfall and to be green. At relatively low humidities vegetation tends to dry up and turn brown. Humidity is simply a key feature of the environment that the insect uses to determine the appropriate response to the environment.

Temperature Regulation by Color Change

Color changes may optimize the thermal relationships of both homeotherms and poikilotherms. Poikilotherm color changes have in fact been considered relative to heat exchange, but hypotheses relating homeotherm coloration to heat exchange are largely lacking.

Many terrestrial poikilotherms undergo daily and seasonal thermoregulatory color changes. This involves darkening during cool intervals and blanching when heat loads become excessive. In these poikilotherms, dark coloration prevails at emergence in the morning, when body temperatures are well below maximum (and optimum) levels. Many lizards, such as the desert iguana (Norris, 1953) and the desert chameleon (personal observation), perform in this way. These same lizards blanch when body temperatures reach or exceed preferred levels. This coloration response should provide an ideal means for determining thermal optima. For poikilothermic maxitherms, the predicted level for color change should be near 40°C, and according to the maxithermy hypothesis the level should in no case exceed 42°C. The best applicable data is based upon studies of lizards, which are notable both for their propensity to change color and for the propensity of biologists to probe their anuses with temperature-measuring devices. As long ago as 1899, Krehl and Soetbeer made the appropriate measurements for the lizard uromastrix. They found that it blanched at 41°C. Norris (1967) has studied the relationship of color change to thermoregulation in a number of species of American lizards. He found that color change from dark to light takes place over a range of temperatures. The most heat-tolerant species studied by him, *Dipsosaurus dorsalis*, has exhausted 50 percent of its color-change potential at 40°C. At higher temperatures the pale color is lighter than any of the substrates where this animal occurs naturally. These limited data agree well with the maxithermy hypothesis, but these measurements should be extended to other species.

Morphological color changes of a more durable sort may also serve a thermoregulatory function. Black gregarious-phase grasshoppers molt to a yellowish color in the next instar if they are reared at 40°C (Carlisle, 1964). This shift is clearly advantageous since dark coloration can no longer provide any thermal advantage above this level. Other grasshoppers, for example, the Australian grasshopper *Kosiuscola tristis*, undergo daily color changes, but the actual thermal relationships have not been determined (Key and Day, 1954a, b). The temporal pattern of this color change is summarized in Table 4-1.

Dark forms of other insects develop only at low temperatures. The bug *Habrobracon juglandis*, a parasite of the meal moth ephestia, is darker when bred at low temperatures (Schlottke, 1926). Another bug, *Microbracon brevicornis*, a parasite of the cotton bollworm platyedra, is black when it develops at 10°C but brown following development at 25°C (Narayanan et al., 1954). The same is true of developing locusts (Goodwin, 1952). These relationships of coloration to temperature emphasize that the value of any particular adaptive configuration depends not only upon the relationship of an animal species with the other members of the biological community but also upon its thermal relationship with the physical environment.

Table 4-1. Color change sequence of the Australian alpine grasshopper, *Kosiuscola tristis* (Key and Day, 1954a, b)

Time	Color	Location	Ambient Temperature	Behavior
Night	Black	Crevices		Not observed
Early morning	Black	Sun		Sunning
Midday	Blue	Shade	>12.2°C	Sheltering
Late afternoon	Black	Sun		Sunning

INSULATION

Insulation drastically alters the value of coloration relative to heat exchange. The thicker the insulation, the less significant environmental heat exchange becomes to thermoregulation.

Insulation Reduction
Birds and mammals are able to manipulate the angle of inclination of their hair and feathers. This ability is used to adjust heat flow from the body in a variety of ways, by:

1 Reducing the amount of insulation
2 Eliminating the greenhouse effect through release of air trapped between the skin and the outer surface of the insulation
3 Exposing the skin or subsurface insulation layers with different reflectance characteristics.

Piloerection by birds may increase the rate of heat gain in the morning. The back of the crimson-throated barbet, *Megaluima rubricapilla*, a small Asian bird, is red at the base and black in the middle. I have observed this bird sunbathing in the early morning, orienting itself so that its back faces and is perpendicular to the sun's rays. During sunbathing, the black heat-absorbing feathers are sleeked, and the more reflective red feathers are held erect.

Insulation Elimination
Insulation reduction has in some instances been taken to the extreme with complete elimination of feathers and hair, at least on limited surfaces. Obviously, birds cannot dispense with their feathers, but large birds can eliminate feathers in limited areas without seriously impairing their flight ability and aerodynamics. The California condor, *Gynogyps californianus*, and some other vultures have no fea-

thers on the head or neck. Under conditions of cold stress, below 15°C, perching California condors raise a ruff of long narrow feathers to cover the neck. This muffler is sometimes lowered at warmer temperatures to expose the uninsulated neck (Koford, 1953). Such an adaptation can serve in both heat gain and heat dissipation, depending upon ambient conditions and the animal's behavior.

Bare surfaces are commonly adapted to heat exchange by mammals. This pattern is highly developed in primates, where insulation is frequently eliminated. Uninsulated portions of primates, other than those on the head and genital areas, are often black. The standing explanation of the significance of these black colors, particularly to man, is that they prevent penetration of hazardous ultraviolet radiation (page 52). Yet, in common with a great diversity of black animals, the primates with black areas are the very species which actively seek sunlight (Chapter 9). Some primate sunbathing postures, e.g., that of the monkey *Langur kasijohni*, even take advantage of the hairless black foot pads, which are held perpendicular to the slanting rays of the morning sun.

BEHAVIORAL ADAPTATIONS TO SECURING SUNLIGHT

Sunbathing

Sunlight generally is considered to be an energy resource for plant life only. Yet many plants require no light energy, and an astonishing variety of animals are absolutely dependent upon it, including representatives of many of those groups which are normally considered to be harmed by sunlight. The North American frog, *Rana pipiens*, basks at the edge of stream banks in full sunlight, when shade may be quite available, and in Mozambique, I have observed tree frogs basking on the upper side of palm fronds throughout sunny days. Fiddler crabs climb out of their burrows to bask in sunlight; fish may waddle completely out of water; mammals bask in the treetops, at the edge of the sea, and about their dens; insects bask on sand dunes, bushes, and in sun flecks on the forest floor. Indeed, sunbathing is of such widespread phyletic occurrence that one is tempted to conclude that the advantage it provides, whatever it may be, is available to all animal life. But a number of phyla (Table 4-2) do not have sunbathing representatives and black coloration adaptations. These groups failed to develop black sunbathing representatives probably because they are composed entirely of marine organisms and, because of the relatively high conductive heat losses in aquatic environments, the potential advantages of sunbathing and an elevated body temperature are not available.

Table 4-2. Major multicellular animal phyla and the occurrence of sunbathing behavior correlated with dark or black coloration.

Phylum	Sunbathing Species	Terrestrial Species	Black or Dark Species Which Sunbathe
Sponges	No	No	No
Coelenterates	No	No	No
Echinoderms	No	No	No
Flatworms	No	No	No
Annelids	No	Yes	No
Molluscs	Yes	Yes	Yes
Arthropods			
Crustaceans	Yes	Yes	Yes
Insects	Yes	Yes	Yes
Chordates			
Fish	Yes	Some amphibious	Yes
Amphibians	Yes	Yes	Yes
Reptiles	Yes	Yes	Yes
Birds	Yes	Yes	Yes
Mammals	Yes	Yes	Yes

Ventral Surface Sunbathing

Mammals and many birds that are deliberate sunbathers tend to emphasize orientation of the ventral surface to sunlight, regardless of the color of the ventral surface. There is a fundamental reason for emphasizing exposure of this surface during sunbathing. During sleep and rest the ventral surface can be protected against excessive heat loss by manipulating the posture (Figure 4-1). Thus, ventral surfaces, on the average, encounter more moderate environmental conditions than dorsal surfaces. Optimum insulation thickness, therefore, need not be as great as for dorsal surfaces, which are more frequently exposed to the full force of ambient conditions. Since environmental heat gain is enhanced by insulation reduction, these relatively thinly haired areas are the natural surfaces to be oriented toward sunlight when heat absorption is to be emphasized.

This relationship is particularly well developed among mammals, which can curl up and eliminate exposure of the ventral surface in the resting posture. But some birds also orient their breasts to the sun while sunbathing. The basis for this use of the ventral surface is related to the fact that for both birds and mammals the ventral surface is subject to less thermal stress than the dorsal surface during the course of normal behavior. A black belly, whether on a bird or mammal, can in most environments be exposed to incident radiation more or less at will. An additional reason for the location of black surfaces that enhance solar heating on the ventral surface is that the dorsal surface is less important to camouflage. When the threat of predation is relatively low and conditions favor sunbathing, it is a relatively simple matter for most animals to adjust their posture to accept sunlight on the ventral surface.

Posture and Postural Changes

There are numerous postural adaptations to thermoregulation other than the simple orientation of dark body surfaces toward sunlight. One common movement involves orientation of the body axis to

Figure 4-1.   Many animals orient the relatively lightly insulated under surface toward the morning sun to maximize the rate of heat absorption. At dawn and in the evening the spider monkey, *Ateles geoffroyi,* curls up (*a*), minimizing exposed body surface. As the sun rises it extends and orients the thinly haired ventral surface to the sun (*b*). Captive gibbons, *Hylobates lar,* often hang for considerable intervals with the ventral surface toward the sun (*c*). The lemur, *Lemur catta,* commonly adopts a posture with the belly toward the sun (*d*).

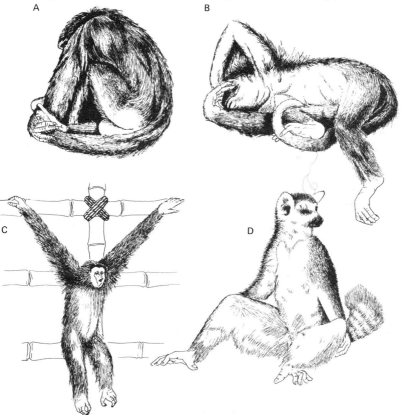

optimize incident radiation input. Frequently, this involves orienting the body axis so that it is perpendicular to the sun's rays in the early morning or late afternoon. In the late afternoon the black-bodied red admiral butterfly carefully taxies to such a posture upon alighting, with the longitudinal axis of the body parallel to the rays of the sun and the body held erect to intercept the rays at as steep an angle as possible. Its movements in this maneuver are remarkably similar to the actions of roadrunners (Figure 2–4) at the same time of day. At other times of day, the elongate bodies of insects may be oriented toward the sun, so that only a small surface area intercepts radiation. On the Sahara Desert, damselflies thrive on the sparse desert shrubs, and are active even at midday, when they point the slender abdomen and body directly towards the sun. Except for a life history that demands free water for larval development, these insects would be highly adapted to a desert environment. Some individuals of the lizard *Liolaemus multiformis* live above 4,500 meters in the Andes. In the cold alpine dawn, with ambient temperatures near 0°C, those lizards can drive the body temperature to nearly 40°C by positioning the body axis perpendicular to the sun (Pearson, 1954).

Many lizards raise themselves on their limbs during periods of excessive heat stress, probably to minimize conductive heat transfer (Norris, 1953). The desert lizard *Holbrookia maculata* may climb into bushes to avoid excessive heat. Near Alpine, Texas, Axtell (1960) observed a gravid female orienting parallel to the sun's rays in bush. The surface temperature of the nearby sand was 50°C. Desert and sand-dwelling tenebrionid beetles often raise themselves on their long legs as far as possible above the hot substrate. The shovel-snouted lizard, *Aporosaura anchietae*, has adopted a unique alternative. It arches the body, limiting bodily substrate contact to a small strip of the ventral surface (Brain, 1962). Another lizard, *Agama sanguinolenta*, avoids ground sands by climbing into bushes that are as much as 28 degrees cooler than the ground. The lizard *Phrynocephalus mystaceus* takes a midday posture such that its legs hold it well off the ground (Kashkarov and Kurbatov, 1930).

Artifacts
Few animals have adopted artifacts to enhance their thermoregulation. Many mammals roll in the mud of drying waterholes at certain seasons, changing their coloration and, inevitably, their heat-exchange characteristics. The actual role of this sort of behavior—practiced by pigs, buffalo, rhinoceroses, and elephants—has never been quantified or evaluated.

Man has been a good deal more resourceful than animals in his use of artifacts to regulate heat exchange, and these adaptations and their relevance to coloration are considered in the concluding chapters of this book.

Social Thermoregulatory Mechanisms
In spite of its significance to heat exchange, the basic body size is probably primarily a response to food supplies, predator-prey interactions, and social interactions rather than to heat-exchange relationships. Many animals are much smaller than the most effective size for maximum overnight or overwinter heat conservation, and aggregation has been a common evolutionary solution to this dilemma. Aggregation of several individuals secures some of the same advantages that are otherwise secured by an increase in body size. Clumping reduces the rate of heat exchange with the environment per unit biomass. On cold winter nights in Europe, tree creepers, tiny birds, gather in groups on the trunks of trees, often in locations so exposed that snow and ice crystals cover the birds. These birds hunt alone or in small bands during the day, and aggregation in the evening appears to be primarily thermoregulatory. On winter nights, bobwhite quail, *Colinus virginianus*, form a circle, bodies touching and heads pointed outward (Stoddard, 1936). However, this category of thermoregulatory adaptation is not limited to winter or even to temperate-region birds. In Kenya, bee eaters gather for the night in tight clusters, and mousebirds also pair off and press against one another, belly to belly, for the night.

Mammals are much more prone to clumping for thermoregulation than are birds. Aestivating ground squirrels huddle together in their underground dens, thus probably minimizing the energy expenditure required to maintain body temperatures above lethal minima. House mice, *Mus musculus*, use less food at low temperatures when they are allowed to huddle together. During bad weather, such as sudden storms, elk formations close ranks (Altmann, 1956). These clustered individuals may continue to graze or may stop eating and take shelter in fir thickets.

Some arctic human populations depend to a considerable extent upon body heat for warmth at night. Inland Eskimos aggregate in a small space in their unheated homes (Rasmussen, 1927). The hardy Siberian Chuckchee people have developed a remarkable cultural adaptation to take advantage of the collective heat of metabolism. Within their reindeer skin houses they construct an inner room, the dimensions of which are suited to the current number of residents. This inner room is simply a fur box, insulated from the floor by willow boughs and thick-furred hides. The top and sides are lined with new furs, sewn together and turned inward. At night the family enter from the lower front edge. In this small room within a room they spend the night, side by side. Perspiration, the plague of arctic and alpine explorers, tends to dampen their cubicle so that by morning the furs may be quite wet. This problem has a simple solution. Every morning the women remove the damp furs and lay them on the snow. A few minutes later they are able to shake out frozen flakes of moisture (Bogoras, 1904) and the furs are dry.

Another thermoregulatory clumping adaptation of man is found in the Kalahari Desert bushmen, who bed with their dogs. These people measure the night as a two-dog or a four-dog night (Tobias, 1964), according to the number of animals needed to warm a man. South American Indians use hairless dogs which maintain exceptionally high skin temperatures as living hot-water bottles (Morris, 1967).

Heat-conserving aggregations are also found among poikilotherms. Overwintering adult insects may use stored fat and food to maintain body temperatures well above ambient levels throughout the winter. Honeybees gather in a mass within the hive during the winter, and their metabolic heat maintains body temperatures several degrees above the temperature of the hive (Milum, 1928). Thermoregulatory clumping mechanisms have probably played a role in the evolution of sociality and group activities. The presence of this behavior in several otherwise solitary species shows the development of a circumstance-specific sociality in which intraspecific hostility and spacing mechanisms may be relaxed even to the extent of permitting physical contact.

ACTIVITY PATTERNS

The most important thermoregulatory behavior patterns are activity cycles. For many animals a change in location within the environmental mosaic can produce a shift in ambient conditions exceeding the seasonal fluctuations in conditions experienced at one point in the environment. The cycle of activity may involve long-term rhythms of activity extending through seasonal or daily regimens, or it may involve quite brief movements from one part of the environmental mosaic to another and back again. A more favorable heat balance can often be readily obtained at modest cost by simply moving from one environment to another. Some details of the particular case of flightless desert beetles are considered elsewhere.

Sorties between Light and Dark Environments

Rhythmical sorties into sunshine and timely retreat following an interval of sunning is a widespread thermoregulatory adaptation. This adaptation has been widely adopted by poikilotherms, but it is not exclusive to them. This tactic is particularly applicable to animals living where there is an opportunity to develop temperatures above 40°C for considerable periods of time. Because terrestrial animals are unable to adapt to persistent body temperatures above 42°C, the thermal potential of these environments cannot be fully utilized. This does not mean, however, that these environments are unusable because of heat-stress problems. Animals adopting sorties to manipulate their body temperatures are often small and able to retreat to cooler environments when the upper thermal limits are approached. Black desert beetles may burrow through sand as warm as 55°C to reach cooler sands only a few centimeters below.

The use of sorties to raise body temperatures is often coupled with color change. Certain fiddler crabs living on mud flats in tropical mangrove swamps, protected bays, and brackish waterways follow a period of exposure and dark coloration by retreat to a cooler burrow (Edney, 1961). Sorties from burrows constitute not only an opportunity to raise body temperatures, but also an opportunity to court and to secure food. Before retreating, these crabs blanch and, as the body temperature continues to rise, retreat to their cool burrows. Following an interval of cooling, they darken and return to the surface to repeat the cycle.

The sortie method of temperature manipulation is most obvious among small animals, particularly desert insects and lizards, where temperature rise is rapid and the cycle is short, noticeable, and predictable.

This sort of thermoregulatory behavior has traditionally been considered from a quite different perspective. Sorties may be interpreted as movements into an unfavorably warm environment, with subsequent retreat to cool environments. According to this view the cool portion of the paired environments is the more advantageous condition. Thus, the crab may be evading the heat, cooling off, then returning to feed and court until he becomes overheated again. Coloration relationships, however, confirm the significance of this behavior in securing the maximum radiant energy as well as extending the opportunity for the obviously significant activities of courtship and feeding.

In the Namib Desert, Neels Coetzee and I had an opportunity to establish the relative value of thermoregulatory behavior for the large vegetarian lizard, *Angolosaurus skoogi* (Hamilton and Coetzee, 1969). These lizards live in the sand dunes, and are particularly adept at plunging into the dry sand and screwing themselves deep into the sand to escape predators and extreme heat. What made the habits of this lizard particularly relevant to the present discussion is the relationship of the basking areas to the feeding places. Basking takes place on the vegetationless sand dune slopes and crests while food is secured at the dune bases and in the interdune valleys, the only place where leaves and blossoms from desert plants are available. Thus, the actions of the lizards on the dunes can be assigned a thermoregulatory and social role. When we observed the daily cycle of these lizards we found that they were spending almost all their above-surface time on the dunes. A few brief visits to the food sources were sufficient to supply their food resource needs. The rest of the day was spent in the sun, first manipulating posture and position to raise the body temperature, then adopting postures and location to stabilize the body temperature near 39°C. To me, these observations demonstrate the relatively great importance of maintaining a high rate of processing of food as opposed to a high rate of raw material acquisition.

Sorties and Man
The sortie method of heat reduction used by such a wide diversity of small animals is also characteristic of man. Human populations are darkest in tropical forests where sorties provide a consistent source of radiant energy and an available retreat from it. In the case of agricultural people, protection from overheating may be less feasible and the daily rhythmicity may involve retreat from solar radiation at midday. However, agricultural conditions are probably newer to man than his coloration characteristics. Tropical agriculture dramatically changes local climates, and the suffocating heat of the tropics is largely a man-made condition, confined to clearings and settlements. Beneath the humid tropical forest canopy a nearly perpetual coolness prevails, and when uncomfortable heat does prevail, it does not approximate the insufferable heat of man-made clearings. These observations lead to the conclusion that man's coloration and his agricultural activities in the tropics are not now in balance. But presumably man pursued quite different trades when his coloration was evolving.

INTERACTION EFFECTS

While certain components of temperature regulation have been considered separately insofar as possible, these parameters seldom if ever function by themselves. The temperature-regulation mechanisms of each individual operate as functional wholes, each parameter affecting the others. This is well illustrated, for example, by white birds, which share a combination of traits probably adapted to minimizing nocturnal heat loss. Heavy insulation, white coloration, and

Table 4-3. General sequence of the activation of thermoregulatory mechanisms of birds.

Cooling	Heating
Coloration, insulation proportions	Coloration, insulation proportions
Postural changes	Postural changes
Sorties into and out of sun	Sorties into and out of sun
Shivering	Panting

a specific relationship to a particular kind of habitat all go together (Chapter 2), each making the animal more efficient in its thermoregulation. Most animals have many thermoregulatory mechanisms. The sequence of their activation usually has been studied by manipulating environmental conditions so that it is difficult for the experimental animal to prevent a rise in body temperature. When this is done, it is found that there is a predictable sequence for the appearance of the alternative regulatory mechanisms. Certain mechanisms, such as postural changes and sorties, are less demanding of metabolic resources—energy and water—than physiological and physical temperature regulatory mechanisms. A basic principle seems to be that the mechanism that demands the least energy—and the least resources—is the first to be put into effect (see, e.g., Table 4-3).

Conclusions
1 The most significant behavioral thermoregulatory mechanism is the rhythm of activity. This may involve a circadian cycle of activity or short-term rhythms of movement within the environmental mosaic.
2 Rhythmical movement within the environmental mosaic may result in sequential exposure to thermal conditions which are more different than the entire annual range of conditions to which an animal would be exposed if it remained at one point in the environmental mosaic.
3 Insulation makes homeothermy possible, but it creates overheating problems when animals are active. Thus, insulation is reduced to a minimum and may be eliminated on certain parts of the body when behavioral thermoregulatory mechanisms are available.

DESERT COLORS

Are deserts thermally hazardous environments to animals living and evolving there? Has anyone observed the heat death of a desert lizard, beetle, or bird in a desert, unfettered by experimental paraphernalia? Do desert poikilotherms ". . . exist in a precarious thermal balance . . . subject to many thermal vagaries in environment" (Cowles, 1958, p. 356)? The long-standing contention that desert animals have more serious problems keeping cool than animals living in more mesic environments is highly debatable. The thermal limits of most of the desert animals noted in Table 1–3 are based upon *laboratory* experiments, performed in situations providing no escape from ambient conditions. Real deserts are a thermal mosaic, and a place of retreat is usually available when the desert surface becomes too hot. Rodents, lizards, and even some birds may retreat to cool semipermanent burrows. Insects, beetles in particular, may burrow directly through the sand, quickly reaching thermally tolerable sands only a few millimeters below the surface. Other insects may climb onto the sparse vegetation, escaping the soil surface and the hot air mass just above it. The fact that voluntarily adopted body temperatures approximate so closely lethal limits when relief is nearby may imply that heat death is a relatively unimportant threat to desert animals living in deserts. It is the opportunity to reach thermally favorable conditions that establishes the thermal suitability of an environment. The opportunity to use the thermal mosaic of each terrestrial environment in a favorable way is in turn related to the size, locomotion capacity, activity cycle, and other characteristics of each animal group and species. Thus, an environment that is favorable for one species may be hostile to another.

THE BLACK BEETLE PUZZLE

There is only one important exception to the generalization that desert animals resemble in colour the soil on which they live, but it is a most remarkable one; in many deserts a number of the indigenous animals are black. This is not commonly known, but is nonetheless fact. Speaking generally, it may be said that any desert creature which is not coloured like its surroundings is black, for bright greens and blues and reds and yellows are very rare; and though black animals are not a dominating element in the fauna, they are sufficiently numerous to be noticeable in many places in the Great Palearctic Desert (Buxton, 1923, p. 150).

Buxton had no satisfactory explanation for this paradox, nor have more recent authors. In comparison with other environments, a disproportionate number of the animal species inhabiting deserts are black. This has seemed to be a paradox because:

1 Excessive heat is a desert problem.
2 Black objects absorb more heat than paler ones.
3 Increased heat loads increase the problem of heat dissipation.
4 Heat dissipation is most effectively accomplished by evaporation of water.
5 Water is scarce on the desert.
6 The number of species and individuals of black beetles and other animals increases on the desert.
7 Since black coloration exaggerates heat gain, it seems maladaptive to desert animals.

This paradox was termed "the black beetle puzzle" by Meinertzhagen (1954). In Jerusalem, Buxton (1923) often saw the black tenebrionid beetle, *Zophosis punctata*, traveling across searing surface soils which measured as much as 63°C. On the Kalahari, Bolwig

(1957) reported black tenebrionids abroad at soil surface temperatures as high as 57°C. By almost any calculation, excessive heat
should be a problem at these temperatures, and if an animal were
exposed to solar radiation black coloration would exaggerate the
problem.

The black beetle puzzle is considered in detail here because of its
relationship to the problem of human skin coloration. Dark human
skin coloration is correlated with low latitude, another apparent
maladaptation. Thus for man, the problem is the same—a dark animal
in a warm climate. If some reasonable explanation of the black beetle
puzzle could be developed, it might also offer an explanation of the
phenomenon of dark human skin coloration.

Solution 1: Black coloration is an evolutionary legacy

Buxton's solution to the black beetle paradox was that black coloration might be an evolutionary legacy which was no longer adaptive:
"Further, we may suppose that *Adesmia* and the other diurnal
Tenebrionidae are black by inheritance, and that they have retained
the family's colours not because it was directly advantageous, but
because it was not disadvantageous" (Buxton, 1923, page 153).

The same argument has been recognized by Lowe and Hinds (1969)
who were concerned with the black coloration of nestling roadrunners, *Geococcyx californianus*. They concluded that for this
species blackness is a maladaptive legacy carried to the desert by
the forest-dwelling ancestors of roadrunners.

Some reasons why this argument is not valid are reviewed in subsequent consideration of hypotheses dealing with human hairlessness (page 174). A central difficulty with this sort of thing is that
diurnal animals are under consideration, and actual measurements
show that black coloration has a pronounced effect upon body
temperature. Thus black coloration can hardly be considered to be
of neutral value to diurnal desert-dwelling animals. Another equally
serious problem with this hypothesis is that the proportion of species
and individuals which are black, especially among birds and arthropods, increases in deserts. Some sort of positive adaptive value to
the color or a correlate of it is implied.

Solution 2: Black coloration provides offsetting advantages

Other solutions to the black beetle puzzle involve the concept of
offsetting advantages. Two additional steps to the logical argument
above are as follows:

8   The characteristics of animals have been shaped by natural selec-
    tion favoring positive adaptations.

9 Since black coloration is not positively advantageous to desert animals, melanin must provide an advantage unrelated to its blackness.

Suggestions for the advantages mentioned in step 9 include nearly all the alternative explanations of black coloration considered in Chapter 1.

Solution 3: Melanin Reduces Water Loss

One way to resolve the problem is by showing that the black coloration is correlated with some other significant benefit that more than outweighs the disadvantages of dark coloration. Meinertzhagen (1954) suggested that insects may be able to increase their impermeability to water only by darkening their cuticle. Melanin is apparently more waterproof than other pigments—a surprising claim, but one well substantiated by comparative and experimental evidence (Kalmus, 1941a, b).

In a more recent test of this hypothesis, Hamilton and Ohmart (personal data) measured the water loss of live black and white beetles of the same size and belonging to the same genus. At the end of 24 hours there was a significant difference between the two species which continued to increase throughout the experiment (Figure 5-1).

Figure 5-1. Weight (water) loss of black (*Onymacris laeviceps*) and white (*O. brincki*) Namib Desert beetles held without food under identical conditions. (From Hamilton and Ohmart, unpublished manuscript.)

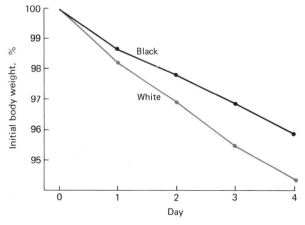

Solution 4: Black Coloration Enhances Heat Loss

The argument that black coloration enhances heat loss suggests that the first assumption of the black beetle paradox is erroneous. If so, the fabric of remaining discussions vanishes. Meinertzhagen (1954) supported this argument, while arguing that the decreased water loss which results from melanization will be less important than reducing heat received from the sun. Evidence for this hypothetical reduction in heat load, supposedly due to some feature of dark coloration, is based upon Buxton's (1924) finding that the body temperature of a black insect was *below* ambient levels. Buxton, however, did not state how long this beetle had been in the sun, and it seems likely that this individual had recently emerged from a cool subsurface retreat. More extensive measurements of the body temperatures of desert beetles (Hamilton, personal data) show that it is unusual for any diurnal desert beetle to have a body temperature lower than ambient temperatures.

Solution 5: Black is positively advantageous in enhancing heat gain

Most studies of desert environments have been made by white men and, consciously or otherwise, assumptions and choices of hypotheses have been biased by personal difficulties in adjusting to the desert. For the alien the thermal harshness of desert environments cannot be ignored, especially in the case of large terrestrial animals such as human travelers who are unable to burrow effectively. For small animals the problem is less difficult in the places and times it is active.

Earlier failures to develop the hypothesis that black coloration in desert-dwelling animals is adaptive in maximizing absorption of solar radiation stem not from any basic misunderstanding of the problems of desert animals and the physical conditions of the desert, but from failure to distinguish between physiological responses to heat stress and adaptive responses to intraspecific competition. The functional machine is best served by leaving a broad margin between body temperatures and thermally stressful temperatures. The response to competition is just the opposite, and that desert poikilotherms press to the edge of their thermal tolerance suggests that competitive forces prevail.

Of course, the restriction imposed by limited water resources of desert environments is real. Dramatic increases in abundance of desert life, including typical desert species, following sporadic rainfall or even the provision of localized water supplies which do not affect vegetation is ample evidence of this restriction. But the problem of water deficits is often effectively countered by behavioral thermoregulatory mechanisms which do not depend upon evaporative cooling. Cooling may be accomplished by any of the numerous behavioral thermoregulatory mechanisms described in Chapter 4. Black coloration may be a positive hazard under some circumstances, but this has not led to its elimination. Instead it has resulted in emphasis upon behavioral rather than physiological thermoregulation.

Black and White Namib Desert Beetles
In 1967 and 1968 I had the opportunity to test some of the above hypotheses in the African deserts, especially in the Namib Desert of Southwest Africa. This little-known desert is distinguished by its diverse diurnal tenebrionid beetle fauna (Koch, 1961, 1962a, b). The most remarkable distinction of this small desert is the presence of several white diurnal tenebrionid beetle species as well as the usual black species. These species provided an opportunity to consider the role of body coloration in thermoregulation and to test the maxithermy hypothesis further.

The Namib is a cool coastal desert (Figure 5-2). Long-term weather records are limited to a few stations, but there is a pronounced east-west climatic gradient across, with the coolest and most predictable weather prevailing along the coast. On any day this transition can be confirmed during a traverse from the coastal bench across the sand dunes to the barren inland gravel plains. Such a course intersects strikingly different climates, from uncomfortably cool to excessively hot. This climatic diversity is critical to the explanation of the coloration of the tenebrionids. Accompanying the great diversity of tenebrionid beetles in this desert, there is a narrowing in the breadth of environments occupied by the component species (Hamilton, in press). This can be demonstrated both for particular genera within the desert and relative to the tenebrionid beetles of other deserts. This habitat breadth is most easily defined in terms of space. Some species are confined to the coastal bench while others live well inland in regions which ordinarily are much warmer. If lethal temperatures and temperature preferences are related to ambient conditions, the species living nearest the coast should have considerably lower lethal and preferred body temperatures. If, on the other hand, these species are maxitherms, the lethal and preferred body temperatures of all the diurnal species should be about the same. Actual body-temperature measurements of these insects in the field demonstrate that there are, in fact, only slight differences among species (Table 5-1).

Black coloration does indeed exaggerate radiant heat gain, and

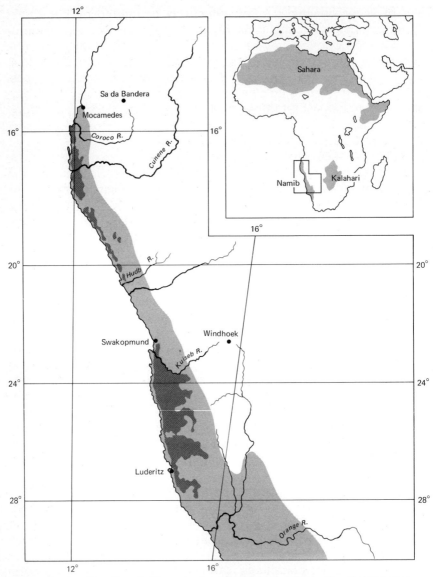

Figure 5-2. The Namib Desert of southwestern Africa. The lighter area receives less than five inches of rain per year. The darker areas are vegetationless dune areas referred to in the text.

white coloration is maximally effective in deflecting solar radiation (Table 5-2). If these beetles are adapted to maintain a body temperature between 36 and 40°C and if it is also advantageous to remain active as long as possible at these temperatures, then the ambient temperatures of specific environments become critical. While behavioral thermoregulation may be effective in manipulating heat exchange involving convection and radiation, it is completely ineffective in modifying heat exchange by conduction from the air. Thus a small poikilotherm quickly comes to equilibrium at or above ambient temperature levels. In the Namib, as in all deserts, ground surface temperatures quickly rise above ambient temperatures soon after sunrise, and by midday I have measured desert sand surfaces as much as 25.5°C warmer than air a meter above the surface. The hot substrate creates a narrow band of heated air just above the surface (Figure 5–3), and because of their small size and flightlessness, this is where the beetles must live. Because of their relatively small size, minimum body temperatures are determined by ambient conditions. Body temperatures are frequently much higher than ambient conditions; they are almost never lower. For this reason environments are habitable only when ambient temperatures are near or fall below 40°C. On many days such moderate conditions prevail in the space occupied by desert tenebrionid beetles only in the morning

Table 5–1. Mean lethal body temperatures and maximum voluntarily tolerated body temperatures of several Namib Desert (Southwest Africa) tenebrionid beetles (Hamilton, personal data). These sand-dwelling insects can attain lower body temperatures at any time simply by burrowing.

Species	Color	Habitat	Maximum Tolerated Body Temperature	Lethal Body Temperature
Onymacris laeviceps	Black	Inland sand dunes (vegetationless)	42.5°C	47.5°C
O. unguicularis	Black	Coastal sand dunes (vegetationless)	42.6°C	47.6°C
O. (undescribed)	White	Inland sand deposits (sparsely vegetated)	42.9°C	48.0°C
O. brincki	White	Intermediate sand dunes	43.8°C	47.8°C
O. bicolor	White	Intermediate sand dunes	40.9°C	48.7°C
O. candidipennis	White	Intermediate sand dunes	41.8°C	49.0°C

Table 5-2. Average body temperature relative to ambient temperature of live black (*Onymacris unguicularis*) and white (*O. brincki*) Namib Desert tenebrionid beetles matched for size and exposed to sunlight. These are the pooled results of paired experiments under natural conditions (Hamilton, personal data). Radiation and wind conditions change constantly, and hence the experiment is not precisely repeatable.

Color	Temperature in sunlight (sample size)	Temperature in shade (sample size)
	Experiment I	
Black	+4.18°C (8)	−0.71°C (8)
White	+2.16°C (8)	−1.26°C (8)
	Experiment II	
Black	+4.68°C (50)	
White	+2.08°C (50)	

and afternoon.   At midday soil surface temperatures may exceed 60°C, and ambient air temperatures just above the surface may rise well above 40°C. At this time, retreat to shade or beneath the soil is mandatory.   Under such conditions activity *must* be restricted to the beginning and end of the day, as in fact it is (Figure 5-3). At other times during the day, these beetles are shaded or have burrowed to cool subsoil environments and their coloration is irrelevant to heat exchange.   The maxithermy hypothesis predicts that in the morning activity period a maxitherm would benefit most by developing maximum temperatures as early as possible and maintaining them until ambient temperatures force it to retreat.   Black coloration combined with behavioral thermoregulation makes this possible. A black beetle in sunlight can develop a body temperature of 36°C when air temperatures have just passed 20°C. Thus, by behavioral means (Chapter 4) the beetles are able to attain and sustain an elevated body temperature for a considerable interval in the permissive morning activity period before they are required to retreat in order to escape the excessive heat.

   In the afternoon, activity becomes possible once more as ambient temperatures decline below lethal levels, i.e., below about 42°C. Thus, when the beetles finally do emerge for the period of afternoon activity, it is to an environment which is optimal, and maximal body temperatures are easily sustained.   However, this is but a point in time, and from this time on, the environment becomes thermally increasingly less favorable, i.e., cooler.   Thus a beetle can use all available heat, and maximum heat gain from radiation is advantageous during this activity period.

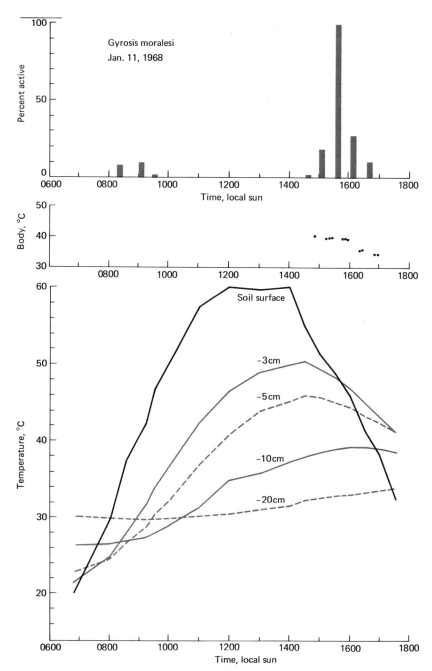

Figure 5-3. The black flightless beetle, *Gryosis moralesi,* is active above the surface of the desert sand during times when the body temperature can be maintained at a relatively high level, but below 40°C.

Thus, in this situation, where thermal environments become excessively hot in the middle hours of the day, black coloration is advantageous to poikilotherms. Since the 42°C limit is the same for all these animals, regardless of the environmental severity, and since almost all deserts are characterized by high heat, the widespread adoption of black coloration by desert poikilotherms is not surprising. In fact, the hotter the environment becomes, especially in deserts, the greater the advantage of black coloration, because in deserts high temperatures are extremes of drastic fluctuations in ambient temperatures rather than uniformly hot conditions (e.g., Figure 5–3). For a diurnal animal such conditions permit only short active intervals which can, however, be taken full advantage of by accepting almost all incident solar radiation.

This is my solution to the black beetle puzzle.

Let us consider the white Namib Desert beetles. How can these conclusions concerning black coloration be reconciled with the fact that, *on the same desert*, there are also chalky white beetles? During the course of the field investigation of this problem, several hypotheses were developed and tested. Most of these failed the test of evidence and are peripheral to this discussion. The most obvious suggestion is that the white coloration buffers its possessor from excessive desert radiation and overheating. If this hypothesis were acceptable, it would raise serious doubts concerning the adequacy of the solution to the black beetle puzzle already expressed. The Namib, however, is not as hot as other deserts which have only black or camouflaged beetles. Thus, adaptation to excessive heat as an explanation for white coloration is contradicted by the absence of white species in these other deserts. The inadequacy of this explanation is compounded when the environmental conditions these beetles encounter are compared with those of black relatives living on the same desert.

The white species are living in somewhat less rather than more extreme thermal environments. The intermediate nature of their environment apparently explains their unique coloration, as follows: There is one circumstance in which white coloration is effective in maintaining a maximum body temperature—under conditions where daily heat loads approximate but do not exceed levels that induce lethal body temperatures at midday. Under these critical thermal conditions, activity may be maintained through the middle of the day if the radiant heat load can be minimized. This is exactly what these white beetles do. Examination of their normal activity cycle shows that they are active at midday when the black species have already retreated. Thus, the most plausible explanation of the white tenebrionids is that they are adapted to intermediate heat loads which approximate but do not regularly exceed upper tolerable levels.

This solution, however, leaves unanswered the question of why there are no white tenebrionids on the other deserts of the world. Several other deserts have climatic gradients from the coast to the interior, producing conditions climatically favorable for white coloration. Why are there no white beetles on these deserts? One possibility is related to the extraordinary species diversity of Namib Desert tenebrionids. With the narrowing of spatial niches on the Namib (Hamilton, in press), new climatic conditions favor white coloration. Other deserts have fewer species and broader niches. Optimal adaptation to specific regions, such as those favorable to white coloration, may be evolutionarily impossible due to extensive gene flow which, considering the range of distribution as a whole, will favor black coloration and the appropriate behavior patterns to optimize thermoregulation relative to it.

The possibility that white coloration serves to reflect solar radiation was rejected earlier by Bolwig (1957), who found that these white tenebrionid species could not withstand higher temperatures than black species. His conclusions are irrelevant, for two reasons. Since the upper lethal temperature of most diurnal Namib Desert tenebrionid species is nearly identical, the fact that the lethal temperatures of white and black species do not differ is not surprising. Coloration differences do not need to influence lethal levels to be adaptive. In any case, in Bolwig's experiments the subjects received no light. A radiator was used as a heat source, apparently under the mistaken impression that it was an adequate substitute for the sun. It is true that the reflectances of these black and white beetles are little different at the infrared frequencies emitted by a radiator, but if Bolwig had used the sun in his experiments, his results would have been quite different.

Black Desert Homeotherms
The same evidence used above to explain the black beetle puzzle is applicable to desert homeotherms. Desert birds and mammals also tend toward blackness (Meinertzhagen, 1954). Furthermore, their behavior suggests emphasis upon behavioral thermoregulation. For example, the antelope ground squirrel, *Citellus leucurus*, has black skin beneath its background matching pelage. Do these under-colors protect their owners from harmful radiation in the excessive sunlight of their environment? Or are they adapted to optimizing thermoregulation? The same comparisons and lines of evidence, applicable to the problem of radiation protection in other environ-

ments, are relevant here. The behavior of these animals, their orientation of plumage and pelage, involving deliberate exposure to the sun, emphasize the significance of heat-gain adaptations.   For example, roadrunners, *Geococcyx californianus*, are birds of the Sonora Desert which generally have camouflaged contour feathers with black underfeathers.   At dawn on most days and during cold winter days, they deflect the outer feathers to the side, reducing their insulation and becoming black (Figure 2–4).   That this surface is exposed only during active sunbathing identifies the role of this coloration as heat absorption rather than radiation protection.

Is it possible that desert mammals such as the antelope ground squirrel would be *black* if it were not for pressure from predation? A case can in fact be made for this conclusion.   Consider the remarkable black jackrabbits, *Lepus insularis* (Bryant, 1891), of Espiritu Santo Island off the coast of Baja California.   This island is, by anyone's standard, a desert island.   The black jackrabbit of Espiritu Santo is closely related to the mainland jackrabbit, *L. californicus*. What condition on the island favored blackness and the loss of camouflage?   The widespread emergence of melanism on islands appears to be related to two circumstances: cool temperatures and a relative paucity of predators (Chapter 7).   The suggestion is that if predators were not present on the mainland, these homeotherms would also be black.

Desert ground squirrels fall into the same category.   If it were not for the presence of predators, they would probably be black.   There are times and places in the desert when heat is not oppressive, and an external heat source is valuable.   For example, I have observed sunbathing ground squirrels, *Citellus* sp., on the Sonora Desert near Puerto Penasco, Mexico, orienting their white undersides to the sun.   They climb to the tops of the scattered vegetation and retreat to burrows only when disturbed.

Black Coloration and Water Loss: A Fallacy?
Other premises of the black beetle puzzle (page 85) may be challenged.   An assumption of this paradox is that (1) all desert animals have "problems" keeping cool and (2) this cooling is primarily accomplished by evaporation.   Both conditions are true of man, but they are rarely applicable to desert animals.   Evaporative cooling appears to be a relatively unimportant adaptation of desert beetles.

Evaporative cooling by desert animals with limited potential water reserves, such as insects, is an ineffective way to keep cool.   When animals are unable to secure shade or cover and are exposed to environments which require cooling, this may be the *only* mechanism available, but its use is limited to the larger desert animals, especially those able to travel considerable distances. The locomotion capability of animals is relative with respect to microclimate, competitors, and predators. The locomotion apparatus of a grasshopper, for example, is well adapted to escape from a carnivorous mouse and to movement about its home range. But with respect to spatially distributed resources such as free water, locomotion capacity is an absolute. Desert insects, most of them flightless, have limited locomotion abilities and can reach open water only when by rare chance their place in the desert is near it. By comparison, a sandgrouse may depend upon an isolated pool of water 30 km from its nest or foraging grounds, and an oryx may return more than 50 km to a waterhole.

For this reason and because of their small size, evaporation is a poor way for most small desert animals to keep cool. Where water is concerned, the desert is much more of a desert for a flightless insect than for a bird or a large mammal. Instead of relying on evaporation, desert insects tend to emphasize behavioral thermoregulation. Furthermore, morphological adaptations such as the hard, nearly impervious chitinous exoskeleton and the fused sclerites of desert tenebrionid, curculionid, carabid, and cicindellid beetles (Hellmich, 1933; Hesse et al., 1937) emphasize the fact that evaporative water loss is minimized by these animals. Behavioral thermoregulation can proceed quite independently of water gain or loss. Suppose, for example, that our desert beetle were merely a sealed water-filled glass vial. Such an ampule will retain its water for centuries. If we wish to maintain the temperature of this vessel at 40°C, we have only to expose it to the sun until the desired temperature is reached, and then move it into the shade or soil. If this vessel were provided with legs, blackened, and given a will of its own, it would become a desert insect, predisposed to burrowing or seeking shade when the thermal optimum was reached. No water would be required beyond the initial supply.

The same considerations of locomotion capacity relative to water are applicable to shade. Diurnal desert birds may range miles into shelterless space in the early and late hours of the day and still be able to secure shade when necessary. I have seen the wide-ranging pied crow, *Corvus albus*, travel 30 km from shade on the vegatationless Namib Desert gravel plains; but this is less than an hour's flight to potential cover. The same is true of the ostrich. I have often seen black male ostriches in barren desert environments which offer no shade for such a large animal, but generally they retreat during the heat of the day, seeking the shelter of a thorn tree along some dry creek bed or a rocky outcrop. During the day the female, who is paler and better camouflaged than the male, broods the eggs.

In a group of desert birds, wheatears, Buxton noted:

> In some species the blackening has proceeded further in the male than in the female, in other species both sexes are equally black. It appears therefore that these birds have evolved their blackness because in some way it fits them to a desert existence. . . . This is the more remarkable because within the limits of the same genus (*Saxicola*) there are birds which inhabit the same deserts and which are coloured like the soil on which they live; examples are the Isabelline Wheatear (*S. isabellina*) and the Desert Wheatear (*S. deserti*), both of which are widely distributed in the Great Palaearctic Desert, and occur side by side with various black and white congeners. The habits of the black and white Wheatears closely resemble those of the other members of the genus, that is to say that they are wary birds, given to perching on upstanding rocks and, at any rate to my eyes, easy to see when they are sitting still, and extremely conspicuous when they move (Buxton, 1923, pp. 154–155).

Meinertzhagen's (1954) observations offer an answer. He noted that the black desert birds generally occur where some shade is available, and this shade is utilized in the hottest part of the day. By contrast, the paler cryptic species seldom shelter, even in the heat of the day. This agrees with my observations of the coloration-habitat relationships of arid region birds. The black species live at the desert edge, where some vegetation persists. This vegetation is well utilized for cover in the heat of the day. Conditions which provide radiation protection for one group may not be adequate for another. In vegetationless regions of extremely low rainfall where black insects flourish, there are no black birds. This is instead a region of pale cryptic species, hues which also are highly reflective. In general, we can conclude that a particular environment is less of a desert in terms of heat-exchange problems and water loss for one animal group than it is for another, and the extent of each group's adaptation can in part be measured by the severity of the environment occupied by the black species belonging to that group. These species are living under optimal thermal conditions, not under conditions of persistent thermal stress.

Metabolic-strength Hypothesis

The metabolic-strength hypothesis for black coloration (page 87) may be applicable in any environment. It is perhaps especially relevant to desert beetles which travel about at ground level where sandstorms are commonplace. On the Sahara near Cairo, I have seen the black tenebrionid beetle *Pimelia angulata* walking at right angles to moving sands that strip the lacquer from an automobile in an hour. The bodies of these beetles showed no signs of wear, but the legs of older specimens were often broken or missing. The abdomens of dead individuals likewise show little evidence of erosion and may blow about on the desert sands for months after death. Because of the relative longevity of these insects, a durable structural material would have a high adaptive premium, and the strength of melanin probably adds to its adaptive value on the desert. Perhaps the information most relevant to this hypothesis comes from the black and white Namib Desert beetles. The white species, particularly *Onymacris candidipennis* and *Onymacris brincki*, are commonly dented, and it is not unusual to find a living specimen with a hole worn completely through its carapace. By comparison, the black beetles are rarely dented, and I have never found them with worn spots. These observations would seem to further support the metabolic-strength hypothesis.

Conclusions on Black Desert Coloration

The preceding discussions support the hypotheses that: black desert coloration (1) is an adaptation to thermoregulation, (2) prevents water loss, (3) strengthens the integument, and (4) may secure radiation protection. Are we left to conclude that the prevalence of melanism on deserts has several adaptive bases, and that it is impossible to distinguish the relative significance of each? This is overcompromise. That melanism has emerged in completely independent phyletic lines suggests that there is some leading variable in this convergence common to each phyletic line. The several hypotheses are not equally applicable in all cases. For example, radiation protection is probably irrelevant to well-insulated animals such as mammals and birds. The amount of dangerous ultraviolet radiation reaching the skin surface and vital internal organs is surely minimal. The role of black pigmentation in conserving water is more important to arthropods, but it is an unlikely explanation for the coloration of birds and mammals, which also show the tendency toward desert melanism. The same logic may be applied to the metabolic-strength argument. There is no reason to suppose that birds and mammals have more serious wear problems on deserts than elsewhere. Of all the hypothetical explanations of desert blackness, only the heat-exchange hypothesis has general applicability to all the desert groups which have become black.

ADAPTIVE CONSTELLATIONS

The evolution of black and white coloration by Namib Desert beetles and the absence of intermediates between these extremes illustrate a phenomenon which will be considered in several contexts in this book. This phenomenon concerns the adaption of a group of characteristics which serve to optimize another characteristic. Such groups of traits are referred to collectively here as an "adaptive constellation." This term evades the question of which traits have led and which have followed in an evolutionary sequence.

In the case of the black and white Namib Desert beetles, a group of mutually reinforcing characteristics, behavioral and morphological, can be identified (Table 5-3). The two groups of traits are essentially opposite, and the adoption of any one trait predisposes the species toward adaptation of the other attributes. In the case of the adaptations summarized in Table 5-3, it is apparent that, given a maxithermy, the other traits follow.

Additional examples of adaptive constellations, particularly with respect to man's convergence with other large animals upon a syndrome of characteristics, are considered in later chapters.

COMMUNICATORY DESERT COLORATION

Black, white, and pale shades of sandy grey and ochre are the most frequent desert animal colors (Pradhan, 1957). There are few brightly colored birds on the desert, and bright colors are completely lacking in desert mammals. In a survey of North African desert homeotherms 24 of 47 bird species and 39 of 50 mammals matched their backgrounds (Heim de Balsac, 1936). Most of the rest were black, white, or black and white. That this should be true of desert mammals is no surprise, since they are nocturnal and must rely upon olfaction

Table 5-3. The adaptive constellation of traits correlated with coloration in black and white Namib Desert beetles, genus *Onymacris*.

Trait	Adaptation	
Coloration	Black	White
Activity pattern	Diurnal bimodal, beginning and end of day	Diurnal, single peak of activity, middle of day
Behavioral response to overheating	Burrow when overheated	Seek shade or climb when overheated

and audition in most of their communication. Thus they would gain little by adopting colorful visual signals. Nor is black coloration of much value to a nocturnal animal in heat exchange. But there are many diurnal birds on the desert, and some explanation of their failure to develop brightly colored species is required, especially since the properties of light seem well suited to visual communication in the open desert environment. In deserts, however, plant resources are reduced due to water limitations, and as a result the overall biomass of the fauna is diminished. This results in a paucity of individuals of each species and an expansion of the individual's space. Song perches are more scattered, and in many desert environments they may be lacking altogether. The pyramid of numbers is still operative, but the absolute abundance of species and individuals is much reduced, increasing the spatial domain of each individual. This in turn increases the relative significance of vocalization in territorial defense. Under this circumstance, loud vocalizations are characteristic (Hamilton and Hamilton, 1965), and the attention-getting value of morphological-visual displays may be reduced because of the small part of the visual field they subtend. Even if song posts were available, they would not only announce to competitors the individual's exclusive rights but also announce his presence to potential prey. Visual signals are uncoded messages. If the preponderance of additional selective forces upon desert birds can be assigned to energy colors and camouflage, the relative value of each is automatically elevated by the exclusion of sexual coloration. This situation contrasts sharply with jungle and forest understory, where the potential value of black coloration to thermoregulation is generally excluded, and the balance shifts to sexual and cryptic colors.

DESERT CAMOUFLAGE

Predation and Desert Coloration—An Old Fallacy
Many of those who are most familiar with deserts minimize the role of predation there (Buxton, 1923; Bodenheimer, 1954; Meinertzhagen, 1954). These men have lived in deserts; their collective years observing predatory birds, the most common predators upon other small birds, should place them in a position to comment on the significance of desert coloration—and they minimize the role of predators. In spite of their familiarity with deserts, however, their conclusions are probably in error. Their mistake stems not from unfamiliarity with desert animals but from a failure to appreciate the mechanism of natural selection. The evidence, so convincing to these masters of desert biology, is assignable to three general categories:

1 Predacious birds are rare on the desert and show little interest in other birds as prey items. Predation is rarely observed on the desert, and the predation rates seem noticeably lower in deserts than in other environments (Buston, 1923; Meinertzhagen, 1954).

2 The actions of these cryptic species give them away, destroying any possible protective value of surface coloration (Etchecopar and Hüe, 1957, among others). This general argument has been advanced as a challenge to the camouflage hypothesis for animal coloration in all environments.

3 The colors of these desert animals do not precisely match their backgrounds, and the match is not as good as in other environments where it is often quite precise.

The first argument is based on the fallacious premise that mortality rates and the strength of natural selection are synonomous. Selection must be measured in relatives rather than absolutes, and to analyze coloration in these terms requires that the adaptive alternatives—sexual, cryptic, and energy coloration—be measured against one another rather than separately. Selection does not operate upon traits as discrete entities. The absolute value of selection is relative to all other selection values operating on different traits and structures. Relative interdependence of these characteristics varies. Because the surface of an animal can only be one color, the relative values of the several bases of coloration are absolutely interdependent. Furthermore, selection must be evaluated relative to avoidable rather than absolute mortality. Some mortality is unavoidable and, affecting all members of the population indiscriminately, does not represent selection. Other sources of mortality are partly avoidable. But it is quite possible that in the desert the absolute value of all selection pressures upon surface coloration is reduced. Because of the relative nature of selection, intuitive interpretation of the significance of selection in any particular situation or environment may be misleading. Even an intimate knowledge of desert conditions and a lifetime spent in the study of the habits of animals may lead to erroneous conclusions concerning the role of coloration unless this experience is measured against an understanding of the mechanisms and limitations of evolutionary processes. Undoubtedly, as knowledge in this field continues to expand, there will have to be continuing reinterpretation of what we see in nature.

While this may seem obvious, they have nonetheless proved to be the flaw in certain relatively recent arguments. Mayr (1963), for example, repeats Buxton's (1923) conclusion that certain prominent characteristics of animals, such as the colors of desert animals, have no adaptive value per se, and he remains puzzled about their adaptive significance.

Critics of the predation-protection interpretation of desert coloration also fail to take into account that selection operates on factors other than mortality; selection for productivity and energy efficiency may play a role in establishing the direction of selection. It does not take a lethal attack by a predator to induce selection for camouflage. If a prey species must flee or is induced to expose its eggs, selection will ultimately be involved.

The second argument, that the movements of protectively colored species give them away, assumes that animals have a single line of defense against predation. As with most adaptive processes—temperature regulation, for example (Chapter 4)—there are many adaptive responses to predation. Camouflage is only one of them. When it fails, other defenses—flight, distress calls, and biting—come into play. But this does not mean that camouflage is ineffective as an adaptation to predation evasion.

Given this combination of misconceptions about the operation of selection and a failure to appreciate one of the relative values (radiation colors), it is not surprising that these earlier workers were perplexed by desert animal coloration.

Gene Flow as a Constraint upon Selection
The third argument concerns the inaccuracies of desert camouflage and failure of the expectation that selection should lead to nearly perfect camouflage if it is based upon predation. The homogenizing action of selection may account for this inaccuracy. There may be genetic exchange throughout the geographic range of an animal species. The effect of natural selection upon each population will be to adjust that population to local conditions. However, the mosaic of environmental conditions upon which the galaxy of species populations exists may be arranged so that genetic interchange between adjacent populations prevents precise adaptation to local conditions. Elsewhere, Ehrlich and Raven (1969) have emphasized the small amount of gene flow between certain plant and animal populations. Their examples emphasize small disjunct populations. But certain populations of animals may have relatively large, mobile, and wide-ranging populations, and gene flow may occur across broad geographic expanses. According to this concept, gene flow may be a constraint upon adaptation when:

1 The environmental condition to which adaption is related is spatially or temporally heterogeneous relative to the constituent populations

2   Barriers to genetic exchange between adjacent populations are
    weak or lacking

The desert may be a singularly difficult environment in which to
avoid the limitations imposed by free gene flow (page 21). Sparse
or lacking vegetation exposes soils and rocky backgrounds. Unlike green or dried vegetation, these backgrounds may vary extensively in coloration from place to place, often over relatively short
distances. Norris and Lowe (1964) have shown that the effectiveness
of the camouflage of Sonoran Desert lizards is correlated with background homogeneity.

Another constraint imposed by free gene flow upon coloration
adaptation of desert birds concerns the general lack of geographic
isolating mechanisms in these environments which are relevant
to birds. The discussion of coloration failures by desert birds has
generally dealt with open-country species, larks and wheatears in
particular. These species may occur over vast areas. With unre-
stricted gene flow between adjacent populations living on soils
of various colors, there may be limited opportunity to adapt precisely
to the local conditions of observation (page 21). The same principle
may be applicable to other animal groups. On the northern Namib
Desert there occurs a small flightless tenebrionid beetle, *Zophosis
sexcostata*. This insect has an unusual reddish-pink pubescence
over its black cuticle. Koch (1962b) observed this reddish beetle on
white coastal sand dunes near Porto Alexandre. There it is a poor
match with its background, and Koch concluded logically enough
that camouflage could not explain its coloration. In 1968 I visited this
area and observed the situation near Porto Alexandre: the pink
beetles do indeed stand out against their white background. Later,
however, I discovered additional populations to the interior, many
miles from the coast. There the sands are a remarkable pinkish red,
the same color as *Z. sexcostata*. Investigation of an extensive part
of the Angolan Namib, which is the range of this species, showed that
most of its habitat was in previously unexplored pink sand dunes.
Thus the coloration of this species throughout its range is understandable in terms of camouflage and gene flow from the area of
population center to a peripheral area where the color is not adaptive [see Figure 1–5b, where population A_4 would represent the Porto
Alexandre conditions and A the inland populations of *Z. sexcostata*].

The same principle almost certainly is applicable to a diversity of
animal adaptations. For example, colorful reef-type fishes extend
into deep waters where it is doubtful that there is enough light to
produce their colors. These fishes generally are species that are
more numerous in shallower waters where their colors are visible

and biologically relevant to communication. That light is necessary for coral growth emphasizes the presence of light in the evolution of reef fishes (Hamilton, personal data).

Reality of Desert Predation
The argument that predation evasion has not produced cryptic coloration in the desert must be accepted if visual predators are altogether lacking in desert environments. This is not the case. The desert kestrel, *Falco sparverius*, captures insects, and roadrunners prey upon lizards. There are a host of other desert hawks, predatory mammals, and insect-eating lizards. While Buxton (1923) argued that cryptic coloration does not secure predator protection to small birds in the North African desert, he acknowledged the considerable role of predation and predators during the nesting season. Many desert birds are incubating during the warmer season, and protection of eggs from overheating is imperative. Many nesting desert birds sit tight and permit relatively close approach before flushing. This habit exposes them to additional predation hazard, increasing the advantage of camouflage. The question, therefore, seems to be concerned with the amount of predation rather than its presence or absence. Once the discussion takes on this frame of reference, the arguments already developed must be reconsidered.

A review of the literature leads to the disappointing conclusion that evidence dealing with desert predator-prey relationships is confined to comparative analyses and is devoid of long-term quantification that would permit life-table analyses. The requirements for such a study would be: (1) that it involve nongame (unexploited by man) species; (2) that the species investigated live in the desert and not migrate to more mesic regions; and (3) that the study include several years of measurements, not only of density but also of sources of mortality. This means that such investigations must be done by teams or individuals living on the desert and making continual measurements. The general pattern of investigators in deserts has been to explore local areas intensively for short periods, then retreat to moderate regions, a performance which obviously precludes development of long-term life-table material. Thus, actual measurement of the impact of predation upon desert animals has never been made.

Cryptic Coloration and Behavior
Some desert animals respond directly to background coloration, actively seeking substrates which match their own coloration. Certain Saharan larks are reluctant to leave the soils they match, even when hard pressed by man (Buxton, 1923). Other species fail to show

this response, and if an animal does not by chance happen to seek cover in the appropriate background it may, in spite of its stillness and protective coloration, be conspicuous. This difference between species presumably is related to the probability that a particular species will by chance reach a background matching its color.

Physiological-correlation Hypothesis

Another hypothesis advanced to explain the pale colors of desert animals is that they represent a response to some environmental condition influencing coloration, but that coloration is not the actual adaptation. This hypothesis seems to be supported by the demonstrated role of throxine and other body chemicals which influence the intensity of pigmentation when experimentally manipulated. Mayr (1942), for example, appealed to this logic in attempting to interpret the knotty desert coloration problem for birds: "We must rather assume that the inheritance of general size or of the degree and kind of pigmentation is correlated with some organ (let us say the thyroid or pituitary) the variation of which is of selective value" (p. 88).

There are certainly physical traits which result from some other adaptation, and Mayr's statement may indeed explain many of the subtle characteristics of animals. But traits such as coloration are not likely to be derived so casually. That developmental mechanism relies upon a certain pathway provides no evidence that these inner workings are the adaptive basis of the trait in question.

Direct Effect of Background on Coloration

A related hypothesis is that the pale colors of desert animals are the result of some direct effect of the environment upon the colors of its inhabitants. Etchecopar and Hüe (1957) contend that the pale coloration of desert animals is often the result of bleaching in the desert sun. They conclude that background coloration is based upon the climate, the nature of the soil, and food, and that somehow it is a defense against excessive heat. Bodenheimer, another lifelong inhabitant of and traveler in Old World deserts, concluded:

> Mammals and birds show prevalently buff, sandy, pale grey, or spotted colours and remain hidden during the day; or when they are diurnal, their chief enemies are nocturnal. Buxton, Heim de Balsac and Morrison-Scott have thoroughly destroyed the legend that this type of colouration is primarily protective. We have to be satisfied with the statement that this "adaptive" colouration is primarily a physiological effect of dry heat on the development of pigments (Bodenheimer, 1954, p. 165).

But now that it is apparent that coloration adaptations to radiation almost inevitably involve the adoption of black, white, or black and white coloration, this argument seems implausible. It is always possible that some unidentified physiological factor or factors, yet to be identified, have not been included in the present analysis. Where known components and combinations fail to make sense and fail to explain the variance of the system, additional explanations and phenomena must be sought.

OLD ARGUMENTS AND OLD PROBLEMS

They Are Nocturnal Anyway

It is widely stated that background-matching coloration of desert animals secures no protection from nocturnal predators, particularly for rodents such as kangaroo rats and gerbils, and that their colors, which closely match backgrounds, must be explainable on some basis other than predation. It is assumed that the colors of these animals cannot be seen by visual predators. The same argument was advanced years ago by workers concerned with interpretation of the pelage coloration of ground-dwelling rodents such as pocket gophers. Some of these questions were relevant, but Dice's experiments (1945, 1947) conclusively demonstrated the ability of night-hunting owls to select rodents visually against color-matched and color-mismatched substrates. He showed that visual discrimination of prey species by owls was possible from 6 feet at light levels as low as 0.0000007 footcandle. Nocturnal illumination from the moon and zodiacal light is based largely upon reflected sunlight. Thus, the color spectrum of nocturnal illumination is similar qualitatively to daytime conditions. Hence camouflage can best be achieved by nocturnal prey species by matching the color spectrum of background materials. However, since the visual acuity of nocturnal animals is scotopic, i.e., shifted in the direction of red light range, selection for background matching may extend to the near infrared. The whole matter of background matching by nocturnal animals and the color vision of nocturnal predators has been little studied. One tacit assumption is that visual discrimination at these low light intensities is based entirely upon contrast rather than color. However, the precise match of some nocturnal rodents to the soils on which they live would seem to imply that predators have color vision nearly to the limits of visual sensitivity. The question of the nocturnal vision of predators is essentially an unexplored area of investigation and one particularly relevant to hot deserts where nocturnal life predominates.

POIKILOTHERMY VERSUS HOMEOTHERMY
ON THE DESERT

Thermal Lability of Desert Homeotherms

The relative merit of thermal lability versus thermal constancy in deserts has received considerable attention. Schmidt-Nielsen (1964) has argued that the capacity of homeotherms to maintain a nearly constant body temperature is an effective adaptation to desert life. The validity of this argument is debatable. Given the problem of excessive heat gain, poikilothermy provides a wider margin between thermal limits because the body can absorb heat at the same rate longer before reaching sublethal levels. The partial poikilothermy exhibited by the camel (Schmidt-Nielsen et al., 1957) is an uncommon adaptation for mammals, and its adoption by an arid-zone animal emphasizes the advantage of using the body as a heat sink. A number of the large diurnal east African mammals also show exceptional thermal lability (Richard Taylor, personal communication) and, while they are not ordinarily considered to be desert animals, some of the plains species share the exposure problems of large desert mammals. When it becomes too hot there is no place to go. Thermal lability may also permit a considerable savings in overnight energy expenditure, since body temperatures can be dropped at night and raised again during the day, saving energy which would otherwise be required to maintain body temperature. Another important advantage of thermal lability is water economy, since evaporative cooling can thus be deferred or circumvented. By comparison, unyielding temperature constancy requires homeotherms to expend water for cooling as soon as ambient temperatures exceed a species' thermoneutral level when behavioral thermoregulation is inadequate.

Hot and Cold Desert Animals

The definition of what constitutes a desert is based primarily upon rainfall and vegetation. Thermal conditions are not included in the definition, and thermal conditions vary markedly from desert to desert. These differences include two general sorts: the amount of seasonal thermal change and the mean thermal level. Most deserts are not tropical and undergo extensive seasonal climatic fluctuations. A few smaller deserts are equatorial, coastal, or both, but even these deserts are affected, as tropical forests are, by seasonal fog or cloud cover.

The general nature of the climate has profound implications for the characteristics and habits of the resident fauna. These differences, particularly in temporal patterns of activity, can be explained only by the maxithermy hypothesis. If animal physiology systems had limitless adaptability to thermal environmental conditions, the adaptations of the animals of each desert would be similar. But, especially for poikilotherms, this is not the case. In hot deserts such as the North American Sonoran Desert there is probably much more biomass tied up by nocturnal animals than in cool deserts such as the Namib. This difference is related to prevailing thermal conditions. Conditions permit maximum body temperatures, 35°C and higher, to develop daily on the Namib, and such thermal conditions may persist for several hours. In the Sonora Desert, particularly in the summer, such thermal conditions are fleeting during daytime. On the other hand, because of the hot nights, these body temperatures can be sustained for considerable periods at night. If there were no limit to thermal adaptability, the Sonoran fauna would not have emphasized nocturnality to such a degree. The faunal patterns of other deserts may be interpreted in similar ways. Animal life systems on the Sahara Desert are highly seasonal. Temperatures are moderate in winter and hot from late spring through fall. Diurnal activities of lizards and ground-dwelling beetles prevail in the cool seasons. In summer heat the system shifts to nocturnal species and forms whose specialization is to life in the shade of vegetation.

The degree to which each faunal component responds to the climate depends upon the degree of buffering from the environment. Ground-dwelling poikilotherms such as lizards and tenebrionid beetles take the full and immediate impact of the environment. Other diurnal animals such as some insects, birds, lizards, and small mammals may avoid the full impact of the environment either by aerial flight or by living in vegetation.

CONCLUSIONS

Lethal and preferred animal body temperatures are no higher in desert environments than in more moderate conditions. Many desert animals prefer body temperatures a few degrees below lethal levels, at approximately 40°C. Small desert animals cannot maintain life conditions at ambient temperatures above 40°C, and must secure shade, burrow, or climb into vegetation to reach cooler conditions when this temperature is exceeded on the desert floor. Since this preferred level generally is present during only a small part of the day and it is advantageous for a poikilotherm to maintain high body temperatures for as long as possible, behavioral thermoregulation often emphasizes radiative heat gain. Black coloration enhances this process.

PART 2   POPULATIONS

Comparative studies of animal behavior dealing with the question of the role of man in nature inevitably draw upon a limited part of the available evidence. Often the limitation is quite deliberate. For example, people study wolves or chimpanzees and ask how they are different from or similar to man and what these relationships tell us about man. Or the comparison may be broadened, perhaps to include all primates, or at least all the primates for which there is a significant body of knowledge. These more general comparisons are common in the contemporary literature, and they are legitimate as long as the limitation of the approach is recognized. It is possible to deny the validity of any animal-man comparison and to suggest, as Niko Tinbergen has done, that if studying comparative animal behavior has anything to offer to our understanding of man, it is the methods we have developed in such studies. Thus, Tinbergen is suggesting that direct observations involving free-ranging human subjects belonging to different populations and with different histories are the stuff for conclusions about man's past and present nature.

There is still another approach which has been widely used. This is to make comparisons on the broadest possible scale, including the entire animal kingdom insofar as it is known to the comparative analyst. When the extension to man is made, the results may differ to an astonishing degree. Thus, in the early part of this century, Kropotkin and then Alee came to the conclusion that man was and is a fundamentally cooperative and peaceful species. The same approach led to a different conclusion when the practitioner of the comparative art was Ardrey, Lorenz, or any one of several other contemporary advocates of primitive aggression. Different conclusions based upon similar data emphasize the dangers of this approach. A well-informed artist can weave a web of apparent evidence that to the uninitiated is both interesting and convincing.

The approach taken in this part is a variation on this latter scheme. Evidence is carefully selected and broadly comparative. What, it is hoped, gives these comparisons a certain validity is that they are applied to the principles and processes of life rather than directly to the phenomena of man. But inevitably the comparison comes down to an extension of the analysis to a single species, man, and the method becomes strained beyond its valid limits. The strength of the comparative method is in distinguishing evolutionary trends and the sorts of environmental factors that are correlated with them and may have caused them. These trends are best distinguished when a group of organisms are under consideration. In the case of man the placement of a single species with a particular group is a hazardous conceptual extension, subject to the synthesizer's entire collage of cultural biases. Thus, the reader should realize that although the comparisons that follow may be satisfying to the author, they are bound to be unacceptable and sometimes even offensive to skilled and well-informed analysts with different experiences in science and life. This is the nature of the method and its conclusions. Secure conclusions concerning man's present are hard enough to come by, and an unequivocal reconstruction of his past is impossible.

TRADES, TOOLS, AND MAN

Predators are organisms which capture and devour other organisms. The effectiveness of predators in prey capture and the effectiveness of prey species in avoiding predators has a considerable influence upon the coloration options available to predator and prey when the hunter, the hunted, or both can distinguish colors. When prey species are able to avoid or minimize the impact of visual predation in some way other than camouflaging themselves, there is an increased relative value to other adaptive bases of coloration. For this reason the significance of predation to coloration begins with a review of some of the ways that animals avoid being preyed upon.

Predation Evasion

It is this recurrence of blackness, in widely separated groups of animals, which is so remarkable. If we may postulate that the Raven has no predaceous enemies, that *Eugaster* [a grasshopper] is protected by its oily secretion from whatever enemies it has, and that the Wheatears evade the hawk by quickness and watchfulness, then we can understand that desert-colour is not necessary to these animals. But at once we are faced with their unanimous choice of black: If they are freed from the necessity of being buff, why are none of them green, or red, or blue? (Buxton, 1923, p. 167.)

Thus Buxton answers a question he could not pose: If black coloration is potentially advantageous to all diurnal animals, why haven't they all adopted it? Buxton understood the relatively slight significance of predation to certain desert animals, but it seemed obvious to him that black coloration was disadvantageous. Some possible reasons why heat and black coloration are valuable to desert animals have already been considered in Chapter 5 (page 88). An animal's coloration is often a living record of the most important basis of selection relative to predation, communication, and metabolism. Energy colors are adopted only when predation by or upon a species or morph is less important than other selection pressures influencing coloration. This relationship is shown diagrammatically in Figure 6–1. In this example the potential adaptive value of camouflage, communication, and energy coloration is compared with the amount of body surface actually allocated to that adaptation. In (a) the potential adaptive value of energy coloration exceeds that of communicatory coloration and camouflage combined and most of the body surface is denoted to energy coloration. A small surface area is allocated to communication, approximately in proportion to its potential adaptive value. In (b) the potential adaptive value of energy and camouflage coloration are equal, but, because energy and communicatory coloration are compatible, the actual allocation of body surface area is to these adaptations which are in sum greater than that of camouflage. Relative values of potential adaptations surely change in the course of evolution, and the balance may tip from one adaptation to another.

The relative value of predation can be minimized in many ways. Reduction or elimination of the need for camouflage is most commonly achieved by adopting a particularly effective defense mechanism. In addition, the animal must not be an active stalking predator or a sentinel hunter (page 117), since these hunting tactics often depend upon camouflage. Once an animal has, by whatever means, reduced the relative value of camouflage, the relative value of other coloration adaptations increases.

Animals range from complete palatability to toxicity so great that

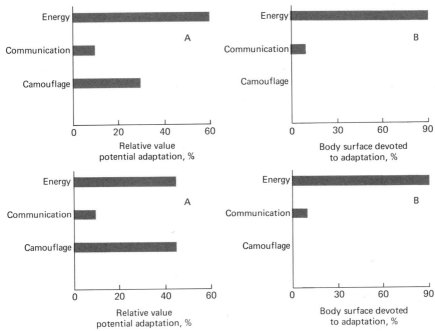

Figure 6-1. Two examples of the relationship of the relative value of different coloration adaptations to the actual colors adapted. The relative values of the different adaptive bases of coloration together is 100 percent, but they are not necessarily expressed in proportion to their potential value because the expression of camouflage and other adaptations are incompatible with one another.

small amounts of their flesh are lethal to large animals. The examples from insects are numerous; many beetles are highly distasteful (Eisner and Meinwald, 1966), and the flesh of birds varies in palatability (Cott, 1940), with relatively conspicuous species tending to be the least palatable.

Animals lacking morphological and biochemical adaptation to predation avoidance may defend themselves from predators by behavior patterns alone. Many animals that have adopted energy and communication colors compensate for their relative conspicuousness by being extremely alert rather than depending upon well-developed defensive weapons. Several animals with no obvious defenses other than aggregation are far more wary than their cryptic relatives. Alertness is a difficult attribute to measure, but the watchful wariness of black birds such as crows and ravens is well known. Beebe's (1926) comments on the conspicuous white Himalayan pheasant, *Crossoptilan tibetanum*, emphasize a difference in demeanor between this conspicuous species and a well-camouflaged relative, *C. manchurium*:

> I was impressed with the difference of action of this White Crossoptilan as compared with that of the browneared Pheasant in the presence of a bird of prey. The latter crouched at once, merging their somber forms with the surrounding rocks and grass. These birds stood erect, ready for instant movement, but without a hint of attempt at concealment (Beebe, 1926, p. 120).

An aggressive attitude may represent an effective defense, particularly when it is a group activity. The long-tailed drongo is an aggressive black bird that often attacks other considerably larger birds (Ripley, 1964). This bird is otherwise without notable adaptations for defense, although the flesh of all the drongos is said to be of poor flavor. The aggressiveness of North American blackbirds is astonishing. These birds may gather to mob potential predators in the vicinity of their nests, and commonly pursue aerial predators such as crows and hawks far beyond the boundaries of their breeding territories.

Further recitation of the relative effectiveness of the defences of uncamouflaged animals could be extended to diverse organisms from a variety of phyletic groups. But the point seems best made in consideration of specific instances (see Table 6–3 in particular).

KINDS OF PREDATORS

There are several well-defined, mutually exclusive kinds of hunting patterns. Evaluation of hunting tactics is helpful in establishing the role of coloration in predator-prey relationships. Certain predators shift from one hunting pattern to another according to circumstances, but most of them are committed to a single hunting pattern for life, not only because of their morphology but also because it is behaviorally impractical to practice several predatory trades efficiently.

Stalking
Modern duck hunters gun their prey in two distinct, mutually exclusive ways. They may hide in the brush or at a blind and wait for birds to fly within range, or they may take the initiative and stalk their prey, moving along water courses or slowly skulling across open water in a camouflaged punt. Like the wildfowler in the stalking role, certain animal predators actively stalk their prey, relying upon stealth

and camouflage to move within range before making the final assault. In this predation pattern the sequence of actions by the predator is:

1 Search while moving through the environment.
2 Sight prey.
3 Stalk prey.
4 Make final rush to prey, seize, kill, and eat prey.

Stalking predators include most of the large cats, a few birds and fishes, certain spiders, and a smattering of other animal species. Animals belonging to this category of predators generally depend upon camouflage (Table 6–1) to make successful attacks. When man functions as a stalking predator, he often adopts some artifact to enhance his camouflage during phase 3 of the sequence outlined above. This fact seems incompatible with any interpretation of the role of man's coloration as camouflage (page 204), at least in environments where this expedient is necessary.

Sentinel Hunters
A considerably more common predatory tactic than stalking is to behave like a duck hunter in a blind, waiting either to launch a short assault or to seize directly the prey which blunder within range. Some animals employ lures to entice the prey, as does the duck hunter who uses decoys or as do angler fishes and snapping turtles that employ morphological lures. Once an attack has been launched by a sentinel hunter, the predator's presence is known to the local population of prey, and some time must elapse before conditions stabilize and another attack can be attempted. For this reason, and because of the relatively long interval between successful attacks, the capture of prey items that are small in relation to the size of the sentinel predators is not worthwhile. The American cuckoos *Coccyzus ameri-*

Table 6–1. Camouflage requirements for various hunting tactics. Double plus (++) indicates camouflage is an indispensible ingredient, plus (+) that it is useful, and minus (−) that it is superfluous.

Hunting Tactic	Camouflage Requirements	
	During Approach	**During Attack**
Stalking	++	++
Sentinel hunting	Not applicable	++
Scavenge hunting	+	−
Fodder feeding	−	−
Trap building	−	−

canus and *C. erythropthalmus*, in their predation upon large insects, amphibians, and reptiles, employ sentinel-hunting tactics (W. J. Hamilton and M. E. Hamilton, 1965) and, when given a choice, choose the larger of two prey items (W. J. Hamilton and M. E. Hamilton, personal data). They are remarkably patient in their hunting actions, spending long intervals, sometimes 20 minutes or more, waiting motionless for some prey to move.

The sequence of predatory actions by sentinel hunters is:

1 The predator takes a position.
2 It sights its prey.
3 It makes a rush towards its prey, or lashes out with its morphological weaponry.

Morphological camouflage may be less important to sentinel-hunting predators than to stalking hunters because the sentinel hunters are motionless during the critical phase of prey activity. Also, in the case of birds and lizards preying upon insects, the sensory acuity of the prey species may be poor at the range from which the predators launch attacks.

Predatory coral reef fish depend to a particularly great extent upon sentinel hunting. This is because effective camouflage on coral reefs is possible only when animals live on or close to the substrate. When a fish is away from the substrate in the generally clear waters of shallow coral reefs, visibility is so good that prey species are usually able to detect predators approaching from open water in time to retreat to the protection of the reefs. This relationship is well illustrated by the reef fish *Chromis caeruleus*, which lives in groups in branched coral. From this coral they go into the adjacent open water to snap up microscopic plankton. When predators approach they retreat toward the protective coral, and if the attack is direct they return to the interstices of the coral branches. Thus predators approaching from open water tend to be relatively ineffective in their attacks. The principle observed here can probably be generalized: Coral reef fish are relatively immune from attack by the usual open-water sorts of predators.

By comparison, the sentinel-hunting fish of the reef lurk on the substrate and their intricate patterns often blend precisely with this background. When a prey passes nearby, a sudden attack is often successful. Thus, most diurnal predation upon reef fish is by predators employing sentinel-hunting tactics.

Many human predators, past and present, have functioned as sentinel hunters, but almost exclusively with the help of thrown or launched weapons. It is not easy to imagine how a man could be successful as a sentinel hunter unless he did throw weapons. This creates a problem, because it seems improbable that weapon throwing was a first step in the evolution of hunting man (page 130).

Scavenge Hunters

Scavenge hunting is active predation in which the predator makes little or no attempt at concealment or stealth while hunting. These hunters exploit prey which may or may not be cryptic. For scavenge hunting to persist, it is essential that at least some members of the prey populations make no attempt to flee or, if they do, that their locomotion ability be poorly developed relative to that of the predator. Most scavenge hunters are capable of short bursts of speed, but are unable to overtake large prey that are in full flight. They may capture fleet prey when they discover them before the prey abandon the ruse of disguise to take flight. Scavenge-hunting predators may prey upon animals attached to the substrate or otherwise incapable of rapid flight. Black oystercatchers, *Haematopus bachmani*, prey upon beds of the black mussel, *Mytilus edulis*, that are permanently attached to the substrate (G. W. Salt, personal communication). The coloration of neither predator nor prey is relevant to the predator-prey relationship, and both predator and prey are black.

The sequence of actions in scavenge hunting is:

1   The predator moves through the environment searching for prey.
2   It detects potential prey.
3   It seizes the prey item and eats it.

Scavenge-hunting predators may do large amounts of scavenging. Their diet also often includes vegetation, particularly items of relatively high food value such as seeds and fruit. This predilection to secure a diverse diet differs considerably from the narrower herbivorous and carnivorous habits of grazers and sentinel hunters respectively, which tend to be more restricted in the character of their dietary intake.

Scavenge hunting depends much less upon stealth in the approach to prey than does sentinel hunting and stalking. Scavenge hunters often collect relatively small prey that have little or no chance to escape once they are discovered. Certain reef fish, for example, prey upon crabs they nip from the substrate. In the heavily populated reef environment where prospective predators abound, any crab that fled before the approach of every predator would not survive for long. Camouflage is not relevant to the predator role of scavenge hunters, and the relative value of other bases of coloration is thus enhanced.

The starling *Sturnus vulgaris* is a good example of a scavenge hunter. Many of its actions are those of a predator, and when given a choice it prefers insect food. This may be taken from the air in sweeping swallowlike flight, or by sitting on a lookout perch in the manner of a flycatcher, thus performing as a sentinel hunter. However, most of its food-gathering actions take place on the ground. Its terrestrial prey are small, and prey capture rarely involves a chase of more than a few centimeters. Starlings also take selected herbaceous vegetation, seeds, and fruit, and at times each of these foods may be the nucleus of an individual starling's diet. In these actions camouflage is relatively unimportant, and both sexes are black.

Fodder feeders (Ivlev, 1961) are another kind of scavenge hunters. These animals may not even see their prey. Aquatic animals, from fishes to whales, are particularly predisposed to this tactic, which involves straining food from water with great efficiency. Camouflage probably is also irrelevant to this category of predators.

Trap-building predators are another special kind of scavenge hunters. Some, like the web-spinning spiders and aquatic caddis fly larvae, fabricate nets and wait for prey to become tangled in them. Most trap-building predators retreat to a crevice and are not visible while they tend their traps, so that camouflage is unimportant to them. Other species, certain spiders, for example, are more attentive in the tending of their snares and may fabricate elaborate camouflage to conceal their presence.

Scavenge hunters share a group of common characteristics setting them apart from other predatory animals:

1 They generally are not camouflaged. Their coloration is adapted to radiation mediation or communication.
2 They are often more common than the stalking and sentinel hunters within most animal groups and within each ecosystem.
3 They readily and voluntarily adopt dietary diversity.
4 They take smaller prey items relative to their body size than stalking and sentinel hunters.
5 They spend more of their time moving in search of food than stalking and sentinel hunters.

The reason for making these comparisons is to establish a basis for evaluating the coloration of man relative to his predatory activities. Most of modern man's predatory activities involve the operation of traps, nets, and snares. This is the case whether we are considering mechanized fishermen or men functioning closer to an appropriate evolutionary context, as in African forests, plains, or elsewhere. Vastly more forest antelopes are killed today with braided wire snares, and were killed formerly with fiber ropes or vines, than with thrown weapons. Far more fish are and were taken by tribal men with nets, traps, and wires than by stalking them with bow or spear. These scavenge-hunting tactics shaped and continue to dominate most human cultures which depend to any degree upon undomesticated animal resources.

Group hunters

Group hunters operate in packs, overwhelming large prey which are often widely ranging nomadic herbivores. These pack hunters generally are committed to group hunting tactics and may be unable to attack successfully until a critical number of individuals has gathered (Salt, 1967). While camouflage may be advantageous to group hunters in their initial approach to prey, there often is no stalking phase to the attack. The very presence of a pack reduces the possibilities of a stalk for effective camouflage, as does their predilection for open terrain. These group hunters often possess bold and conspicuous patterns and colors (Table 6-2). The significance of these piebald markings to certain pack hunters, such as hyenas, hunting dogs, and killer whales, may be positively advantageous in herding prey. Some group hunters have great stamina and are able to press their prey to the limits of endurance before making a kill. This strategy depends to a considerable degree upon the site tenacity of their prey

Table 6-2. Some pack hunters and their coloration.

Group	Species	Color	Hunting pattern
Birds			
	Starling (*Sturnus vulgaris*)	Black	"Overlapping" flocks capture prey startled by other flock members.
	Pelican	White	Groups form a living "seine" which is closed around fish schools.
	Cormorant	Black	Groups dive together to pursue schools of small schooling fishes.
Mammals			
	Wolf (*Canis*)	Grey	Packs harry isolated hooved animals (Mech, 1966).
	Killer whale	Black and white	Packs hunt by terrorizing sea lions, and cooperate in herding them.
	Porpoise (*Phocaena*)	Dark	Groups hunt together for fishes (Fink, 1959).
	Hunting dog (*Lycaon pictus*)	Piebald	Packs chase hooved mammals until they are exhausted.
	Striped hyena (*Hyaena hyaena*)	Piebald	Packs chase hooved mammals until they are exhausted.

—its unwillingness to flee indefinitely away from familiar terrain. The flight of any animal is seldom along a straight path for long distances and a determined pursuer or group of pursuers may eventually be able to overwhelm their victim. These hunters may gain a positive advantage from their conspicuousness by revealing their presence to the prey. When the prey species realizes it has been sighted, a fundamental change in the predator-prey interaction takes place. Locomotion of predator and prey become locked on one another. The prey animals may attempt to break sensory contact with the predator by a variety of tricks, but for large prey animals this may be quite impossible. It may be advantageous for the predator to facilitate the maintenance of sensory contact by the prey, especially if this visual stimulus induces continued flight. Movements of the prey animal become more predictable, and the effectiveness of cooperative hunting strategies increases. Anyone who has herded sheep or other livestock in brushy country knows the importance of letting the herd know where the herdsman and his dogs are, a relationship that can be facilitated by conspicuous clothing, shouts, and whistling. The peculiar and clearly conspicuous patterns of some pack hunters may serve the same role. They may also facilitate group coordination by providing conspicuous signals enabling members of the pack to keep track of one another's identity and location.

Aggressive Mimicry
A few animals mimic harmless or less harmful animals and are thus able to enhance predation on commensal relationships with other species. These relationships are most extensive and elaborate among insects, where they are accompanied by extensive morphological adaptations. A wide variety of animals—spiders and particularly fish—mimic background objects, such as flowers, leaves or other vegetation, or pebbles, objects unattractive to potential predators. Many of these mimics are themselves predators.

Man appears to be the only mammal that is an aggressive mimic. Hunting men, because of their ability to modify artifacts and their large size, have commonly adopted the tactic of aggressive mimicry. They pull hides or skins over themselves to mimic their intended prey or some harmless associated species. This strategy was used by Africans who donned the skins of the harmless ostrich to stalk antelope and by American Plains Indians who used the hides of animals such as wolves to approach within bow range of buffalo. The latter case is especially interesting because it points out how phases of attack and responses to them differ with predatory style. In open country, pack hunters sometimes are continuously within sight of their prey. If the prey species fled before the sight of each potential predator, life would be impossible. But these prey species know the habits of predators and respond only when flight is absolutely necessary. The Indian wearing a wolf skin took advantage of this circumstance to approach within striking range.

These observations of the hunting tactics of man emphasize that, in the environments where they are employed, the coloration of man is inadequate camouflage.

STEPS TO MAN

Man has undergone an accelerating development of occupational diversity. Hunting, agriculture, fishing, trading, and a host of other occupations are all well developed. With each of these transitions, man secured a greater part of the available energy and increased his population and range as well. By comparison, even limited occupational diversity is uncommon among animals, and certainly would not have been characteristic of emerging mankind. Man's trades were added one by one, each innovation setting the stage for the development of other new skills. Upon what beginnings were these innovations based?

In recent years there has been a common tendency to interpret modern man's behavior as that of a somewhat transformed predatory ape and territorial titan (Ardrey, 1963; Lorenz, 1966; Morris, 1967; others). These popular accounts reflect serious and widely held scientific attitudes for which supporting evidence is not altogether lacking. In his preference for meat and in his modern food habits, man does not closely resemble the other apes. The difference, however, is one of degree rather than kind. A number of primates, like the starlings noted above, will increase the portion of meat in their diet when given the opportunity. This reflects what seems to be a general principle for omnivorous animals—that food items of high caloric content and those relatively efficiently converted to usable energy are preferentially selected when the opportunity arises. Man's emerging technology provided this opportunity, and it is reasonable to conclude that the dietary change which accompanied the development of sentinel and stalking hunting in man did not represent a fundamental transition in diet but rather the fulfillment of man's dietary potential. As a stalking hunter, man is a unique primate. That he has indeed moved away from the typical primate diet is unarguable. But when the broad picture of man compared with other animals is developed on the basis of the concepts of predation and coloration already considered, the interpretation of man's ancestry as a specialized predator finds little substantial support. In a comparative analysis of coloration relative to trade, man is like the large, dark, uncamouflaged African mammals that are herbivores, scavengers, and scavenge hunters (Table 6-3). Preman and emerging man probably belonged to one of the less specialized predation categories. Versatility and plasticity of diet, social organization, and habitat utilization accompanied this way of life, and have been expressed in the subsequent adaptive radiation of the tribes of mankind.

Who's the Slowest of Them All?

"The full list of man's physical superiorities, when compared with other mammals, must include his ability to run rapidly and to run long distances. One need only cite the conquest of the four-minute mile and the long-distance running of various Indian tribes" (Laughlin, 1968, p. 312).

This statement expresses the widely held assumption that man's

Table 6-3. The defense mechanisms of the large dark uncamouflaged mammals of open terrain in Africa compared with the characteristics of some camouflaged species.

Species	Defense	Hairiness
Dark or Black		
Elephant	Tusks, large body size, herd structure (mutual defense)	Hairless
Rhinoceros	Tusks, large body size, herd structure	Hairless
Buffalo	Horns, large body size, herd structure	Sparse hair
Wildebeest	Weak horns, large herds	Moderate
Man	Spears, shields, groups, shelters	Hairless
Camouflaged		
Gazelles (several spp.)	Flight, groups, camouflage	Completely haired
Forest antelope (several spp.)	Flight, camouflage	Completely haired
Zebra	Flight, groups, camouflage	Completely haired
Giraffe	Camouflage, groups, size	Completely haired

physical prowess is competitive with that of other large mammals. This conclusion lies at the heart of many additional interpretations of emerging man's adaptation to prey capture. It follows from this conclusion, for example, that men may have been able to use their first weapons to club fleet prey. But attacks with such weapons would have been possible only if preman were able to challenge free-ranging animals by lying in ambush or stalking and then dashing to the attack. To do so he would have had to be either faster or more durable than his prey. However, judging from the best performances of modern man compared with large mammals (Table 6–4), the first of these alternatives is not possible. The only large animals man approximates in footrace competition are the same species, rhino, elephant, and hippo, that he also resembles in other ways (Table 6–3). These brutes were and still are too big, too strong, and too dangerous to be successfully attacked with any regularity by individual men armed only with simple hand weapons. A man or even a group of men could not one day have seized sticks or stones and clubbed an elephant to death, nor is it something they would have attempted. And the less dangerous birds and mammals simply were too fast for them.

The main reason the conventional wisdom, which assumes that man began his carnivority by clubbing large mammals, has remained unchallenged is the widely held belief that the physical attributes of speed, stamina, and strength, which permitted man the steps from clublike tools to more sophisticated thrown or launched tools, vanished when these attributes no longer were needed. One of the most compelling reasons for rejecting this argument is that there are human populations living today whose economies still depend upon physical performance. Most hunting peoples can, on occasion, employ every bit of stamina and speed available to them, and selection for the improvement, or at least retention of, traits permitting this level of performance remains relevant. Yet it is a remarkable fact that the outstanding individuals of each of the races of man, however different they are in their current occupational specialties, perform nearly equally in track events. For example, the current world high-jump record, 230.5 cm, is shared by a white American and a Chinese. In any case, racial and population differences in performance between populations of man, if they really exist, do not alter the observation that no population of man includes individuals that exceed the capabilities suggested in Table 6–4.

Man fares no better in a comparison based upon long-distance performance, and in fact, his staying power deteriorates more rapidly than that of his prospective prey, as shown in Table 6–4.

Table 6-4. Maximum sprint and sustained speeds of some mammals and man in miles per hour. Sustained speeds are average speeds for the entire distance indicated. Thus actual speed will be somewhat slower near the end of that distance.

Species	Sprint Speed, MPH	Sustained Speed, MPH (distance run)	Source
Man	22.4	13 (6.2 miles)	Lloyd, 1967
Elephant, African	25		Howell, 1944
Rhinoceros, black	25		Poppleton, F., personal communication
Hippopotamus*	30		William M. Longhurst, personal communication
Patas monkey	34		Tappen, 1960
Coyote	35		Howell, 1944
Ostrich	35		Hill, 1950
Greyhound	39		McWhirter, 1968
Hare (*Lepus alleni*)	41		Howell, 1944
Wild donkey (*Equus hemionus*)	41	31 (16 miles)	Howell, 1944
Horse	43		McWhirter, 1968
Giraffe†	45		Poppleton, F., personal communication
Antelope, pronghorn	61	30 (7 miles)	Einarsen, 1948
Gazelle, Mongolian	62	41 (10 miles)	Howell, 1944
Cheetah	70		Hildebrand, 1960

*Longhurst's measurements were made by pursuing hippopotamuses in eastern Africa with a vehicle. His observations are based upon numerous measurements. Hippopotamuses maintain this maximum for at least 1/4 mile.
†In spite of the figure of 28 to 32 mph quoted in Howell (1944), Poppleton has paced giraffes at this speed with a motor vehicle.

If those performances are indicative of preman's relative capacity, his only effective predatory strategies were to:

1 Capture prey while they were asleep or before a chase began
2 Operate in relay teams while the quarry circled
3 Capture very small prey items or poikilotherms that were cool and unable to run rapidly

4 Work in teams to herd animals until they could be clubbed or otherwise captured

Man's poor locomotion capability is closely comparable with that of the large, dark, conspicuous African mammals (Table 6-3) which depend upon physical prowess rather than locomotion speed. This emphasizes the fact that man could not have employed a "lightning dash," as Morris (1967) has suggested, to prey upon large mammals when he was shifting to a predatory style. The only possible circumstance where such a dash may have been applicable to preman was a lunge to strike stalked prey before they sensed danger and made a move to escape.

To be properly comparable with animal locomotion capacity, the figures for man in Table 6-4 need to be reduced considerably. The maximums for man provided there are based upon the outstanding performance of outstanding individuals, highly trained for particular events and selected from a population of tens of thousands of individuals. These individuals are performing under optimum and artificial substrate conditions, and their performance traction is enhanced by the use of track spikes and other special equipment. If a sample size more comparable to that from which the mammalian data are derived were applied to human populations, still including only well-conditioned individuals, 11.0 seconds for 100 yards or 19 mph would be a more appropriate figure. Thus, a very ordinary elephant would easily pull away from an especially fast man.

There seems to be no information concerning the top speed of man's nearest living relatives, chimpanzees, gorillas, and orangutans. These are basically forest apes, and the chimpanzee and gorilla do most of their traveling on the ground, but there is no obvious way to time them under natural conditions. Certainly the most vigorous man is no match for either a gorilla or a chimpanzee in a footrace through the forests where they live, even when the substrate is relatively even and clear. The same is probably true of performance in open terrain. This I know from my own observations of these animals in the forests of Africa. But we need actual measurements of the top speeds of these animals to help determine the price man has paid for his bipedal stance.

The emphasis of these comparisons does not need to be modified by the observation that man's mammalian middens are composed mainly of young animals. In eastern Africa, antelope of some species calve through much of the year, and small groups of hunting people could have depended upon the calves for a food supply. Except for infants only a few days old, however, the young of most mammals are nearly as fleet as the adults. Newborn antelope of some species may depend upon immobility rather than flight, and it is in this attitude that they are most likely to be taken by man in his scavenge-hunting role rather than in his stalking-hunting or sentinel-hunting role.

An alternative explanation of Table 6-4 and its extension is that man may have shaped the nature of the table. This he could have accomplished by simply eliminating the species he could overtake, with the result that only species faster than he would remain. In the New World, compelling evidence suggests that this was the case. At just the time when the first record of man in the New World emerged, large numbers of mammals became extinct. It is possible that the same thing happened in the Old World, and that it was the slower and less wary species that early man exterminated. If this were the case, significant modification of the conclusions I have drawn from the data of Table 6-4 might be necessary. But in the absence of a detailed analysis of appropriate data, consideration of the possible alternative explanation that would result does not seem warranted.

Scavenge Hunting and Tools

The hypothesis I favor is that preman was a scavenge hunter, an occupation that requires neither particularly well-developed loco-motion ability nor camouflage. This hypothesis agrees with man's extraordinarily broad diet. In the evolution of human tool-using capability, tools have played diverse roles. Initially a narrow pattern of tool use must have been involved. Were the original human tools potentially lethal weapons that could be used to kill game and other man as well? In what capacity is man likely to have used tools originally? One might suppose that the archaeological record would provide a clear answer. One approach to this problem might be to determine when the first tools were used. But the unmodified tools which probably preceded modified tools, whether unmodified stones, sticks, or whatever, left no trace.

An analysis of the tools used by birds and mammals in obtaining food (Table 6-5) shows that without exception the known tool-using birds and mammals are scavengers and scavenge hunters. They use those food-getting tools in scavenging activities, not as missiles, and never in association with stalking predation. This result of a comparison of tool-hunting animals with hunting tactics is understandable when possible evolutionary sequences leading to man's most sophisticated tool-using tactics are considered. Development of thrown weapons from tools used to assist scavenging activities provides a more probable evolutionary sequence than the direct adoption of sentinel-hunting tactics that were dependent upon weapons.

Table 6-5. Animals using tools in food getting and their occupations. Emphasis upon scavenge hunting by nonhuman tool users suggests that man's tools may have been originally correlated with his omnivorous habits and subsequently adapted to more active hunting tactics.

Species (Source)	Tool and Use	Hunting Method
Birds		
Black-breasted buzzard	Stone, dropped on emu eggs to break them	Scavenging
Buzzard	Stone, hurled from bill to break ostrich eggs	Scavenging
Galapagos finch (Millikan and Bowman, 1967)	Cactus spine, to probe in crevices for insects	Scavenge hunting
Brown-headed nuthatch (Morse, 1968)	Bark chip, to lift bark on tree trunks to reveal insects	Scavenge hunting
Mammals		
Sea otter (E. M. Fisher, 1939; Hall and Schaller, 1964)	Stone, to break sea urchins to expose edible soft parts	Scavenge hunting
Chimpanzee (van Lawick-Goodall, 1968; Jones and Pi, 1969)	Stick, to excavate termite mounds; bark, to obtain water; grass, to obtain edible mound termites	Scavenge hunting
Cebus monkey	Peeled twigs, to pry free concealed insects	Scavenge hunting
Man	Stick, to pry for roots, club prey	Scavenge hunting Stalking hunting
	Bow, to kill game	Lookout hunting
	Net, to capture fish	Scavenge hunting

Thrown weapons could have developed from scavenge-hunting tools, but an initial phase of sentinel or stalking hunting seems improbable. It seems more probable that scavenge-hunting tools were pre-adaptations to man's thrown weapons.

It has been suggested, largely on the basis of observations of captive primates, that the initial development of tools by primates and man stemmed from displacement activities and redirected aggression in frustrating food-gathering contexts (Hall, 1963). These conflict situations supposedly led to throwing movements. From these undirected actions, offensive and defensive tool use supposedly developed. Once these activities were well developed, food-getting applications were then secondarily derived. According to this logic the hypothetical sequence in tool use would have been:

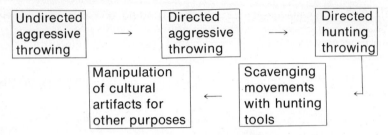

However, van Lawick-Goodall's (1968) extensive observations of free-ranging chimpanzees, the primate most dependent upon and versatile with tools in natural situations, provide little support for this hypothesis. She found that chimpanzees manipulate a variety of tools in various feeding contexts, particularly to obtain termites for food. The tool-using actions she observed are all typical scavenge-hunting actions. Chimpanzees do occasionally throw things—rocks, sticks, and fistfuls of vegetation. These actions may be aimed at other chimpanzees, baboons, men (van Lawick-Goodall, 1968), and sometimes even leopards (Kortlandt, 1965). However, the movements are weak and their aim generally poor, so that the tool does not travel far. These behavior patterns are limited to certain individuals within a group, and they have never been observed to result in an injury to another animal (van Lawick-Goodall, 1968). By comparison, scavenge-hunting actions by chimpanzees with tools are well developed. It seems likely, therefore, that if these two kinds of tool-using behavior by chimpanzees—one in agonistic encounter and the other in food-getting—do bear any evolutionary relationship to one another, it is the scavenging actions that are likely to have been the antecedents.

There is thus an alternative evolutionary sequence to that suggested by Hall:

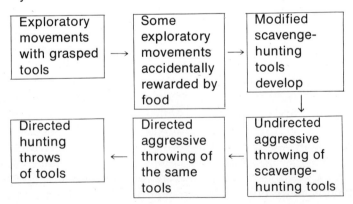

Those hypothetical steps to hunting tools provide less complex transitions and are in closer agreement with the context of van Lawick-Goodall's extensive observations of tool use by chimpanzees. This sequence is also more easily related to the comparisons of the context of food-getting tool use by other kinds of animals (Table 6–5).

The comparative analysis of tool use will be enhanced by the study of more populations of tool-using primates. Terrestrial primates seem disposed to adopt local traditions of tool use, and study of a spectrum of these populations is bound to provide much useful evidence concerning possible sequences in the development of tool use. The most extensive studies of chimpanzees have been in the highlands at the eastern edge of the range of these animals (e.g., van Lawick-Goodall, 1968). In the lowland forests of Africa, Jones and Pi (1969) found that chimpanzees use sticks somewhat shorter than a meter to probe rain-softened termite mounds. This was the only context in which they observed tool use. Where the particular species of termites that these tools are used to exploit are not present, tool use appears to be lacking. Thus local tradition in tool use may be influenced by environmental conditions.

The camouflage requirements of the several categories of non-mimetic hunters are summarized in Table 6–1. Man's use of artifacts as camouflage during stalking and sentinel hunting emphasizes the fact that in the context of these hunting styles he is a poorly camouflaged species. The step to more specialized hunting tactics was made by use of artifact camouflage and missile-type weapons. This development, coupled with the use of artifact weapons, permitted new populations of man to occupy environments where preman scavenge-hunters could not function.

These new and more specialized hunting men did not give up their scavenge-hunting tactics altogether. The females of nearly all human populations, past and present, continue to perform scavenge-hunting activities and food processing, rather than actively participating in stalking and sentinel-hunting activities. Stability of human females in their occupational role is accompanied by a remarkable and little-discussed fact: Most of the morphological features of racial diversity in our species are limited to males, and when racial differences in proportions and stature of man are discussed, data are based upon measurements of males. Occupational diversification in man was superimposed upon a scavenge-hunting ancestry, and as diversification of man took place it was the men that were mainly concerned with the process of adaptive radiation.

CONCLUSIONS

1   Predacious animals have basically different hunting tactics which influence the relevance of coloration to them.

2   Active stalking predators and sentinel hunters, which strike from a perch or post, require camouflage to make good their attack.

3   Scavenge hunters, which attack relatively small and defenseless prey, do not require aggressive camouflage, and their coloration is likely to be based upon some other potential advantage.

4   Scavenge hunters tend to have a broader spectrum of kinds of food items in their diet than the more specialized stalking and sentinel hunters, and to include the generalists in other aspects of their adaptation.

5   Potential prey species may evade predation in a variety of ways. When relatively great immunity is secured, camouflage may be unnecessary, and it is possible to adopt a coloration pattern based upon another adaptive basis.

6   Man living in savannah environments in Africa is similar to several large mammals in his capacity to defend himself from predation and in his conspicuous and dark coloration.

7   The few animals that use tools to obtain food are all scavengers or scavenge hunters. No animal uses a thrown tool to obtain resources. The steps to hunting tools by man probably involved a gradual transition from tools such as digging sticks used to make his scavenge-hunting operations more efficient.

8   On a comparative basis, man's physical prowess, especially his locomotion capacity, is poor by comparison with that of other large terrestrial animals. The upright stance appears to have cost man much speed, and arguments that suggest that populations of man may have initiated a hunting existence by sprinting to run down prey depend on the additional conclusions that man was faster in the past or there were slower animals.

POPULATION AND ECOSYSTEM DYNAMICS

The analysis of the relationship of animal coloration to animal abundance has been mainly restricted to mimic-model ratios. Some other less known density-coloration relationships are considered here. These relationships may help explain certain enigmatic phenomena, phase polymorphism in insects particularly, but also seasonal changes in animal coloration and cyclic population phenomena.

The value of animal coloration to prey species is determined not only by the relative values of advantages that might be secured by the alternate coloration adaptations of social coloration and metabolism, but also by the extent to which predation evasion colors are *effective* in securing immunity from predators. Predation rates also depend upon the abundance of prey species relative to prospective predators and upon the abundance of other prey species which may partially buffer the impact of predation upon a species. In many instances animal coloration has been influenced by these numerical relationships.

DEMOGRAPHY AND DENSITY

Longevity

A corollary to the axiom that animals must have adequate defense mechanisms in order to adopt energy and communication-enhancing coloration (Chapter 6) is that, once an adequate defense has been secured and one source of longevity restriction relieved, longevity increases and new bases for population regulation take the place of those that were operational. Increased longevity may have other effects such as the adoption of social organizations and systems emphasizing learning, less rigid behavior patterns, and emphasis upon parental behavior.

Demography and Energy Coloration

Animal populations seldom are completely free of predators. But many animals are able to minimize the impact of predation, and because immunity from predation is a prerequisite for the development of an energy color, black and white animals are relatively long-lived. Black and white animals differ from camouflaged and to a lesser degree from brightly colored species belonging to the same groups in a series of additional characteristics. Among terrestrial vertebrates these include:

Energy-colored Animals	Other Animals
Greater longevity	Shorter longevity
Lesser fecundity	Greater fecundity
Larger body size	Smaller body size

Where is the causal relationship in these correlations? Why should large animals live longer than smaller ones? There is no obligate physiological relationship, because some small animals are quite long-lived. The tiny cavernicolous vespertilionid bats may live more than 10 years while mice of similar size live only a year or two at the most. The most probable explanation seems to be that a combination of characteristics have developed together when predation protection became available. A population which is relatively free of predators is more likely to be limited by available resources, food in particular, than one more limited by predators. Resources for reproduction will thus be less available to the resource-limited population. High reproductive rates have less value for a resource-limited population, and there is greater emphasis upon infant survival. As populations press the limits of available resources, the proportion of adults increases. Juveniles are less likely to survive to maturity because there is no place for them. They must occupy marginal environments and enter intraspecific competition more fully equipped to compete with adults of their species. Thus there is a premium upon enhancing juvenile survival through parental care, allowing a juvenile to be shepherded by its parents until it is more capable of competition. This often includes provision of additional embryonal material with each offspring, and larger eggs and young are produced. The energy available to each reproductive female is thus divided into fewer and larger shares.

MAN'S DEFENSE MECHANISMS AND HIS LONGEVITY

Man agrees with a group of black and white animals in his exceptional ability to defend himself against predation and in his great longevity. In Chapter 6, I drew the conclusion that two basic requirements for the adoption of energy colors are the possession of a reasonably potent defense against predators and that an animal not be a stalking hunter itself. Now we shall consider what man's defenses were when he was developing his coloration.

Defenses

Man can be grouped with several large African mammals possessing particularly potent defenses (Table 6-3). His special capacity for defense is largely cultural—tool use and group defenses. Sharpened sticks, clubs, stones, and thorny brush to give protection from nocturnal predators probably provided the critical defenses from an early stage in man's history. If preman developed his unique characteristics in the open country of eastern and southern Africa, it would be revealing to compare his coloration and defenses with those of other large diurnal mammals (Table 7-1) living in the same regions today. These recent mammals shared an evolutionary history with man on the plains of eastern Africa. In the excavations at Olduvai with the remains of man's prehistory lie also the ancestors of the modern representatives of the same animals that range these high plains today. My own observations of these animals in their modern colors suggest that the most conspicuous animals are also those most capable of self-defense (Table 7-1). Man's conspicuousness is further enhanced in a plains environment by his upright stance, for most of his body rises above the sparse plains vegetation; and a black man on the savannah is a conspicuous sight indeed.

Table 7-1. Comparison of conspicuousness, coloration, and defense mechanisms of some large African mammals and man. Conspicuousness is compared with man, based upon categories ranging from 1 (most conspicuous) to 5 (least conspicuous) to the human observer. Defense mechanisms are based upon a graduated scale from 1 (least capable of defense) to 5 (most capable). The species tabulated include several species of antelope, monkeys, apes, cats, canids, the rhinocerus, hippopotamus, elephant, warthog, and hyena. Zebras are excluded from this analysis.

Conspicuousness	Brown	Grey	Black	Defense Mechanism
1	6	0	0	1.0
2	5	0	0	1.4
3	11.5	.5	0	2.1
4	2	1	2	3.4
5	0	2	3	4.8

Longevity

Increased longevity relative to camouflaged species of the same group is a common characteristic of energy-colored animals. One basis for this longevity is apparent in the case of adult rhinoceroses and elephants: They are relatively immune from predation. The same must also be true of man. With nearly complete immunity from predation, the permissive state for longevity is achieved and physiological adaptations to longevity can develop. Selection for longevity is related to the usual characteristics of survivorship curves and the relative contribution that each segment of the population makes to its own progeny or potential progeny. As the curve becomes thinner and the contribution of survivors fades, the strength of selection for the physiological traits that sustain long life declines. Cultural adaptations have also been associated with man's long life, the trend already well developed among the highly social primates (Table 7-2). The main lines of defense among the social primates are their large size, particularly that of the adult males, and the function of these males in defense against predators. The longevity so gained has in turn placed a premium on physiological durability, assuring maximum reproductive potential of each adult and his or her offspring through the contribution of information (i.e., the maintenance of traditions) by postreproductive adults to their descendants.

Another basis of human longevity has been proposed by Dart (1964). This is that use of tools and utensils prevented wear of

Australopithecine teeth, permitting relatively great longevity and an extended period of infancy. Considerable evidence supports this argument. All primates have rooted teeth, and when the adult teeth are gone no replacements develop. This contrasts with many other animals, from shark to porcupine, which continue to produce new teeth or to grow unrooted teeth throughout their lives. Roots impose a fixed limit on the amount of wear a primate tooth can withstand in a lifetime. The use of tools and the development of cooking to soften foods may allow man to overcome this limitation and extend his potential reproductive life considerably.

Man's conspicuousness and general freedom from predation, and his poorly developed powers of locomotion (Chapter 6) raise the question of his relative palatability. Louis Leakey, in an article in the *San Francisco Chronicle* (February 12, 1967), has suggested that man is relatively unpalatable to large carnivores, and that this is the reason he is avoided by potential predators. This hypothesis seems plausible when man's other adaptations—such as great longevity, potent defense, and sluggish locomotion—are considered. Like other energy-colored animals, man's defense mechanisms are diverse, and distastefulness might be a second line of defense. Palat-

Table 7-2. Mean and maximum longevity of some primates in captivity.

Species	Color	Mean Longevity, years	Maximum Longevity in Captivity, years
		Man	
Man	Diverse	♂66.5 ♀73	100 +
		Black and White Animals	
Chimpanzee	Black	15–20	37
Gorilla	Black		26
Gibbon	Black or brown		23 +
Colobus	Black and white		18
		Camouflaged Animals	
Patas	Brown		20 +
Cercopithecus	Brown		19
Macaque	Brown	10–13	29
Baboon	Brown	9–11	25
Cebus	Brown	10	31
Mandrill	Brown		26

ability to most cannibals is, of course, irrelevant evidence because of man's tendency to cook his food. The cooking process may destroy distasteful substances and obliterate the action of the chemical protective mechanism.

Conspicuousness – Defense-mechanism – Proportionality Hypothesis

Most experimental studies of predator-prey relationships tend to be concerned with the interaction of a single predator with a single prey species. Few natural predator-prey systems are so simple. Most predators take several, often many, prey species, and most prey species are attacked by several kinds of predators. Because of this complication the impact of predation upon animal species in nature depends not only upon the defense mechanisms of that species but also upon the defenses of alternative prey species and their respective numerical abundance and availability. This relationship is well illustrated by studies of several species of sawfly larvae and their avian predators (Prop, 1960; Tinbergen, 1960). In their natural environment, the needles of pine trees, these larvae cannot easily be categorized as either conspicuous or inconspicuous. Instead, there are several intermediate degrees of conspicuousness. Experimental determination of the relative palatability of these larvae, by supplying them to insectivorous birds that normally would prey upon them, showed that the subjectively determined conspicuousness of each species is inversely related to its palatability (Figure 7–1). Studies of predation by the same birds upon the same sawfly larvae species in nature showed that the most conspicuous species, *Diprion fructetorum* and *D. virens*, are not as regularly targeted by their avian predators as are the other related but less conspicuous species (Tinbergen, 1960).

What is the significance of this relationship? Presumably, conspicuousness is determined by the adequacy of the defense mechanisms of each species relative to buffer species, or species which are taken in preference to the species in question and which thus deflect predation from it. Buffer species need not necessarily be close relatives, but related species or other members of the group to which a species belongs are more likely to bear a relatively constant spatial relationship to one another, and the probability of mutual evolution in this case of distinguishable conspicuousness gradients is probably greatest for close relatives.

When the conspicuousness – defense-mechanism relationship is considered relative to the animal species of the world, some possible explanations of natural coloration phenomena emerge. Many ani-

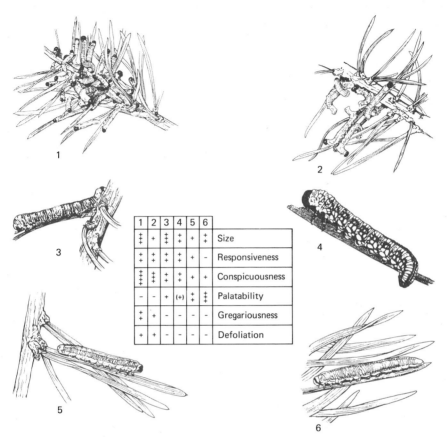

	1	2	3	4	5	6	
	‡+	+	‡+	++	+	++	Size
	++	++	++	++	+	-	Responsiveness
	‡++	‡+	++	++	+	+	Conspicuousness
	-	-	+	(+)	++	‡+	Palatability
	++	+	-	-	-	-	Gregariousness
	+	+	-	-	-	-	Defoliation

Figure 7-1. The conspicuousness and palatability of six species of sawfly larvae are inversely related to one another. Other behavioral characteristics are related in a predictable manner to these traits. (After Prop, 1960.)

mals are not as well camouflaged as they might be, if we can base a judgment upon comparison with other species living in the same area. These apparent flaws in the perfection of camouflage may be attributable to the adaptive relationship described above. The same relative values for defense mechanisms and colors apply to other groups, although no data approximating Tinbergen's studies of the pine forest sawfly larvae and their interactions with birds have ever been reported. Meinertzhagen (1954) describes a situation for Southwest African bustards. These large birds, *Afrotis afra* and *Eupodotis ruppelli*, live together in the same general habitat—sparsely vegetated brush and grassland. *Afrotis* is black and white and quite conspicuous; *Eupodotis* is cryptic. Of the two, afrotis is conspicuous in habit as well as pattern, and seems to actually advertise its presence. By comparison eupodotis crouches when disturbed or slips away, while afrotis seldom travels far. When Meinertzhagen subjected both to a stewing, eupodotis was found to be barely edible, afrotis "disgusting."

Warning Coloration

In the case of the sawfly larvae studied by Prop and Tinbergen, the range in conspicuousness of the several species is relatively narrow. None of these sawfly species are really highly conspicuous when compared with conspicuous insects in general; all are at least partially camouflaged. The two bustard species Meinertzhagen observed and tasted extend the range further; but again, compared with the potential range of avian coloration, the ends of the conspicuousness spectrum are not attained. However, the conspicuousness-defense-mechanism–proportionality relationship probably covers the full spectrum of animal coloration. This range includes bright colors such as the most conspicuous reds, blues, and yellows. The effectiveness of the defense mechanisms of insects possessing all these bright colors was determined experimentally by Jones (1932, 1934), who provided captive wild birds with trays of insects. Under these circumstances the difference between camouflaged and conspicuous insects was reduced, and the results are unlikely to have been biased to any great extent by the ability of the captive predators to locate prey. The result of these experiments was that the cryptic species—those that were green or brown—were most acceptable and presumably most palatable. The species most frequently shunned were yellow, red, orange, or of metallic coloration. Black, white, pink, and pale yellow forms were *intermediate* in acceptability. Thus the relationship of conspicuousness to defense mechanisms, at least insofar as palatability is concerned, seems applicable to the full range of insect coloration.

NUMERICAL FLUCTUATIONS IN ABUNDANCE AND COLORATION

Many animal populations undergo great fluctuations in abundance over relatively short time intervals. If the density of any prey species increases relative to the population of predators, the selection pressure upon each member of the prey population declines. The hypothesis that energy colors depend upon the relaxation of predation may therefore be further tested by evaluating the coloration relationships of species which fluctuate in numbers. Where there are color changes associated with changes in density, there should be a greater tendency to adopt energy and communicatory colors at the phase of the population cycle that is subject to the least predation.

While most animals are the same color regardless of their density, some, particularly those which undergo changes in abundance regularly and rapidly, have evolved coloration adaptations to density fluctuations.

Phase Polymorphism

Insects provide the best examples of density-related coloration changes. The color change with density of the migratory locusts *Schistocerca gregaria*, *Locusta migratoria*, and *Nomadacris septem-fasciata* is well documented. These polymorphic species may be either a brownish or a green camouflage color or may be a dark, nearly black color. The mechanism for expression of the dark color form is associated with the circumstances of development. If an egg mass from a single female is divided and some hoppers are reared under conditions of isolation, the isolated individuals develop the camouflaged coloration. The other hoppers from the same egg case raised in groups develop the dark or black pigmentation. The herbivorous cricket *Gryllus bimaculatus* behaves in much the same way. At low densities they are brown, but as their abundance increases they become black (Fuzeau-Braesch, 1960).

The dark form of the migratory locust differs in a number of behavioral ways from the solitary form. The dark hoppers are gregarious and remain so throughout their lives. Those reared in solitary conditions remain solitary by choice. Individuals of the gregarious dark form are nomadic. At maturity they may launch migrations that take them great distances, plaguing agrarians and accounting for the fact that their biology is so well known (reviewed in Uvarov, 1966).

While these density-coloration relationships are well established, the circumstances of the morphs relative to predation are poorly understood. According to the hypothesis presented here, the coloration of dark insects implies a reduced predation rate at the higher density levels. However, since high densities and aggregation make these swarms conspicuous anyway, predation rates per se might remain unchanged, while the potential advantage of coloration in securing protection from predators declines. Predators encountering and following grasshopper swarms seem to have little difficulty obtaining their fill. There is thus no evidence to support the suggestion by Key (1957) and Kennedy (1961) that the dark coloration of the nomadic forms serves to warn predators that they are unpalatable. This warning coloration hypothesis also appears to contradict evidence from field studies (Albrecht and Ellis, unpublished, cited in Kennedy, 1961), suggesting that there is no difference in the palatability of morphs of different colors. Huddleston (1958) has observed that small birds are reluctant to attack the swarms of black hoppers. They seem to pick off only the stragglers. Perhaps these predators are frightened by the unusual sight of a hopper band. There is ample evidence that both gregarious and solitary locusts are taken regularly by predators. The African stork, *Sphenorhynchus abdimii*, hunts both dark and light migratory grasshoppers by walking in parallel ranks across the savannahs where they graze (Jackson, 1938). When the migratory hordes take flight, they may be attacked by blocks of wattled starlings, *Creatophora carunculata*, which adopt special flocking maneuvers to seize them (Stark, 1900).

The role of the coloration of the dark morphs of phase polymorphic insects in raising body temperatures has been confirmed experimentally. Strelnikov (1936) found that the body temperature of dark third-instar nymphs of *Locusta migratoria* rose more rapidly than green nymphs at the same stage. Other experimental measurements of body temperature differences between dark and light locusts are reviewed on page 40.

The correlation of dark coloration with relatively high densities is not confined to orthopterans. Certain moth larvae follow a similar pattern. Gregarious species are particularly prone to phase polymorphism, also becoming darker at high densities. The adaptive characteristics accompanying the shift with density have been demonstrated by Iwao's studies (1962, 1963, 1968) of noctuid moth larvae. One group of the seasonal Japanese species which he studied, *Parnara guttata*, *Naranga aenescens*, *Maliattha signifera*, and *Leucania placida*, are camouflaged and do not regularly undergo extensive population fluctuations. Other related species, *L. separata*, *Prodenia litura*, and *Trachea atriplicis*, are their opposites. These species periodically undergo massive population explosions, in some cases becoming agricultural pests. Individuals that develop during these irruptions are darker and relatively conspicuous. Their metabolism and developmental rates increase, survival is greater given equal conditions, and they eat more vegetation per unit of body mass per unit of time. These adaptations (Table 7-3) are possible because of the relaxation of predation pressures at high densities. Increased metabolic and developmental rates are nearly always advantageous, but they may not be possible because of other factors such as the availability of food or the relative cost of predation.

The relatively high metabolic rate of the high-density morphs of the moth larvae occurs whether or not the dark body coloration con-

Table 7-3. Constellation of adaptive traits in phase-polymorphic noctuid moth larva relative to density (after Iwao, 1968).

	Density	
Characteristic	**Low**	**High**
Coloration	Greenish to brown, with whitish band	Velvety black, with white and reddish band
Coloration interpretation	Camouflage	Energy and/or warning coloration
Development	Slow and variable	Fast and synchronized
General behavior	Sluggish	Active and irritable
Response to mechanical stimuli	Immobilization	Active movement
Fat content	Low	High
Metabolic rate	Low	High
Resistance to starvation	Weak	Strong
Tolerance to unpalatable plants	Low	High

tributes to an elevated body temperature. High metabolic rates characterize even a ground homogenate of the larvae. Thus the system appears to be geared to a higher rate of operation whether or not the sun shines. This does not mean that the color is not an adaptation to securing heat, but simply that a combination of adaptations have evolved, which secure a particular advantage when the organism operates as a functional unit. Under the usual conditions of life of these moth larvae, some sunlight will be intermittently available, and relatively higher body temperatures are to be predicted.

Dark noctuid moth larvae, like dark locusts, exhibit distinctive behavior patterns. The pale low-density larvae drop to the ground when disturbed, where they tend to remain coiled and motionless. The dark, more conspicuous larvae drop to the ground only when more severely agitated, and once they drop, they immediately begin to move (Iwao, 1963).

In a sense, adoption of dark coloration under crowded conditions seems paradoxical. If crowding increases competition, food supplies should be more rapidly depleted, and a low metabolic rate minimizing energy needs would seem to be the more advantageous response to the circumstances. But this would be true only if all other individuals in the population also slowed down. This would represent a form of cooperation that is inconsistent with known evolutionary processes (see Williams, 1966, for a review of the conditions under which group selection and altruism are likely to occur). Each individual (genotype) gains maximum evolutionary advantages by maximizing developmental rates, whatever the existing or potential state of resources. Serious resource depletion occurs commonly in species that regularly undergo sharp cyclical changes in abundance. In the face of potential famine, it will be advantageous to mature and reproduce early.

Seasonal Changes in Coloration
Seasonal changes in the relative abundance of predator and prey may also cause shifts in the relative intensity of predation. Many tropical butterflies are more cryptic in the dry than in the wet season. Most tropical insects breed at the end of the rainy season, and their larvae take advantage of the abundant vegetation available only at that time. The coloration evidence suggests that during the rainy season butterfly predators are more relatively abundant than during the dry season. Later, during the dry season, predation per prey individual increases, and the role of camouflage is enhanced. A comparable situation probably occurs in the insect faunas of temperate regions. Conspicuous insect species tend to emerge only during seasonal increases in insect populations. The abundance of insects relative to predators decreases in the late autumn, winter, and early spring so that predation pressure per prey individual increases. Insects that remain vulnerable to visual predators at these seasons are almost completely confined to cryptic species.

Color Changes with Age
Some of the most interesting color changes are those which accompany development, especially when they involve shifts from one adaptive basis to another. These situations may demonstrate the relative significance of alternative adaptative strategies during the life cycle. For example, black coloration is more common among young animals than among adults. The pelage of young baboons is black when they are born. At this time, they ride slung beneath the mother, clinging to her breast, and in the context of predation, when the mother is fleeing, the black youngster is not a serious legacy in terms of coloration. In the open savannahs of Africa where baboons live, detection by predators is from considerable distances, and the position of the young under the female minimizes the hazard to both female and infant. When young baboons become more mature, they shift to a jockey-style posture on the mother's dorsal surface. At about this time the young baboon's coloration changes to match his mother's cryptic brown. Many young birds, especially those frequenting open environments, are black. Nestling roadrunners, desert

birds which make open nests in desert bushes, are black, while the adults are cryptic. These young roadrunners are able to minimize the cost of thermoregulation by taking advantage of radiant solar energy when the parent is away from the nest (R. D. Ohmart, personal communication). When the parent is at the nest and can shade the offspring, the black coloration is irrelevant. The same coloration conditions apply to many other birds, which nest where filtered sunlight reaches the nestlings. For example, baby Virginia and sora rails, coots, and gallinules are black, whereas the adults are well camouflaged. These black infants are another example of the relationship between black coloration and cover at night (page 55), but in this case the cover is provided by the parent.

Many newborn insects are black. The small larvae of the clearwing moth, *Hemileuca*, a herbivorous willow-infesting and cottonwood-infesting caterpillar of southern California river bottoms, are black from birth. Later instars develop a more cryptic color (personal observations). In the case of poikilotherms, there is little advantage to be gained from conserving the relatively small amount of heat from metabolism, but it is advantageous to raise body temperatures and thus to expedite growth and potential longevity. Once an animal has attained adult size, rapid growth is less significant, but growth energy may be transferred to reproductive energy and a premium upon maximum rates of energy transfer retained.

CONSEQUENCES OF REDUCED PREDATION

A number of adaptations follow from the development of a relatively high degree of immunity from predation:

1 Energy colors become relatively more valuable and are more likely to be adopted. Coloration may be the least important of the several additional adaptations described below, but it is noticeable, and suggests that where the adaptive basis of coloration differs within any group of animals, developing quantitative data relative to the parameters will be worthwhile.
2 The relative value of parental care increases and develops in groups which have ways to provide such care effectively.
3 Brood sizes are reduced, and the size of eggs or newborn young increases.
4 Learning becomes more important in adaptations for securing a suitable food supply and to other aspects of life.
5 Play assumes greater adaptive value in its role of enhancing the effectiveness of learning.

6   Tradition assumes a greater role in the social organization of the
society.
7   The potential contribution of postreproductive individuals to their
progeny increases.

Kramer's Adriatic Island Lizards
Gustav Kramer is best known to biologists for his investigations of
the significance of the sun in the orientation of migrating birds.
Some years earlier Kramer described in a series of papers (summarized in English, 1951) the population characteristics of the ruins
lizard *Lacerta serpa* which lives on the offshore islands of the rugged
Mediterranean coasts of Yugoslavia and the Sorrento Peninsula of
southern Italy.   Kramer compared several aspects of the biology of
the island and mainland populations.   These investigations are of
particular interest because they provide a unique opportunity to
compare the responses of the same species to island and to mainland existence following the Pleistocene glaciation, 9,000 to 18,000
years ago (Kramer and Mertens, 1938; Kramer, 1946).   Thus there
had been a massive experiment lasting thousands of years.   Differences between mainland and island populations of these lizards must
have developed during that interval.   The island populations were
derived from and are closely related to mainland populations.   By
comparison, the island lizards are relatively little differentiated, and
crosses in captivity between these populations result in fertile offspring.
     A point of particular interest here is Kramer's report that the island
lizards are nearly black, whereas their mainland relatives are camouflaged.   Was relaxation of predation pressure the permissive condition that enabled this adaptation to develop?   While strictly quantitative data are lacking, general descriptive data are available (Kramer,
1946).   The most important predator upon the mainland lizards is a
snake which does not live on most of the islands.   Mammalian predators are also absent on most of the islands though present on the
mainland, and the only significant island predators are crows and
ravens. Predation pressure upon this lizard thus seems to have been
relaxed on the islands.   The abundance of lizards has increased and
exceeds comparable densities per unit of suitable habitat on the
mainland (Kramer, 1946).   These more numerous populations should
be less subject to regulation by predators, and social factors do
appear to play a greater role in regulation of the density of the island
populations. The ruins lizard is territorial.   Males establish territories
and defend them against all trespassers, including juveniles.   When
the opportunity arises, and especially when the usual insect food
supply fails and pressure for the most suitable space is greatest, the

adults do not hesitate to supplement their food supply with the young of their own species.   Under these circumstances, with the role of social factors in population regulation expanded to a considerably greater extent than on the mainland, territorial behavior and adaptations to securing a territory are relatively more valuable.   Visual stimuli adapted to territorial encounters are more highly developed. On the mainland the underparts are white, but on the Sorrentine Islands blue belly coloration (Kramer, 1949) has been developed, a color widely used by other lizards in visual displays.

The shift to emphasis upon coloration and behavior emphasizing control of social space effectively limits the opportunities for juveniles to successfully establish themselves.   This is confirmed by the age structure of the population.   The mainland population is young; on the islands it is much older (Figure 7-2).   This emphasizes the importance of establishing a territory on the islands.   Once an individual becomes established on the islands, considerable longevity is probable.   On the mainland, the constant pressure from predation provides no such prospect, and population losses to predators continue to open new space.

An additional consequence of these special conditions for island

Figure 7-2.   Adriatic island lizards, *Lacerta serpa,* are much older on the average than mainland representatives of the same species. The classes 1, 2, and 3 are categories of increasing age.   (After Kramer, 1946.)

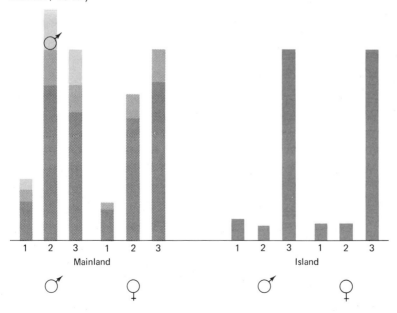

existence is that the reproductive rate of island lizards is reduced. This is due in part to the smaller number of broods per year, the result of a shorter reproductive season. The average number of offspring per brood is also lower on the islands. On the two Sorrento islands where Kramer worked, there were 3.0 young per female, compared with 5.1 on the mainland. As reproductive rates decline on the islands, the size of eggs and newborn young increases. There is little difference between the two populations in the amount of reproductive material produced per unit time. However, the island lizards emphasize individual survival, while on the mainland there is greater emphasis upon numbers. On the mainland, where predators maintain the population below levels that allow social factors and intraspecific competition to become critical, there is a greater evolutionary advantage in numbers. On the islands, competition for space and cannibalism create conditions where the survival of young and their subsequent reproductive success may be greatly enhanced by relatively large size, enabling them to compete more effectively.

ISLAND LIFE

Kramer's observations and the conclusions I have drawn from them can be extended to principles generally applicable to island life. The animal residents of islands, like deserts, are particularly prone to melanism. Several unique features of island environments, physical and biological, may underly this blackness, which appears in widely separated animal groups, notably reptiles, birds, and insects. Among these unique features are (1) the climate of islands, especially small islands, which tend to be cooler than the nearest land masses, (2) the general absence of or reduction in diversity and numbers of stalking and sentinel hunters, and (3) a lower diversity of species by comparison with inhabitants of mainland land masses.

Islands and Predators

Island diversity does not include many large vertebrate predators. As a result, there has been a general loss of fear responses by animals belonging to groups, which are considerably more wary on the mainland. On the Galapagos Islands, there are no mammalian predators, although a number of small mammals have spanned the 600 miles from South America. The requirements for initial colonization of islands are not the only restriction upon island predators. Many islands near the mainland also lack predators or have reduced predator densities. When predators reach these islands, they may quickly eliminate the island's entire population of prey species or reduce the population to densities that cannot continually sustain the predators. On the mainland, predators often respond to depletion of food resource by emigration. Also, as prey are locally depleted, the vacuum is refilled by immigrants from adjacent areas. This situation probably also accounts for a common discrepancy between laboratory and natural environment studies of predator-prey relationships. In nature, predators and their prey coexist; in the laboratory, predators annihilate their prey and then perish (Gause et al., 1936; Huffaker, 1958). Only on islands large enough to permit populations of predators and prey to fluctuate can there be successful colonization by predators.

Island Climates and Black Coloration

An entirely different possible explanation of the widespread emergence of black coloration on islands is that, due to relatively cool island climates, dark coloration has greater adaptive value. The relationship of cool and extremely hot ambient temperatures to the evolution of black coloration has been discussed in the earlier evaluation of the significance of dark desert coloration (Chapter 5). The applicability of this argument to island life is related to the well-known cooler climates of coastal areas and islands. The adaptive basis of dark coloration on islands is probably the same as it is for high-altitude animals, which also tend toward melanism—for example, the lizard *Sceloporus graciosus* in the Sierra Mountains of California (Stebbins and Robinson, 1946). The coolness of coastal islands and coast regions in the summer, when most temperate-region animals are active, is well documented, and certain coastal mainland animals have probably also adopted dark coloration due to this circumstance. In the case of mainland animals, however, coastal species adopting black coloration are largely restricted to the species with exclusively coastal distributions. Other more widely distributed species that interbreed with inland populations may, as a result of homogenizing selection (page 21), have no opportunity to adopt this characteristic even though it might be locally more adaptive than a camouflaged form.

Island Bird Plumage

There may seem to be no positive advantage to drab plumage (Mayr, 1963; Grant, 1965) of island birds which do not closely match their background. This conclusion needs to be examined carefully, however, because it and related observations are the cornerstone of a hypothesis concerning the relevance of natural selection to the characteristics of island animals. Mayr has argued that, because a small number of individuals inevitably colonize each island, the reduced genetic material and genetic drift unrelated to natural selection may account for the subsequent direction taken by the genetic characteristics of that population.   A related suggestion is that genetic drift, in the absence of selection, is the basis of these traits.

In general, the diversity of physical and vegetative environments occupied by animals is inversely related to the diversity of sympatric species occupying a region. Since the diversity of habitats occupied by birds is closely correlated with the diversity of vegetation types, and vegetation diversity is in turn correlated with diversity of soil conditions, it follows that the less diverse avifaunas of islands will tend to be found on relatively diverse substrate colors than their mainland counterparts. Thus they may be less able to adapt as precisely to match substrate conditions. In any case, it is not legitimate to conclude that there has been no adaptation to background conditions when the coloration of an animal is relatively imprecisely matched to its background. The potential to match background conditions precisely differs from species to species according to numerous features of its basic biology, including patterns of microgeographic distribution, the visual system of the relevant predators, and patterns of population fluctuation (p. 140). A basic premise of this book is that most if not all animal coloration can be explained by allocating the coloration of animals to one of the three fundamental pressures determining animal coloration. It is my contention that the diverse body of information supporting this conclusion presented in this book is adequate to establish the validity of this premise. Given this conclusion, the first approach to the explanation of apparent exceptions such as the problem of island bird coloration is to force an explanation based upon one of the alternatives. The alternative, as noted in the Mayr quotation above, often depends upon some nonadaptive explanation of the observed coloration.

Direct Effect of the Environment
A classic explanation of island melanism is that high humidity and salt spray have a direct and nonadaptive effect upon coloration. This explanation has, for example, been used to explain the black populations of the land snail *Cochlicella acuta* in western England and Wales and on offshore islands (Aubertin et al., 1930). The hypothesis is inadequate. While melanism is more common on islands surrounded by salt water, it is by no means confined to them. A number of islands in lakes have melanic forms. No causal evidence linking melanic species to salt spray and trace elements has ever emerged. This hypothesis appears to confuse a simple correlation with a causal relationship.

CONCLUSIONS

1 Conspicuousness is proportional to the effectiveness of defense mechanisms. This generalization crosses broad phyletic lines, but is most clearly demonstrated when close relatives are compared.

2 A number of animal species, particularly certain large herbivores, are relatively immune from predation. They have achieved this immunity through the evolution of particularly effective morphological weapons and also simply as a result of their large size.

3 These predation-free animals tend to adopt conspicuous colors adapted to optimizing radiation exchange and communication.

4 Phase-polymorphic insects tend to emphasize energy colors during the high-density phase. This suggests that camouflage is relatively less important at high densities.

5 Seasonal changes in abundance are a special case of population cycles. The seasonal coloration changes emphasize that predation pressures per prey individual are less at times of peak prey abundance in temperate regions than at other seasons.

6 Island animals tend more toward blackness or darkness than mainland representatives of the same groups. One explanation of this circumstance is that there are few or no sentinel and stalking predators on islands. This may be due to the improbable dispersal of these animals to islands. Another possibility is that islands, because of their relatively small spatial dimensions, have limited opportunity for emigration, which is a major basis of population continuity in mainland situations. This may allow the predators which reach islands to overeat their prey and become extinct.

7 Islands tend to be cooler than adjacent mainland land masses. This also places a premium on dark coloration in island environments.

8 Relative immunity from predation increases mean longevity.

9 Predation immunity leads to an increase in emphasis upon learning and the maintenance of traditions.

10 In savannah environments, particularly in Africa, prehistoric black man shared a series of characteristics with a group of large dark African mammals that are not well camouflaged and that tend to have especially effective defense mechanisms.

VISUAL COMMUNICATION

Visual communication is a third major function of animal coloration. Some general principles of visual communication among animals are considered in this chapter, and these principles are then related to possible interpretations of the communication morphology of man. A central concern in this book is to develop an understanding of man's coloration, and this analysis leads inevitably to an evaluation of the role of several features of man's morphology in communication with his fellow man.

Persuasion Displays

Visual signals have two distinct functional roles: persuasion and coordination. Persuasion displays concern signal receivers that must be convinced, while coordination displays deal with more receptive individuals or groups. Response to a persuasion signal provides a greater advantage to the signal sender than to the receiver. Coordination displays provide approximately equal potential benefits to the sender and the receiver of the signal.

Visual signal characteristics differ extensively relative to this dichotomy. Persuasion displays tend to be dynamic, coordinating displays static (Table 8-1). Coordinating displays include the most complex signals. If persuasion signals are complex they tend to be redundant, and thus to provide less information than coordination displays. These relationships can be elucidated by a consideration of signals relative to specific circumstances.

Social Organization and Persuasion Displays

Persuasion displays serve to maintain territories in courtship, mate attraction, the maintenance of dominance relationships, and certain forms of warning. In each case an imbalance exists in the potential gain to the participants in the communicatory interaction. This relationship is well illustrated by the courtship process. Once the sexes establish contact, whether as the result of mate-attracting displays or by chance, it is adaptive for the male to induce the female to mate with him. When males are easily located, and are continuously available for mating as is the usual case, the potential benefits from communication are not as great for the female. Female reproductive potential is limited by the number of offspring she can produce. Hence the courtship process has less meaning to her, and she is generally the less colorful of the two and less concerned with the courtship process. By comparison, the courting male is constrained by metabolic considerations related to gaining access to mating rights with one or more females.

Communicatory imbalance favoring male persuasion reaches its extreme among certain polygynous animals. Emphasis upon mate-attracting signals increases with the number of potential matings, and polygynous males may mate with several females. The peacock is a notable example. Males persistently court relatively passive females. Several features of their incredible display are notable— the pattern is extremely complex. Each feather has a spectrum of stimulus characteristics, and the pattern is highly redundant. The basic pattern, a multicolored bull's-eye, is repeated again and again throughout the display plumage. The actual display is presented in a highly dynamic manner, with the male facing the female, plumage erected and expanded, thus increasing the volume of the signal. The visual field intercepted is further increased by the movements of the male as he taxies in front of the female. The tail feathers are moved rapidly, producing a rattling sound and adding more movement to the signal. During the courtship process, which may last

Table 8-1. Characteristics of persuading and coordinating visual displays.

Persuasion	Coordination
Functions of Signals	
Establishing territoriality	Recognizing individuals
Courtship	
Establishing dominance	Coordinating group movements
Attracting mates	Maintaining dominance
Warning coloration, based on real or counterfeit counterattack	Warning coloration, based on distastefulness and isolating mechanisms
Characteristics of Signals	
Movement	Static
Anterior position	Anterior, flank, and other positions
Little information	Much information
High stimulus value	Low stimulus value
Typical intensity	Graded intensity

for several hours and be repeated day after day, the females remain for the most part seemingly unmoved by the display. Often a female will remain busily at work searching for food while a male courts her at full vigor.

Territorial Signals

Visual signals concerned with the establishment of territories and dominance relationships also are persuasion displays. The signal received must be convincing, and this is accomplished by supporting the signal with aggression. These signals would not need to be as elaborate or as specific as courtship displays if spacing were their only function. Their primary function is to establish the reality of a willingness to fight. Signals that support the establishment of territories and dominance relationships must be proportional to the ability of the animal to defend itself. The most vigorous and largest individuals of many species displaying territorial colors also tend to be the most highly colored individuals. Do these aspects of fitness lead to a heightened color, or is a heightened color responsible for the fitness? The latter seems improbable, but Marler's (1955) experiments with the breast coloration of chaffinches, *Fringilla coelebs*, suggest that this is a possibility. In those experiments, Marler determined the dominance relationships of male and female chaffinches at feed trays. The redbreasted males normally dominate the females, but when the dull breasts of the females are painted red, they are better able to dominate other females. It seems that the conspicuousness–defense-mechanism–proportionality relationship (page 138) can be extended from predation relationships to intraspecific aggressive encounters.   Intraspecific coloration may vary so that brilliance is proportional to the offensive capability of each individual.

As with courtship, there is no limit to the degree to which it is useful to stimulate the receiver of aggressive signals. Thus, territorial signals, like other persuasion displays, must be dynamic. These signals are on particularly movable body parts and generally are located in an anterior position to emphasize their role in head-to-head encounters.

Warning Coloration

Partitioning of signals to persuading and coordinating functions establishes a dichotomy in warning coloration relationships. The communication of information to potential predators may operate on a coordinating or a persuading basis. The warning signals of prey species able to counterattack or pose the threat of counterattack are based upon persuasion displays. Some examples are the exaggeration of body size by owls when disturbed, chest beating by gorillas, and shouting and arm movement in man. These displays announce to an adversary a defensive capability based upon a real offensive potential. When these signals are used in interspecific encounters they communicate an imbalance, since the interests of intruder and defender differ. Signals serving this function are dynamic. They involve color and volume changes, extensive movements, and highly conspicuous colors (Table 8–1).

PERSUASION DISPLAYS BY MAN

Interpretation of the superficial morphological features of man is critical to this analysis of the significance of the coloration of man. The central hypothesis proposed here relates man's coloration to his hairlessness, so that both man's hair and his lack of it need to be evaluated. Alternative hypotheses to explain man's coloration and hairlessness tend to emphasize the role of body features in communication, and so in order to interpret the interrelationship of communication and physiology adequately it becomes necessary to consider all man's surface aspect.

Reversal of Sexual Signal Roles in Man

The human female is a remarkable exception to the situation that is almost universal in the animal world—that where there is sexual dimorphism in coloration it is the male that is the more highly colored sex. In daily life and to a considerable extent in other contexts as well, the female human in most contemporary and historical societies tends to adopt artifact coloration that is more conspicious than that of the males. The female breasts seem to be another adaptation to sexual signaling, for two reasons: first, that the comparative evidence shows that the human female is unique among primates (Morris, 1967) in the development of external breasts, and second, that women lacking well-developed breasts have no serious problems in nursing infants.

These relationships suggest that in human beings it is the female who gains the advantage from persuasion. What possible basis is there for this circumstance? It is apparent that, for the human female, there is no more advantage in securing multiple matings than for any other female animal. Prostitution is the obvious exception, but this is hardly a trait of general evolutionary significance, and conspicuous visual signals are not confined to this situation. Within the context of female monogamy there seems to be only one feature distinguishing man from other monogamous vertebrates—that there are extensive differences in the value of establishing a bond with any particular male. Most mature male animals are essentially alike in terms of the maximum resources they can provide for a female and her offspring, and so it makes relatively little difference which male she associates with as long as he has secured a suitable territory. Man, however, is distinguished from the animals by his ability to maintain and inherit power and wealth. Both power and wealth influence to a considerable degree the probability that a particular female's offspring will have food in time of shortage. This point is emphasized by the willingness of females in certain societies to associate voluntarily with a wealthy polygamous male, in spite of the fact that this may mean giving up some communication, persistent courtship, and other forms of attention. According to this hypothesis, polygamy in man should be associated with the individual males who have acquired a disproportionate share of the power and/or wealth of a society, and it should be less frequent in societies such as those composed of low-population-density hunter-gatherers where resources are relatively evenly distributed among members of the society.

Penis Size

A central feature of Desmond Morris's (1967) analysis of the role of man's communication morphology is his conclusions (1) that man is fundamentally monogamous and (2) that there are numerous morphological adaptations which reinforce the relationship between members of a pair. This line of reasoning led Morris to the conclusion that the evolution of a much larger penis in man than in any other primate was an adaptation to reinforcing the pair bond. According to this hypothesis, man's large penis provides sexual rewards to both sexes commensurate with its dimensions. This argument is internally inconsistent. If a structure functions to reinforce a pair bond, it is serving a coordinating function, and there would be no selection for exceptionally large size or for other characteristics of persuasion displays. Magnification of stimulation is not a primary function of coordination, and the argument thus lacks support in just that area from which it supposedly derives its strength—interspecies comparisons.

If man were polygynous, and if copulation served a primary role in the courtship process, then the function of the giant penis as a persuader would be more plausible. This is not to say that man is not in fact polygynous, but that he is polygynous was not the basis for Morris's conclusions. We must either reconsider man's fundamental social structure, or reevaluate the adaptive basis of the large penis. The ubiquitous nature of the pair bond in most living human populations supports Morris's arguments concerning monogamy and pair bonding as a fundamental feature of human social organization, and given acceptance of this aspect of his biology, his explanation of man's giant penis must be rejected.

Another problem with this hypothesis is that it assumes that sexual rewards are correlated with penis size. The limited information of an objective sort relating penis size to sexual gratification suggests that these characteristics are unrelated to one another (Masters and Johnson, 1966). The reason seems to be that vaginal contraction adjusts to the size of the erect penis, regardless of its size. Thus Morris's apparent source of information, the locker room and cocktail party lore relating penis size to sexual pleasure, seems to be unsubstantiated by physiological or comparative evidence.

Given these objections to the Morris hypothesis, some alternative explanation of man's giant penis is called for. One such suggestion has been offered by Guthrie (1970)—that it is an adaptation to visual communication with other males. The evidence is as follows:

1 The penis, the testicles, and the surface area near the genitals are brightly colored in a number of primate species. The function of these signals seems to be concerned primarily with male rivalry (Wickler, 1967). The upright posture of man would be a logical preadaptation for emphasis upon the genital area in visual communication.

2 In human societies it is a common practice to decorate the penis
in the context of male rituals (Figure 8–1). The cultural emphasis
upon the penis suggests a role in agonistic male encounters.

These comparisons with primates also suggest an objection to the
interpretation that the size of man's penis is an adaptation to male-to-
male visual communication. None of the primate species that have
well-developed visual signals in the genital area have particularly
large penises. Instead, communication is emphasized by coloration,
discontinuities, and other signal characteristics. Perhaps the difference between these primates and man is related to man's compre-
hension of the communicatory significance of the penis, and that this
conceptualization of the relationship of the penis to the significant
process of copulation modified man's behavioral response to the
signal. This relationship of signal to behavior could set the stage for
selection to modify morphology, in this case an increased penis size.

The role of the penis in visual communication varies from society
to society according to the character of social interactions, patterns
of dress, etc. Nevertheless, a thread of continuity that shows widespread agreement across cultural boundaries is an emphasis upon
the size of the penis in male-to-male verbal communication. Within
any race these comparisons deal with relatively minor size differ-

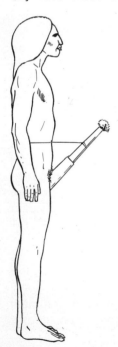

Figure 8–1. New Guinea hill tribesmen cover the
penis in a decorated sheath. The length of this sheath
increases with individual status in the society.

ences. However, among the New Guinea hill tribes it is customary to shield the penis with an erect sheath (Figure 8–1), the size of which varies greatly from individual to individual. Size identifies the status of the male in the society, so that the dimension of the signal agrees with position in the heirarchical order.

The graded size of these penis sheaths and the behavioral response to the heirarchical order they connote has a parallel in the weaponry of certain horned animals. Mountain sheep, *Ovis dalli*, react to one another according to the size of the horns. The rank of these animals is directly correlated with the size of the horns, and the response to a stranger can be predicted by the observer on the basis of horn size alone (Geist, 1966). In the case of the ram the signal and the means of its maintenance are the same, while the penis and its sheath are not weapons. But the message seems to be the same: "This is my level in the society."

Axillary Hair
An explanation of axillary hair offered by Hingston (1933) is that man's dark underarm hair tufts are an adaptation to threat display. This signal would function in the context of arm gestures, together with the shaken fist, as preliminaries to overt aggression or as threats that minimize the need to fight.

Such displays would have minimal stimulus value to human populations with dark skin colors, since dark hair viewed against dark skin shares few of the characteristics of visual signals. Yet black men too —all men for that matter—possess axillary hair. If the first hairy armpits were on black men, any value of axillary hair tufts as visual threat displays would probably be secondarily derived and confined to depigmented men. However, it is also possible that depigmented men were the first men (page 182), and the threat-display hypothesis becomes more plausible from this starting point.

It has also been argued that the axillary hair tufts are an adaptation to trapping and holding the secretions of apocrine glands, which in man are concentrated in the axillary and pubic areas (Morris, 1967; Guthrie, 1970).

These alternative hypotheses are not based upon much substantial evidence, and it is even difficult to conceive of a means to develop relevant evidence.

Beards
Another hairy part of the human anatomy that has been considered in the context of communication is the beard. One possibility is that beards have a threat function, a conclusion suggested by the fact

that the beard is limited to sexually mature males. Beards share the characteristics of many aggressive threat displays—expansion of the area subtended by man's primary signaling area, the face. Beard hair tends to be curlier, coarser, and darker than the hair on the head, and is thus the antithesis of what appears to be the sexually more attractive hair on the rest of the head.

Comparative analysis of the facial features of primates shows some close parallels with man's beard (Guthrie, 1970). Many primates, particularly males, have well-developed hairy expanses in the facial area (Figure 8–2). So far there has been no experimental analysis of the role of these facial signals in primate communication, and their role as agonistic signals is tentative.

If the beard is a morphological threat, an explanation for the remarkable and nearly ubiquitous habit of removing it is available. As human populations came to be organized to an increasing degree upon verbal communication, and as status came to be divorced to an increasing degree from physical prowess, morphological signals came to be less valuable. The transition to this level of organization happened in the recent moments of man's existence, and the biological responses of this inappropriate or imprecise morphological signal were not eliminated as rapidly as the new forms of communication developed. However, the problem could be neatly solved by cultural removal of the signal. This hypothesis may explain the reduced beards of Orientals and their derivatives, the indigenous people of the New World. The crowded conditions typical of urban existence are probably older in the Orient than anywhere else in the world, and the adaptive loss of beards by these populations may have proceeded apace.

The threat-signal hypothesis also agrees with the current cultural role of the beard in many stable human societies where beards are retained only by chieftains, elders, and individuals who have attained high status. This hypothesis may also explain the greater tendency for older men to wear beards in most societies. Age and status are often closely related, and the need to reduce the threat display is diminished.

An alternative hypothesis, also in agreement with the correlation of the bearded state and sexual maturity, is that the beard is a sexual attractant (Darlington, 1969; and numerous earlier authors—all male). But the physical characteristics of beard hair (see above) argue against this interpretation as the adaptive basis of beard hair. The considerable part of the female population that is particularly attracted to the bearded male has probably come to this preference secondarily.

Figure 8-2. Facial hair and pattern of some primates. (a) Celebes ape, *Cynopithecus niger;* (b) crab-eating monkey, *Macaca fascicularis;* (c) marmoset, *Callithrix jacchus;* (d) baboon, male and female, *Papio hamadryas;* (e) Brazzae monkey, *Cercopithecus neglectus;* (f) hoolock gibbon, *Hylobates hoolock;* (g) patas monkey, *Erythrocebus patas;* (h) saki, *Chiropotes satanas;* (i) diana monkey, *Cercopithecus diana;* (j) guenon, *Cercopithecus ascanis;* (k) mangabey, *Cercocebus aterrimus;* (l) tamarin, *Saguinus mystax;* (m) orangutan, *Pongo pygmaeus;* (n) howler monkey, *Alouatta seniculus;* (o) uakari, *Cacajao rubicundus;* (p) *Colobus guereza.* (After Guthrie, 1970.)

Two rather more prosaic additional hypotheses deserve consideration. One is that the beard actually represents thermal protection for
a part of the body not easily protected by simple clothing. This hypothesis may also agree with the development of beards at sexual
maturity, since it is at this time that males in hunting societies take
on a serious hunting and long-distance foraging role. This hypothesis also agrees with the sex-limited nature of the beard, since the
more prolonged forays away from shelter are, in almost all societies,
exclusively male adventures.

An associated hypothesis is that the beard is a form of camouflage,
disguising what otherwise would be the well-defined outlines of a
man's head. The same evidence applicable to the preceding hypothesis can be applied here, i.e., that the beard is a male attribute emerging at the time of physical maturity and adoption of a hunting role.

Pubic Hair

The traditional hypotheses dealing with the explanation of pubic
hair concern its role in holding olfactory stimuli.

An alternative is that the pubic region is a focus for aggressive
visual signals, and that pubic hair is a part of this display. The secondary role of male genitals as a threat is well established for primates, including man (Wickler, 1967). It is conceivable that pubic
hair enhances this signal.

In the case of the female, pubic hair may also serve a significant
role in the repulsion of sexually aggressive males. If human society
is basically a monogamous one, and there are numerous compelling
reasons for believing this to be the case, then it would be advantageous to conceal the primary sex organs, reducing the stimuli reaching uninvited males. If dark curly hair has taken on a threatening
function on other parts of the anatomy, the male face in particular
(page 160), it seems possible that the same function might be associated with female pubic hair. That removal of pubic hair is a common
and widespread practice among prostitutes lends some support to
the contention that this hair has a repelling role, since it is clearly
advantageous for prostitutes to bypass preliminary hostile relationships to males as rapidly as possible.

According to this line of reasoning an interpretation of the early
and widespread development of the loincloth emerges, similar to that
suggested above for beard shaving. This is that loincloths are an
adaptation to the reduction of aggression in a species which moved
culturally from low to high densities. It would be advantageous to
conceal morphological threats of whatever sort, and the cultural
adoption of an artifactual cover would serve this function.

There seems to be no evidence whatsoever to support the widely cited hypothesis (e.g., Darlington, 1969) that pubic hair serves to prevent mechanical friction during intercourse. The actions of prostitutes, noted above, would seem to demonstrate that a hairless pubis can accommodate considerable friction without serious chafing effects.

COORDINATION DISPLAYS

Unlike persuasion displays, the basic objective of the sender and the receiver of a signal in cooperative behavior is the same. The sender of the signal wishes to convey certain information; the receiver wishes to receive that information. Establishment of appropriate information transfer is thus beneficial to both sender and receiver.

Kinds of Coordination
This category of signals includes communications favoring parent-young interactions. It is advantageous for parent and young to coordinate their activities, so as to enhance the survival and the evolutionary progress of both. This category of signals also includes markings facilitating the maintenance of fish schools and flocks of birds. Signals that are adopted to facilitate individual recognition clearly belong to this group of signals, and it would appear that isolating mechanisms do also.

Before proceeding with an interpretation of these several categories, it is necessary to point out that the principles enunciated below, with respect to the characteristics of signals (and summarized in Table 8-1), refer only to visual signals. Other kinds of signals, because of their physical nature, are not as extensively separable, although casual analysis suggests that many of the same principles are obtained. But there is, for example, no such thing as a static auditory signal.

Isolating Mechanisms
It is advantageous for all members of a population to avoid, to an equal degree, mating with another species. A popular practice in the analysis of isolating mechanisms is to detail temporal, spatial, and behavioral characteristics which distinguish a group of species, and to conclude that these differences are responsible for maintenance of species integrity, i.e., that together they represent the relevant isolating mechanism. There are, however, surprisingly few experimental demonstrations of the actual function of any of these parameters as isolating mechanisms.

In the case of a closely related group of Arctic gull species, genus

Larus, Smith (1966) found that the sexual isolation was to a large degree dependent on differences in eye iris coloration. These large, basically white birds thus utilize little of the body surface in communication, and the pigmentation may serve other important physiological functions which depend on the covering of the entire heat-absorbing surface (Chapter 2). Behavioral interactions leading to pair formation during the breeding season take place at close range, and since this is a coordinating rather than a persuading behavioral function, there is no need to devote an extensive body surface area to the signal.

As the number of potential alternate species with which to mate increases, the complexity of the visual signal may also increase. For example, in coral reef fish the complexity of body surface coloration, as measured by the number of different colors per individual, increases with the number of potentially sympatric species belonging to the same family (Table 8–2, Hamilton, personal data). This calculation is based upon an analysis following the elimination of coloration and pattern that are clearly assignable to other hypotheses. The failure of the relationship to hold at the generic level (Table 8–2) is probably the simple result of the relatively arbitrary nature of this taxon.

Warning Colors
Unlike warning colors which announce counterattack possibilities, warning colors advertising distastefulness tend to be static. This is particularly true of the colors of insects. In the case of distasteful and poisonous insects, it is equally advantageous to the prospective predator and the prey to have the signal properly interpreted.

COMMUNICATORY COMPROMISES

Many coloration adaptations involve a compromise between the need to communicate and other requirements. These compromises will be considered here for two specific circumstances; suboptimal social colors and the conflict between communication and concealment.

Compensation for Suboptimal Social Colors
Energy colors and camouflage are not the most effective colors for visual communication. The species which have adopted this garb must thus either compensate for this limitation on their visual communicatory system or settle for less effective visual communication. When background-matching colors are adopted, prominent visual signals may give away the ruse.

Table 8-2. Number of colors other than silver per individual Indian Ocean reef fish, ranked by family and genus.

Number of Colors (number of fish species)	Mean Number of Species per Family	Mean Number of Species per Genus
0 (8)	6.2	3.8
1 (5)	29.2	6.2
2 (13)	32.1	14.3
3 (11)	39.1	13.5
4 (6)	39.8	10.0
5 (2)	54.5	19.0
6, 7 (3)	65.0	6.0

Relatively somber animals have adopted a number of alternatives for communication. These include the use of artifacts and iridescence. Inflatable devices that accompany vocalizations are generally brightly colored and have taken on a prominent role in visual communication. Their transitory nature reduces the amount of space committed to signals which might otherwise make them highly conspicuous. For example, the umbrella bird of the South American jungles, a large black bird of the jungle canopy, inflates a brilliant red air sac. Another large black bird, the frigate bird, *Fregata magnificens*, a bird also living in the canopy of vegetation during the breeding season, has evolved a similar adaptation. There are evolutionary difficulties in shifting from energy colors to other adaptive types.

The shift from energy colors to sexual colors is probably less difficult than the shift from energy colors to background matching, because an immediate advantage could accrue from a small patch of bright coloration. It is particularly easy to visualize the steps when one considers the basis of iridescence (Greenewalt, 1960) and the manipulation of small structural components to secure otherwise unavailable brilliance. There is a striking correlation of iridescence with groups of birds that have black representatives, and many black birds are iridescent. Iridescence on plumage tends to occur most commonly on just the colors which are, by other criteria, least stimulating. Green coloration in particular, so common among the canopy birches of tropical forests, is especially likely to be iridescent.

Another way of compensating for the lack of bright sexual or other social colors is the use of artifacts. A partial list of species using artifacts in their social interactions (Table 8-3) emphasizes that these are animals which have energy or cryptic colors and that the artifacts used frequently have the conspicuousness and therefore the stimulus value of displays. In the case of the visual displays of man, a wide

Table 8-3. Animals using artifacts in their social interactions.

Species	Body Color	Interpretation	Artifact	Artifact Color	Authority
Birds					
Great crested grebe *Podiceps cristatus*			Weeds in beak	Brown, grey	Huxley, 1914
Brown towhee *Pipilo fuscus*	Brown	Camouflage	Piece of leaf in mouth	Green	Author's observations
European starling *Sturnus vulgaris*	Black	Energy	Piece of leaf in beak	Green	Author's observations
Bowerbird	Brown	Camouflage	Display scene	Pink, blue	Gilliard, 1963
Bowerbird	Black	Energy	Display scene	Blue	Gilliard, 1963
Bowerbird *Chlamydera nuchalis*	Brown	Camouflage	Berry in mouth	Green	Gilliard, 1959
Mammals					
Gorilla	Black	Energy	Leaf in mouth	Green	Schaller, 1963
Man	Black	Energy	Body pigments, clothing, feathers, etc.	Red, yellow, blue, orange, green, black, white, others	Numerous
	White	Metabolism			

variety of objects are used including colorful clothing, paints daubed on the body, mud applied to the hair and body, and objects thrown, held, and used in almost every imaginable manner. The extensive role of such objects in communication emphasize man's relatively uncolorful structure and extends the evidence aligning man with color-disadvantaged creatures.

Compromises surrounding the development of sexual colors raise the question of why the coloration-stimulation relationship has not taken the potentially more adaptive step of simply matching the color pattern most advantageous in other contexts—i.e., black, white, grey, brown, or green—to the maximum stimulating value at the level of the central nervous system. Why, for example, have females not simply evolved a maximum responsiveness to browns, greens, and greys? The correlation of compensation adaptation with less conspicuous colors, as demonstrated in the preceding analyses, seems to emphasize the *inherent* stimulus value of other colors. Is the stimulus value of these bright colors inherently greater at the receptor level? This hypothesis assumes a limitation on the ability of the visual system to adopt a high responsiveness to colors which are less conspicuous.

A more probable explanation is that the relatively conspicuous colors have been adopted by animal visual systems because they contrast with usual background colors. Greens, browns, and greys have probably dominated vegetated backgrounds from the beginning. Against these substrates, visual communication is most effective if it contrasts with the substrate; and reds, yellows, and blues as well as contrasting patterns of black and white are the logical ways to enhance the effectiveness of communication.

Visual Communication and Concealment

Visual signals often compromise with concealment, and a diversity of animals have evolved adaptations that minimize interspecific communication while enhancing social communication. These compromises involve a number of alternatives:

1 The signal may be restricted in area and so placed that visual communication is highly directional and can be effectively oriented to the desired receiver of the signal. Some signals are on the underside of the body, while the dorsal surface remains camouflaged. Many ground-dwelling birds and lizards have adopted this strategy. Iridescence is most effective when viewed at the precise angle of reflection, and some iridescent animals take advantage of this by orienting their displays to the sun (Hamilton, 1965) (Figure 8-3).

2 The signal may be limited to skin folds, the surface of an inflatable air sac, or underfeathers which can be revealed by erection at the appropriate time. Such adaptations may also help to prevent habituation to a signal. Some birds may erect concealed patches of spectacular crown feathers. Other animals may erect or inflate gular folds, as, for example, most lizards, the throat sacs of gibbons (Hylobates), and the similar gular sacs of birds such as the frigatebird (*Fregata magnificens*).

3 The signal may be seasonally or otherwise temporally restricted to occasions when it will be most valuable. This may be accom-

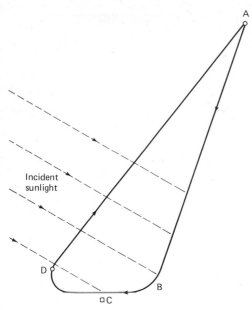

Figure 8-3. Display flight of the male Anna's Hummingbird, *Calypte anna,* oriented toward the sun. The male climbs nearly vertically and stops in midair (*A*), 40 to 50 m above and to the side of the display object away from the sun (*C*). At this point he hovers and then power dives. The flight levels (*B*) a few meters from the display object, and the male passes over this object almost horizontally and in the direction of the sun. Then he slows and veers upward, rises in a hook-shaped course 3 to 4 m above and beyond the display object, hovers and returns to *A* to repeat the cycle. (After Hamilton, 1965.)

plished by rapid color change, plumage and pelage molts, and developmental color changes.

4   A muted color, intermediate between camouflage and colorful, may be employed as the signal. This is probably a widespread and exceedingly common adaptation, but a way to secure relevant evidence to test the hypothesis is not obvious.

PART 3   MAN

Man shares a group of traits with a small number of other large animals, including some large African mammals with which he also shares a common prolonged evolution in arid Africa.

Man is committed to an integrated social life. He clusters even when suitable homesites are distributed throughout environmental space. From these refuges he radiates outward to secure resources—the distance he travels depending upon the nature of the resources he utilizes, the extent to which they have been reduced by his exploitation, and his means of securing them.

Animal species organized on a similar refuging socioeconomic basis generally are long-lived as a result of the development of special defense mechanisms including aggregation, and also as a result of the development of morphological and tool weapons, and group action in times of danger. Longevity has also enabled animals organized on this basis to emphasize learning in their exploitation of resources.

The coloration of black men has been variously interpreted—as camouflage, radiation protection, a preventative to hypervitaminosis, and in other ways. Analysis of the group of traits he shares with other animals—body size, longevity, social organization, and hairlessness —can be interpreted as support of a heat-exchange hypothesis to explain dark human skin coloration. One possibility is that black man's coloration is fundamentally an adaptation to heat absorption, thus minimizing the cost of maintaining a high body temperature. The effectiveness of black coloration in thermoregulation would be enhanced by reduction or elimination of insulation. In man the traits of hairlessness and dark coloration probably evolved simultaneously. This leads to the conclusion that depigmented man was secondarily derived from black ancestors and that the first hairless men were black. But it is also possible that as clothing came to replace hair, an unpigmented skin was uncovered which has secondarily taken on dark pigmentation following the reduction of clothing insulation.

THE HAIRLESS HOMINID

Analysis of human skin coloration is introduced here with a consideration of man's hairlessness. This is because interpretation of man's hairlessness is critical to the interpretation of his coloration and to the development of the characteristics that have led to his biological domination of this planet.

HAIRY MEN

Some time ago an unresolved controversy concerning the origins of man's hairlessness developed in the journal *Science* (Glass, 1966 and later). Details of this discussion are of special interest, not only because of the general interest in interpretations of the evolutionary basis of man's physical traits, but also because they exposed the biases and assumptions of the participating scientists. Subsequently, Morris (1967) advanced another explanation of man's hairlessness. This chapter evaluates these hypotheses and suggests some alternatives.

Primate Hairlessness and Heat Exchange

One of the alternatives to be developed here is that human hairlessness is an adaptation to optimizing radiant heat exchange. Optimiza-
tion implies facilitation of both heat gain and heat loss, i.e., thermoregulation. Many primates have hairless areas on limited parts of the
body surface (Table 9-1). On most primates, these hairless areas are
restricted to the head, chest, genital regions, and hands and feet. In
some species these hairless surfaces are highly colored, especially
in the head and genital areas, and share other characteristics of
effective social signals: They are set off by discontinuities and contrasts, and often they are displayed by ritualized movements in the
context of certain predictable social encounters. These characteristics confirm their role in visual communication.

These brightly colored hairless areas contrast with the black hairless areas of other diurnal primates. In these species the hairless
areas are found about the head, chest, and feet. These surfaces
probably are adapted to maximizing heat exchange. This interpretation is supported by study of the behavior of the species that have
such hairless areas. A visit to any large zoo, in either temperate or
tropical regions, reveals many black primates, furred and furless,
orienting hairless chests, soles, palms, and faces to the sun (Figure
4-3) at the times of day when heat is at a premium.

Fire, Heat Exchange, and Clothing

If hairy preman were confronted today with the heat-exchange problems faced by most primates, he would have limited tolerance to low
temperatures, but he would be able to withstand upper thermal extremes reasonably well. Thus, in spite of his hairy insulation, man
would be unable to forgo the advantages of heat conservation provided by insulation unless he could avoid excessive heat loss at night.
There must have been some adaptation to reduce his need for a furry
insulation at night. Whatever this trait was, its development permitted him to shed his hair and thus increase his thermal efficiency.
Any one of three cultural developments might have allowed the elimination of structural insulation. These are (1) the development of
clothing, (2) the use of fire, and (3) retreat to artificial or particularly
warm shelters at night. Each of these traits would reduce heat loss.
The problem is to determine whether it was one or a combination of
these adaptations that led to man's hairlessness.

Comparative evidence suggests that what might appear to be one
of the simplest routes to hairlessness, the adoption of artificial shelters or caves as nocturnal retreats, is the least probable alternative.

Many mammals live in shelters at least equal to any natural or cultural shelter preman could have secured in terms of thermal protection. Diurnal mammals that burrow at night and surface during the day —badgers, ground squirrels, and hares—live under particularly favorable conditions for heat retention, especially when their use of fine roots and grasses as insulation against damp, cold substrates is considered. This subterranean phase of their life presents few thermal problems. When they are exposed during the day, however, excessive heat loss must be prevented, and a light furry coat is retained. Thus, burrowing diurnal mammals have relatively thin coats which probably are a compromise with the less favorable thermal conditions of their nonburrowing active periods.

However effective a shelter may be in conserving heat, there are still heat-loss problems when the shelter must be vacated, and no one suggests that men ever lived the active part of the daily cycle in caves. Of the unique human cultural adaptations, only clothing offers a solution to this part of the problem. Fire, like shelter, may enhance the effectiveness of thermoregulation, but, also like shelter, it is generally effective only when the animal is present at the shelter or during intervals of inactivity.

Clothing is another unique human attribute setting man apart from the other primates. Clothing enhances thermoregulatory efficiency regardless of location, and it would have given to relatively thinly insulated preman a considerable advantage in extending his range

Table 9–1. Relationship of man's body hair or its absence to preference for or rejection of it.

Cultural State	Adaptive Condition	Man's Preference
Hershkovitz's Argument		
Time No cultural development	Hairy	Would prefer less hairy individuals
Clothing, fire	Hairless	Prefers hairless individuals
Alternative Suggested Here		
Time No cultural development	Hairy	Prefers hairy individuals
Clothing, fire	Hairless	Prefers less hairy or hairless individuals

into otherwise inaccessible environments (Figure 9–1). Thus cloth-ing appears to be the only critical precondition to human hairlessness.

Hairlessness from Loss of Adaptive Value?

Bently Glass (1966), the initiator of the *Science* discussion, also con-cluded that hair became unnecessary once clothing entered man's cultural repertoire, but for a different reason. His conclusion was that hair disappeared as a result of *mutation in the absence of natural selection*. To adopt this position, Glass had to conclude that man reached a point where neither hair nor hairlessness had any signifi-cance to him:

> One may postulate a positive advantage in being hairless, a disadvantage in hairiness; or one may postulate that hairiness simply became incon-sequential to man. The first hypothesis does not seem very probable, because the human species, evolving in East Africa or wherever else, was in the company of other primates who did not become hairless, to judge from their modern descendents. Although the matter must of course remain without conclusive proof, it seems far more reasonable to suppose that man very early in his separate existence as a species (or genus) began wearing clothing (in the form of skins) and later using fire to warm himself. Thus he changed his environment sufficiently to make hairiness an inconsequential feature, except on the more exposed parts of his anatomy (Glass, 1966, p. 294).

Glass was first challenged by Baker (1966), Kraft (1966), and Fentress (1966), who suggested that Glass's attitude was Lamarckian, a "charge" denied by Glass. In the process of these criticisms, each of the offended authors took the opportunity to offer his own sugges-tion concerning the significance of man's hairlessness. These alter-natives, which were meant as substitute solutions to the problem, are discussed below.

There is, however, a criticism of Glass's statement which is more relevant than the charge of Lamarckianism. The aspect of his state-ment which must be questioned is his suggestion that any fea-ture of an organism that is as prominent as its insulation can have neutral adaptive value. An extraordinary deviation from the primate norm, such as hairlessness, must be based upon some powerful driving force. Furthermore, the unimpeached arguments by Fisher (1930) establish the vast improbability that any significant character-istic will develop or disappear as a result of recurring mutation in the absence of selection. Mutations may increase the range of variation within a population if they are not eliminated by selection, but those

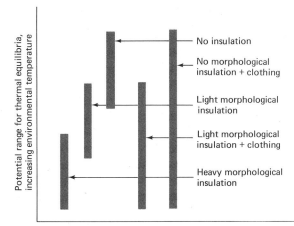

Figure 9-1. Morphological insulation or its absence restricts the range of thermal equilibrium to relatively narrow limits. Clothing is a removable insulation that permits a much broader range of thermal adaptation. The absence of all morphological insulation provides for the broadest range of thermal adaptability, a circumstance which probably accounts for man's hairlessness.

mutations are not directional. Thus, mutation can result in the elimination of a characteristic under only the most improbable of circumstances.

Conservation-of-metabolic-energy Hypothesis

In a second round of letters the *Science* discussion expanded to include more criticism and more hypotheses. One letter contained a traditional explanation of the loss of characteristics where no obvious adaptive basis for the loss can be determined: ". . . every character requires metabolic energy to develop and maintain it, and elimination of a useless character diverts this energy to uses that promote survival . . ." (Hailman, 1966, p. 364).

The same concept has been proposed to explain the loss of pigment and eyes by cave animals (Chapter 7). This view accepts the inevitable influence of almost every conceivable change, however small, upon survival value and reproductive advantage. But the actual energy required to develop and maintain such characteristics has never been determined, and precise evaluation of the merits of this argument awaits the development of real measurements. The values involved here are, however, probably quite small, and demonstration of other significant effects of any sort would seem to eliminate this factor as a variable *leading to* hairlessness.

Hairlessness and Ectoparasites

Another correspondent, Walter Olson (1966), supported the role of hairlessness in minimizing the problem of ectoparasites. Olson noted that primates spend much of their time delousing one another, and he suggested that a mutation resulting in hairlessness antedated the emergence of man. If a more hairless primate were less subject to ectoparasite-borne diseases, it might thrive. Hairlessness would thus have spread, as the more thinly haired members of the population would have been better at surviving epidemics. This advantage, Olson contended, was a compelling reason to invent clothing, shelters, and the cultural use of fire, because otherwise this flea-free preman was also going to be chilly: "The need to compensate for a defective gene may thus have been one of nature's most powerful stimulants for the advancement of mankind" (Olson, 1966, p. 364).

It is reasonable to assume that the significance of ectoparasites to man altered with changes in hair density. However, the freedom that man may have secured from ectoparasites by becoming hairless was lost again when he adopted clothing, and since clothing was a prerequisite for hairlessness, it is not clear how loss of hair could have resulted in an ectoparasite-free existence, even temporarily.

An alternative explanation of man's hairless condition was needed, and in the same issue of *Science* additional alternatives were available.

Multiple-significance Hypothesis

Kennington (1966) introduced a multiple-significance hypothesis in the *Science* hairlessness discussion and described studies dealing with the role of human hair in eliminating trace elements and in serving other physiological processes of the skin. However, he did not offer this as an exclusive explanation of man's hairlessness. To do so, of course, would be to suggest a unitary explanation, a conclusion contrary to his basic premise. Instead, Kennington categorically challenged all standing and all potential hypotheses.

One of the safest arguments concerning any biological phenomenon is to suggest that it has a combination of advantages and disadvantages. It is safe because in the vast majority of cases it is almost surely correct. There are two basic reasons for this. First, all directional causes of mortality, every effect upon energy expenditure, and/or every modification of reproductive success will inevitably lead to an adaptive response if it is not counteracted by stronger selection pressures precluding that adaptation. Second, every adaptation influences the value of all the other adaptations of that organism. But it is for just this reason, the ubiquity of this argument, that this statement provides little in the way of explanation.

Once the multiple-significance hypothesis is stated and agreed upon, the next steps are to ask: (1) What are the several selective pressures? (2) What is the relative value of each? (3) What is the temporal sequence of their evolution? In the case of animal coloration we have seen that the relative value of alternative selective pressures is all-important in determining the surface characteristics of animals. Unless the animal involved is able to undergo color change, the characteristic which is most important relative to alternate selection pressures will be emphasized to the exclusion of alternative adaptations. In most instances, including man's hairlessness, some selection pressure has probably been the most important component leading to the adaptation.

Sexual Selection and Hairlessness

One of the most emphatic responses to Glass's statements came from a taxonomist, Hershkovitz (1966), who advocated a sexual role for man's hairlessness: "Man's long tresses and relatively thinly haired body and limbs are almost certainly the result of sexual selection, with the male selecting for these traits in the female" (Hershkovitz, 1966, p. 362).

In this statement Hershkovitz undoubtedly expresses not only his scientific opinion but also his own personal preference for hairless women. I am in full agreement with this preference. But isn't this because Hershkovitz and I share a long history of common descent and tradition in a hairless tribe? Which came first, our preference for smooth-skinned women or their hairlessness? The argument is summarized in Table 9–1. It is apparent from this tabulation that the critical question Hershkovitz must answer is: Why should hairy preman have preferred more thinly haired individuals? Since we are considering an animal derived from hairy precursors for tens of millions of years, there is no obvious reason that his preference should be other than for this original condition.

Comparison with other primates provides no substantial evidence to support Hershkovitz's claim. Primates, the highly colored mandril for example, limit visual sexual signals to the face and pubic areas. Adornment by adoption of colored fur is a common primate trait, and to suggest that some primordial preman developed a predilection for mating with hairless mutants is unsupported by evidence other than current cultural prejudice. Furthermore, Hershkovitz is on unsafe ground in attributing sexual selection in primates to female signal elaboration. Among nonhuman primates, males are often the more highly colored sex, and extensive behavioral field observations emphasize that in primate societies, unlike most human societies, the choice of a mate is basically a male prerogative. Female primates are limited in their reproductive rate by the problems of prenatal and postnatal energy provision for their infant's nourishment; each female individual must be concerned for the welfare of her own infant; and it is *relatively* unimportant to her which male she mates with. For the male the problems of infant support are not as restraining. Opportunities to mate with several females may arise. Field studies of primate social organization have failed to show that males neglect to serve receptive females. Among nonhuman primates, sexual selection is probably related to competition for females by males, the usual case in most animal societies. Thus, there is no comparative evidence to support Hershkovitz's argument, nor do there seem to be other logical bases for his suppositions.

The sexual selection argument as an explanation for hairlessness is wholly accepted by Darlington (1969); who considers no alternatives. He extends this hypothesis to include the male sex. His argument is that, since hairlessness is a secondary sexual characteristic, there is less rigorous selection for intersexual differentiation than in the case of the primary sexual characteristics. Thus, selection by the male for a characteristic in the female affects the chromosome complement of the species. Therefore, as an indirect and not necessarily adaptive consequence, the male has selected for his own hairlessness. This line of reasoning reemphasizes Darlington's fundamental contention that in the course of recent human evolution—he puts the interval at 1,000 generations in this case—the genetic system has been unable to keep pace with that which would be optimal. While this may be true in some instances, the availability of attractive alternative hypotheses to explain the phenomenon of human hairlessness leaves Darlington's conclusion insecure at best.

Human Hairlessness and Heat Exchange
Several participants in the *Science* discussion considered the role of hairlessness in heat exchange. Some evaluated this aspect of the problem relative to clothing. No one challenged the premise that man's immediate ancestors were hairy.

Loring Brace (1966), an anthropologist, emphasized the relationship of man's hairlessness to heat exchange. Man, he noted, is a biologically unique primate, not only because of his hairlessness but also because of his habit of hunting during the heat of the tropical day. The combination of hairlessness and perspiration could have emphasized his heat-dissipating capacity and been instrumental in the development of this unique hunting tactic.

From this line of reasoning, and assuming that the correlation of hairlessness with the adoption of diurnal hunting habits by early man is established, Brace and Montagu (1965) have suggested that the onset of hairlessness in man can be given a relative date. Since the archaeological record shows middle Pleistocene human hunting habits to be half a million years old, they identify this as the time of onset of man's hairlessness. This is questionable reasoning, depending upon the validity of two premises. The first is that man's hunting habits developed in regions where cooling was the most important aspect of his overall thermoregulatory adaptation. This question was considered in the context of comparative animal thermoregulatory biology in Chapter 4, where a different conclusion was reached. The second premise is that an active stalking-hunting habit (page 116) was a mainline early human adaptation. This conclusion is also vulnerable (Chapter 7). Brace and Montagu extend these conclusions still further by suggesting that man's clothing developed subsequently. They date this event to approximately 100,000 years ago, based upon their original unproven assumption concerning the significance of hunting to heat exchange. If these initial conclusions are indeed correct, the first appearance of weapons in the archaeological record must also identify the onset of man's hairless state.

It seems apparent that the appearance of leather-working tools in the archaeological record coincides with the development of man's clothing. But the state of man's insulation at that time remains questionable. Clothing would have been advantageous to a lightly furred primate (Figure 9–2) and would have induced selection for further hair loss. Immediate advantage that would have accrued from the use of clothing might well have induced the spread of cultural insulation in a furred population of preman.

Another advocate of a heat-dissipation hypothesis, Desmond Morris (1969), subsequently introduced a variation on the theme by suggesting that instead of hunting per se, it was the final rush to prey that led to man's hairless state. His reasons are essentially the same as those of Brace and Montagu, and they emphasize man's need to avoid overheating. Morris expressed with some conviction his conclusions concerning man's early activities:

> The chase was so important to him that he would have to put up with this [extreme physical strain], but in the process he must have experienced

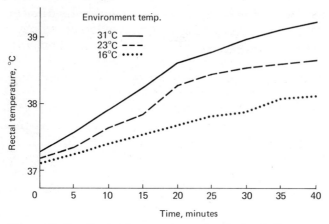

Figure 9-2. Rectal temperature of a trained distance runner with time. (After Costill, 1968.)

considerable over-heating. There would be a strong selection pressure working to reduce this over-heating and any slight improvement would be favoured, even if it meant sacrifices in other directions. His very survival depended on it. This surely was the key factor operating in the conversion of a hairy hunting ape into a naked ape (Morris, 1969, p. 47).

Other evidence indicates that overheating during sprints may not have been a critical limit to emerging mankind. Men seldom take sizable prey species by running them down. If man were to be successful at all in this tactic, it would almost surely be at the very start of the chase, before the surprised prey got underway or later when it reached the limits of its endurance. Body temperatures do not build up in modern (or hairless) man during short sprints, but heat continues to accumulate for several minutes depending upon the pace and ambient conditions—wind, temperature, radiation, and humidity. Body temperatures of man as high as 41.1°C have been recorded by Robinson (1963) for world record runners after racing 14 and 30 minutes under warm (30°C), humid conditions. This same temperature, 41.1°C, was recorded by Pugh et al. (1967) as the maximum temperature of 47 marathon (42 km) runners at the end of a race. The highest value was for the individual who won the race, and Pugh et al. conclude that an ability to tolerate a high body temperature is a requirement for successful marathon competition. This temperature, 41°C, seems to be close to man's limit in competition, which is no surprise considering how close it is to lethal limits, somewhere between 41 and 45°C. These considerations might seem to lend credence to the contention that preman exercising a hunting trade was limited by overheating, especially if there was further restriction by a permanent fur coat. But this would only have been applicable to long runs in the sun, and then only at relatively high humidities. Human body heat accumulation depends upon high ambient temperatures and develops slowly (Figure 9–2), not during sprints. How much more rapidly would these temperatures develop and how much higher would they be if man were furred like other plains animals? This can only be determined by experiments with insulated men. However, these data do suggest that the insulation of a light fur covering such as is typical of savannah animals including primates—baboons and monkeys—would not crowd man to his thermal limits during brief sprints.

Other comparative evidence fails to confirm Morris's hypothesis. Human hunters may drive game with dogs or fire. They may even operate as sentinel hunters (page 117), or utilize a number of other hunting tactics. But all these tactics involve stalking and bush beating, not sprints to the intended prey. When man does attack with a "lightning dash," the quarry is likely to be a sick or wounded animal, a newborn antelope, or some other weakened or very small prey item. The exercise of attack is unlikely to exceed or even approach that of a troop of hairy gorillas fleeing before a leopard, or an impala before a cheetah or lion. There is no evidence to sustain the conclusion that these furred animals ever die of heat exhaustion.

It is noteworthy that other lightly furred or feathered plains animals may run for miles (Table 6–4) without suffering heat exhaustion. Thus, these heat-loss ideas fail to place the argument in the context of the uniqueness of human hairlessness. This requirement, that any argument attempting to account for man's hairlessness take into account his special place among primates, is only satisfied when cultural adaptations are taken into account. With cultural developments such as clothing, fire, and fabricated shelters, man was prepared to enhance his thermal efficiency. At dawn he could be active in the sun or could actually sunbathe, restoring body temperatures to optimal levels. In the heat of the day he could seek shade, and his hairlessness would have been advantageous in evaporative cooling. The cycle was reversed in the afternoon, and, as ambient temperatures dropped, he could minimize the energy expenditure required to maintain his body temperature (Chapter 10). At night, a shelter, fire, and a leather robe would have reduced heat loss and thus kept energy expenditure to a minimum.

Hairlessness and Ultraviolet Light Absorption
In the course of extending the vitamin D hypothesis to explanations of racial differences in human skin pigmentation (page 199), Loomis incidentally advanced a new hypothesis to explain human hairless-

ness: "Having evolved in the tropics, early hominids were probably deeply pigmented and covered with fur, as are most other tropical primates. The first adaptation one might expect therefore to lowered availability of ultraviolet light as they moved north of the Mediterranean would be a reduction of fur . . ." (Loomis, 1967, p. 503).

This hypothesis, which contends that hairlessness is the result of a temperate-zone environment rather than the tropics, encounters extensive logical difficulties. What about the furry black men who were left behind in the tropics? According to Loomis's hypothesis they must have secondarily developed hairlessness after the colonizing populations moved out to the north. If an independent evolution of hairlessness in the tropics were involved, it must have taken place for entirely different reasons because the ultraviolet problem of sub-Saharan Africans, if they had one, was too much vitamin D, not too little, as Loomis points out. Loomis offers no suggestion about what these reasons may have been. Any one of several alternative explanations one could offer would suffice to salvage this argument temporarily. But the coincidence of a dual derivation of such a singular trait as man's hairlessness for two or more entirely different reasons within the same species seems most improbable. In addition to independent derivation of this unique trait, an improbable timing in the sequence of events is required. Black Africans would have had to retain their fur for millions of years of independent tool-using existence, to and beyond the occasion of man's northerly emigration and adaptation, and *then* would have had to develop hairlessness. Other alternatives are equally cumbersome, and the hypothesis probably is best dropped as casually as it was offered by Loomis in the first place. The only reason for considering this hypothesis here at all is that, left unchallenged, it would remain as a building block in Loomis's version (1967) of the vitamin D hypothesis as an explanation of the colors of mankind. The difficulties surrounding this hypothesis are considered in Chapter 10 (pages 199-204).

Thus the hypothetical preman I have been discussing picked up a series of traits in rapid succession, but nonetheless successively. The sequence may have gone like this:

1 Black furry ape—the preman—existed.
2 A bare chest area developed. If it was not already black, it became black.
3 Nocturnal shelter was improved by artifacts (huts of some sort).
4 Fire and clothing were adopted.
5 Morphological insulation (body hair) was reduced.

This brings us to a creature that was, in terms of physical appearance, not unlike modern African man. He was black, and his hair was generally lacking. Comparative evidence, considered as a whole, supports the conclusion that the depigmented races of man were derived from black ancestors such as these.

Extensive clothing minimizes the role of solar radiation in heat absorption. Given this circumstance, the advantage of black coloration in thermoregulation would be greatly reduced. While this may explain the loss of adaptive value for dark human coloration, it cannot account for the loss of pigment.

HAIR

A logical case can be made for the conclusion that man's hairlessness was superimposed upon a creature socially attracted to and stimulated by hair. Certainly there is no evidence that there is anything intrinsically repulsive about hair per se, either to animals or to man. Hair on the human head in particular tends to be a focus of tactile stimulation during courtship. There have never been satisfying physiological explanations of the other areas of residual human hair, the armpits and pubic areas, both of which are highly responsive to tactile stimulation, as is man's hairy chest. We stroke our furry house pets in a manner not unlike that of our manual movements in courtship, and the pleasurable sensation that we receive when we stroke a commercial fur, whether muskrat, mink, or otter, is at least somewhat similar to a sexual response. Thus the conclusion that hair is somehow a deterrent to sexual pleasure is hardly supported by either comparative evidence or introspection.

DEPIGMENTED MAN

European man is not white; he is depigmented. The reflectance of the skin of a group of depigmented men is illustrated in Figure 9–5. Depigmented man's reflectance is high in the visible range.

Maximum Reflectance Hypothesis
Several fairly reasonable explanations of northern man's depigmented condition exist. One possibility is that it became advantageous for nontropical man to extend his active period into the middle hours of the day. This may have been due to the shortened food-gathering season and more marked seasonal fluctuation in food availability at higher latitudes. Summer days in temperate regions are considerably longer than anything tropical man encountered, and man would have come to rely more heavily upon this seasonal burst in exploitable resources. The midday siesta could profitably be eliminated and activity extended away from bimodality. There is,

however, a major obstacle to this hypothesis. According to any consideration, depigmented man was clothed, and bare surface areas, except for those on the head, were probably seldom exposed to the sun. How could a high reflectance over the entire body surface protect such a man from the sun? There are a few occasions during the middle hours of the day when clothing might have been shed to reduce excessive insulation and enhance evaporative heat loss. On such occasions the relatively high reflectance of depigmented skin could have been an asset.

Skin Coloration and Human Heat Loss

Another possibility is that depigmentation minimizes heat loss. This possibility was considered in Chapter 3 with respect to white animal coloration in general. The difficulties related to this hypothesis do not differ materially when man is considered. So far there is no evidence that there is a physical basis upon which to base such an interpretation, in spite of the fact that it continues to be cited as one of several (Darlington, 1969) of the adaptive bases of human skin coloration. Barnes (1963) felt he had demonstrated that body coloration is not correlated with heat loss. His measurements were not, however, strictly quantitative. In fact, there do appear to be heat-loss differences correlated with certain artificial pigments applied to the human skin, and continued evaluation of this problem seems to be called for.

If a correlation between pale coloration and reduced heat loss could be demonstrated, the relationship of clothing to man's depigmentation would fall smoothly into place:

1 Dark human skin coloration, losing heat more rapidly than paler hues, would be advantageous in warm climates where overheating is a problem.
2 As man penetrated cooler regions, the balance of heat exchange would shift to the retention of body heat.
3 Insulation would become more extensive.
4 Other heat-retentive characteristics would be emphasized, including paler coloration.

There is, however, no known physical basis for this conclusion, nor is empirical support for such a hypothesis available.

Could Depigmented Man be the Original Hairless Man?

Another explanation of depigmented man's condition follows quite different lines. This is that depigmented man originated at the same time as or before black man. This argument also begins with the assumption that man's origin was tropical and that he had a hairy progenitor. From these beginnings, range expansion was to cooler regions via the cultural supplements of shelter, fire, and clothing. Now, assume that clothing was superimposed upon a furry covering, so that there was now a hairy man occasionally wearing clothes or simple skin robes. This combination could extricate early man from the tropics. His thermoregulatory efficiency at this point would be improved if he came to rely more heavily upon the more manipulable artifactual insulation (Figure 9-2). If this happened, it would be remarkably simple to devise depigmented man. Suppose the original furry black vagabond from the tropics were not black but depigmented under his hairy covering. Many primates are not pigmented beneath their furry coverings—for example, chimpanzees. If such a depigmented hairy animal were to lose its hair as described above, a depigmented hairless primate would result.

This hypothesis, which has not previously been considered, is one of the few that adequately explain the unique color of the *entire body* of European man. Other hypotheses, such as the vitamin D and maximum-reflectance hypotheses, must assume that much of the body surface depigmentation is due to the fact that surfaces exposed to radiation induced the depigmentation adaptation and that coloration or lack of it on unexposed surfaces is an incidental by-product of the adaptation of the entire system.

Extensive additional implications follow from this problematic hypothesis. The most important of these is that we are left without a link between black man and depigmented man. There are ways to bridge this gap. One would be to derive black man from depigmented man, by reinvasion of the tropics. This alternative, which is not altogether in disagreement with the fossil record (see Coon, 1965) raises the possibility of a nontropical origin of hairless man.

A more probable alternative is that the sequence of events described above leading to a depigmented hairless hominid took place within the tropics. From this starting point, the populations which retained the heaviest clothing would have given rise to the depigmented peoples of the temperate regions to the north. Subsequently, as warmer tropical environments were penetrated, the black-skinned people would develop.

Black Sensory Epithelium Hypothesis

Alfred Russell Wallace (1878) developed an early hypothesis explaining depigmented man's state based upon Darwin's discussion of the comparative olfactory acuity of black and white pigs. Darwin observed that white pigs were predisposed to consume poisonous roots that had no effect upon black pigs. He assumed that the immunity enjoyed by black pigs was associated with a constitutional quality associated with their black coloration which rendered these poisons harmless to them. Wallace provided another interpretation. He suggested that the difference between pigs of various colors might be based upon variation in their ability to *smell* poisonous herbs. If this were true, wouldn't it be more likely that the coloration per se influenced the olfactory sensitivity? This was Wallace's contention, and he was able to support it on comparative grounds. Albinistic mammals of many kinds tend to be susceptible to plant poisoning. When albinistic rhinoceroses eat the poisonous African plant *Euphorbia candelabrum*, they succumb. White sheep are poisoned by *Hypericum crispum*; black sheep are not. White horses may be poisoned when black ones are not. Wallace concluded that somehow melanin directly affects olfactory acuity. Wallace's hypothesis of a constitutional correlation effect which would now be called a pleiotropic genetic effect, might be a relevant explanation for one animal species, but would be less improbable for several.

The next step in Wallace's argument concerned the relationship of black coloration to sensory epithelium in diverse animal forms. If dark coloration were associated with and necessary for optimum functioning of important sense organs, it is logical to conclude that its absence could be associated with a corresponding loss of perceptual acuity. This led Wallace to his conclusions concerning the evolution of depigmented man:

> It is even possible that this relation of sense-acuteness with colour may have had some influence on the development of the higher human races. If light tints of the skin were generally accompanied by some deficiency in the senses of smell, hearing, and vision, the white could never compete with the darker races so long as man was in a very low or savage condition, and wholly dependent for existence on the acuteness of his senses. But as the mental faculties became more fully developed and more important to his welfare than mere sense-acuteness, the lighter tints of skin and hair and eyes would cease to be disadvantageous whenever they were accompanied by superior brain-power. Such variations would then be preserved; and thus may have arisen the Xanthochroic [depigmented] race of mankind, in which we find a high development of intellect accompanied by a slight deficiency in the acuteness of the senses as compared with the darker forms (Wallace, 1878, p. 267).

A considerable discussion of these ideas might ensue, but this is not a book about the history of racial attitudes. Certain basic biological points do require comment. Explaining the loss of a valuable attribute may or may not require directional selection (page 175). Wallace suggested that the lack of a positive adaptive value would suffice to produce the observed structural loss. This seems improbable, based upon comparative evidence. If so, then the fabric of his argument fails, and we are simply left with an interesting series of examples of the deleterious biological effect of massive mutation.

Metachromism and Depigmented Man

Recently Hershkovitz (1968, 1970) developed a hypothesis that dealt specifically with explanations of the diverse coloration of South American marmosets, but which he also applied to the skin or pelage coloration of a diversity of mammals including polar bears and "blond Norsemen." According to Hershkovitz, "The principle of metachromism holds that evolutionary change in cover-hairs, skin, and eye melanins is neither random nor opportunistic, but follows an orderly and irreversible sequence which ends in white or loss of pigment. . . . In all events, the direction of change is toward the elimination of pigment" (Hershkovitz, 1970, p. 644).

If there were a valid principle of metachromism and it were applicable to the skin and hair pigmentation of man, it would follow that depigmented man was definitely derived from black man. However, the evidence Hershkovitz provides in support of his hypothesis is open to serious question (Lawlor, 1969). Applicability of the principle and of the specific quotations cited above seem to be directly contradicted by the evidence provided by New World man, where all archaeological evidence seems to point towards the derivation of the darker tropical New World populations of man from less heavily pigmented ancestors (Chapter 10, especially Figure 10-2 and its interpretation). Thus the principle of metachromism, real or imagined, is not likely to be very helpful in developing an understanding of the color of depigmented man.

OTHER PEOPLE

On page 191 and throughout Chapter 10 various hypotheses dealing with the coloration adaptations of man are considered. It is necessary to emphasize that, regardless of which hypotheses one chooses to favor, the coloration of certain peoples remains unexplained. Two of these exceptions and unexplained phenomena are considered here.

Oriental Skin and Hair Coloration
Throughout much of Asia north of the Himalayas there is little or no gradient in skin coloration. Since all available hypotheses concern climatic gradients, and since there is a considerable thermal and radiation gradient on this continent, some explanation is called for. Darlington (1969) contends that the lack of a gradient can be accounted for by simply supposing that there was no genetic variability upon which adaptation could act. This hypothesis calls for comment, since the contention that genetic constraints have limited man's adaptation to his environment is a central concept in his analysis of the interrelationship of man's biology and culture. In this instance a plausible alternative seems possible. This is that in the part of the Asiatic subcontinent north of the Himalayas there has been a free exchange of genetic material as a result of recurrent invasions, emigrations, and a lack of prominent geographic isolating mechanisms. This might have resulted in a homogenizing action of selection (Chapter 5), so that the overall coloration would be to the center of mass of the population rather than to the entire area occupied by it. This hypothesis seems at least as plausible as Darlington's concept, and thus this evidence, at least, should not be considered a foundation stone for further speculation.

New World Peoples
Darwin was struck by the uniformity of coloration of the peoples of the Americas by comparison with the Old World. Paradoxes such as this must have been considerable hindrance in the development of Darwin's evolutionary theory. We know now that there is a fundamental historical basis for this hemispheric dichotomy. The peoples of the New World have all been derived, in the course of a few thousand years, from Oriental ancestors. At the same time, it is apparent that *some* adaptation has taken place in the New World (Walter, 1958, Figure 10–3). It seems possible to agree with Darlington (1969) in this case that the rate of human adaptation lags behind its full adaptive potential. There is, however, a point of fundamental disagreement concerning the availability of sufficient genetic diversity to permit this adaptation to proceed to its optimum. Darlington's conclusion that no color gene has mutated in 20,000 years of man's New World existence cannot be taken seriously. There is even the possibility that the color of New World man is fully adapted to his environment. Regardless of which hypothesis we choose to entertain, some correlation between amount of radiant energy and coloration is implicated. However, it is not necessarily legitimate to plot gross solar radiation (or ultraviolet radiation, which is generally directly

proportional to it) against human skin pigmentation and expect that people living in different parts of the world will be the same color if they are maximally adapted to their environment. A much greater part of the New World tropics than of the Old World is covered by dense forest, and men, in the course of their daily activities, may receive vastly different proportions of the incident solar energy. What is needed is a sample of aboriginal people wearing radiation badges during the course of their evolutionarily relevant activities, and a comparison of the results of these meter readings with skin pigmentation. Unfortunately, the opportunity for these measurements lies largely in the past.

CONCLUSIONS

1 Development of human hairlessness depended upon the adaption of clothing. Other human cultural developments dealing with heat exchange serve man only while he is inactive and would not have permitted a hairless man to maintain normal activity.

2 Loss of hair made man more versatile and economical in his thermoregulation in both tropical and temperate regions. The trait thus had positive adaptive value when coupled with the use of clothing (Figure 9–1).

3 According to this hypothesis the original hairless man was black, and depigmented (European) man has been derived from black ancestors.

4 A number of hypotheses advanced to explain human hairlessness are concerned with advantages unrelated to heat exchange. The advantages identified by these hypotheses may be real, but probably are secondary to heat-exchange relationships.

5 Hairless human skin became sexually attractive when the hairless trait became physiologically advantageous. Sexual selection would not have induced selection for this characteristic in the absence of a physiological advantage unless emerging man were polygamous or polyandrous.

6 Man develops elevated body temperatures which approach lethal levels after prolonged running at high humidities and temperatures. Loss of hair may have kept man cool and made him a more effective hunter relative to these conditions.

7 Modern man does not develop excessive body temperatures while sprinting, and it is unlikely that overheating as a result of sprinting after animals was a factor in preman's loss of hair.

8 Depigmented man may have been the original hairless man. This hypothesis assumes that furry preman had unpigmented

skin beneath his fur. As he developed clothing a thermal efficiency resulted from hair loss, incidentally exposing the unpigmented skin beneath.

9   This hypothesis to explain depigmented man implies that black hairless man was derived from a hairless depigmented ancestor, rather than the reverse.

10   The hair other than head hair remaining after man's general loss of hair may be interpreted as a signal, adapted to enhance aggressive threat.

11   According to this hypothesis, shaving and loincloths are adaptations to the concealment of morphological threat signals.

12   This concealment or elimination of aggressive signals may have been necessary if man's social organization shifted rapidly from small groups to groups containing several adult males.

BLACK MAN

The spectrum of hypotheses concerned with man's hairlessness and depigmentation is paralleled by an equal array of ideas advanced to explain his tropical blackness. Several of these hypotheses implicate factors influencing modern and ancestral black man's biology. But this does not tell us why black man is black. Here the concern is with the evolutionary factor or factors that have caused man to become black.

RADIATION EXCHANGE IN MAN

If the hypothesis that dark coloration in man is primarily concerned with sunlight absorption is correct, proof should include either (1) the demonstration of a lower metabolic rate in sunlight or (2) a fluctuating daily body-temperature cycle. In spite of the overwhelming number of metabolism measurements that have been reported for man, the critical experiments relative to point 1 above have not been performed. Evidence concerning the stability of man's temperature is available, however, and this evidence is useful in interpreting the relevance of coloration to man's temperature regulation.

Body Temperatures of Man

Human thermal stability varies with race and environment. It would be superfluous here to review the numerous circumstances moderating man's body temperature. Many studies have shown that both depigmented man and black man have deep body temperatures near 37°C under modern conditions of clothing, housing, and choice of climate. A look at man under other conditions reveals a different pattern. The comparative studies of Scholander et al. (1958) and Hammel et al. (1959), both reviewed in Hammel (1964) show that deep body and skin temperatures drop considerably during the night. This heat loss has been demonstrated for Australian aborigines, Kalahari bushmen, and European men used as controls and exposed to similar conditions (Figure 10–1). These values are perhaps more or less characteristic of native human populations that do not depend upon extensive insulation. The heat loss amounts to a considerable deficit. For a small man weighing 50 kilograms (110 pounds) a 2°C drop in deep body temperature amounts to 1,000 calories, which must be replaced by the addition of environmental heat or metabolic energy. Peripheral heat loss, i.e., from the extremities and near the body surface, is considerably more extensive (Figure 10–1), and may amount to 5°C or more. If we assume that this amount of heat loss occurs in approximately 20 percent of the body mass within 1 cm of the surface, this amounts to another 300-calorie loss. This loss obviously must be restored before the following night. Just as there are no precise measurements upon which to base the preceeding estimates, so also there is no information which will permit determination of the proportions of this lost energy that are replaced by environmental heat and by metabolic energy. In many environments, however, there is every opportunity to restore the deficit with environmental energy, especially in the form of solar radiation.

Human Skin Coloration and Heat Absorption

The role of dark human pigmentation in absorbing solar radiation and its heating effect has been confirmed experimentally. When a group of black and depigmented soldiers exercised in the sun under desert conditions, the body-temperature rise of both groups was the same when they were fully clothed. But when the same group of individuals exercised nude in the sun, the average temperature rise of the depigmented group was 0.5°C, while that of the blacks was 0.7°C. The significant difference was unrelated to water loss, which

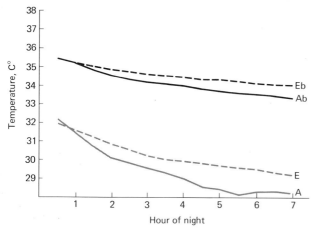

Figure 10-1. On a 5°C summer night the deep body temperature (*b*) and the skin temperature (*s*) of lightly covered Central Australian Aborigines (*A*) and a control group of Europeans (*E*) falls through the night. The Europeans compensate for the heat loss by increasing their metabolic heat production, but the aborigines maintain nearly constant metabolic heat production through the night. (After Hammel et al., 1959.)

was the same for both groups (Baker, 1958a, b) and probably can be assigned to the role of melanin in absorbing radiant energy. The reflectance of the visible solar radiation (Figure 10-2) amounts to 45 percent from a fair-skinned depigmented man, 35 percent from a dark brunette man, and only 16 percent from a black man (Blum, 1945). This temperature rise is an enigma to those who consider the additional "heat load" disadvantageous. It is, no doubt, a heat load, but the question of whether the heat is advantageous or disadvantageous is not so easily settled. Previous opinion has been nearly unanimous in favor of its disadvantageous nature (Blum, 1945, 1961; Loomis, 1967, and others), an opinion seemingly supported by the well-established observation that the degree of skin pigmentation is, throughout the world, inversely proportional to latitude (Coon et al., 1950; Garn, 1961). There is a real correlation between ultraviolet (UV) radiation and degree of skin pigmentation (Walter, 1958). Walter's regression analyses demonstrate a close correlation between skin color and UV intensity (Figure 10-2). This is not surprising, since even the most casual analysis of skin coloration demonstrates a clear gradient of skin coloration from the pale coloration

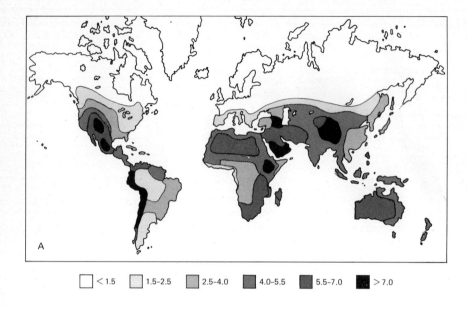

| <1.5 | 1.5–2.5 | 2.5–4.0 | 4.0–5.5 | 5.5–7.0 | >7.0 |

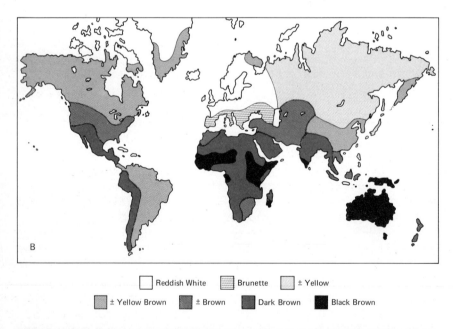

| Reddish White | Brunette | ± Yellow |

| ± Yellow Brown | ± Brown | Dark Brown | Black Brown |

Figure 10-2. The global distribution of ultraviolet radiation intensity (*a*) is closely correlated with the degree of human skin pigmentation (*b*). (After Walter, 1958.)

of the peoples of northern European regions to the very dark skin colors of equatorial Africa. The same gradient is found in eastern Asia, from the near black of Australia and southern India, through the browns of Indonesia and Malaysia, to the pale yellow of eastern Asia, and the trend continues into northern Asia. Failure of New World peoples to correlate as well (Figure 10-2) is probably due to the much more recent origin of these people.

If the heat-exchange-optimization hypothesis is to be extended to man, how has black man avoided the problem of overheating? One solution has been to carefully time sorties from shade to sun and periods of activity in general. Certain human populations may, as Brace (1966) contends, remain active and exposed to the midday sun, but this practice is surely not widespread where high midday ambient temperatures prevail. In many cases, such behavior is a recent cultural development. Aboriginal people commonly limit their activities in exposed environments to the beginnings and ends of the warmest days. Activity commences at daylight and continues until the work is done or heat becomes oppressive. Later in the day, after ambient temperatures have declined, activity may resume. When heat is excessive, sheltering takes place wherever shade is available. Sometimes this is in culturally devised shelter—sheds, houses, or fabric shelters of various sorts. In shade, dark coloration is neutral in terms of heat-exchange relationships, and this part of the day can play no role in shaping the coloration characteristics of the species.

Viewed from this perspective, siestas are neither artifacts nor evidence of cultural deterioration; they are physiological and economic adaptations to hot climates. This conclusion should come as no surprise to anyone familiar with these regions and their people. The consequences of this adaptation to societal evolution may have been considerable. Dark skin is only a part of a widespread cultural adaptation to a relatively passive resource-acquisition existence. Especially in areas of high equability (low climatic variance from season to season and year to year) the need and opportunity to store resources diminishes. Subsistence, i.e., the matching of energy input to output with little or no food storage other than as slight fat reserves, becomes an optimum and optimized strategy.

IS RADIATION PROTECTION A FUNCTION OF MELANIN?

It has often been argued that the melanin functions in animals and man are to protect them from excessive ultraviolet radiation (Thomson, 1955) (page 41). To a considerable extent this argument is based on the difficulties white men encounter when they expose large portions of their body surfaces to sunlight.

> That melanin functions in man primarily as a solar screen is almost indisputable. Melanized epidermis acts as a cloak that shields the underlying dermis by effectively blocking the passage of injurious u.v. rays. In man, melanin-forming cells, melanocytes, are present in small numbers in vestigial loci in the meningeal sheaths of the central nervous system and in abundance in the eyes and skin, where they form a front line of defence against the effects of solar radiation (Fitzpatrick, Seiji and McGugan, 1961). The remarkable resistance of pigmented skin to u.v. radiant energy is attributable to the melanin produced by these cells (Fitzpatrick, 1965, p. 365).

Fitzpatrick's statement summarizes current conventional wisdom; albinos are definitely troubled by exposure to solar radiation. They must carefully protect themselves from direct exposure to sunlight. Carelessness in this matter may result in serious sunburn, eye damage, skin cancer, and other dermal lesions. In addition, excessive occupational exposure to sunlight is more likely to induce skin cancer in normal depigmented men than it is in black men. Thus, circumstantial evidence might seem to support the conclusion that the adaptive basis of pigmentation is to prevent excessive radiation exposure.

It has always seemed a paradox to depigmented man that the heavily pigmented races of man should inhabit tropical latitudes, while light skins are reserved for the northerly districts. The argument, and its usual solution, follows:

1 I am white (depigmented).
2 Warm weather distresses me.
3 Black coloration absorbs more heat than white coloration.
4 Black body coloration must therefore make its possessor even more uncomfortable than I am in the sun.
5 Therefore, black coloration is a positive disadvantage to black men because they inhabit the warmest parts of the earth.
6 Therefore, black coloration must be adaptive in some context other than heat exchange, and this advantage must offset the disadvantage of dark coloration in heat exchange.
7 Ultraviolet radiation is known to be harmful—it causes sunburn and may induce cancer.
8 The evidence from albinos and from comparative studies of dermal lesions due to excessive radiation shows that black people are at an advantage under comparable circumstances.

9   It must be this protection from excessive radiation that is the off-
    setting advantage to the dark races.

This idea was first proposed in 1820 by Sir Everard Home in a paper
published in the Philosophical Transactions of the Royal Society of
London, "On the rete mucosum of the negro being a defense against
the scorching effect of the sun's rays." Sir Home's argument appears
essentially unmodified in the Fitzpatrick (1965) paper from which the
above quotation was taken.

My contention is that this argument falls short because it fails to
take into account man's actual environment, daily and seasonal,
when the characteristic was evolving. There is certainly overwhelming evidence that dermal melanin today provides protection from
excessive ultraviolet radiation to certain human populations. But this
is hardly evidence that radiation protection was the evolutionary
basis for the original *evolution* of melanin. Man did not evolve on a
tractor, or as a roofer, shepherd, or lifeguard, exposed to a full day
of solar radiation. That some individuals earn their livelihood in
such ways in our agricultural and industrial world and, as a result,
that they tend to develop skin lesions has little relevance to the
adaptations of evolving mankind. In relative terms, these habits have
had only an instant to induce adaptation and superimpose their
characteristics upon the legacy of millions of years of another way
of life. The more conservative a trait is in evolution, the less likely it
is to adjust rapidly to new environmental conditions. Tolerance of
ultraviolet radiation must be closely correlated with the evolutionary
history of exposure to it. Temperature tolerances barely exceed
temperatures normally encountered (page 9), and the same principle is likely to be applicable to tolerance of UV radiation. This
explains (1) why mutants (in this case albinos) suffer from exposure
to ultraviolet radiation and (2) why depigmented men suffer when
they are displaced to environments characterized by more intense
radiation than those where they evolved.

Interpretation of Function from Mutation
Interpretations of function based upon mutations deleting normal
characteristics has not been confined to human skin coloration. The
following discussion reveals the emphasis upon the radiation-
protection function of both plant and animal pigments:

> *C. Ellenby*: "Dr. Carlisle points out that copepods 'open' their chroma-
> tophore 'umbrellas' when they rise to the surface waters of the sea and
> suggests that this protects them against the harmful effect of the light.

But they rise to feed on the organisms of the phytoplankton which apparently can manage without such protection."

D. B. Carlisle: "Dr. Ellenby is, I think, mistaken when he says that phytoplanktonic organisms can manage without the protection of pigments. In a number of plants mutants are known which lack carotenoids from the chloroplasts. Such organisms, after emergence from the seed or spore, can survive in the dark as long as their food reserves last, but if they are exposed to the light, they die of 'sunstroke.' In other words the carotenoids are needed to protect them against the damaging effect of the light. Phytoplanktonic organisms then have a permanent 'parasol' of pigment to protect them against solar radiation. Sea water absorbs ultra-violet light extremely quickly so that protection is needed against visible light, not against the ultra-violet" (Carlisle, 1964, p. 65).

The counterarguments presented above as an alternative interpretation of the detrimental action of light upon unpigmented human mutants may be applied to this and any other situation in which interpretation of function is based upon genetic anomalies. That an unpigmented mutant is in trouble when exposed to normally tolerable solar radiation levels cannot be a basis for interpretating the evolutionary basis of pigmentation. Furthermore, there are plausible alternate interpretations of the correlation between pigment expansion and exposure to radiant energy as being a protective adaptation.

The preceeding discussion should not be interpreted as a challenge to the reality of ultraviolet radiation hazards to plant and animal life. These hazards have been well documented (Cole, 1943). But this is not the problem. The evolutionarily relevant question is: Are the radiation levels that induce radiation damage the radiation intensities normally encountered in nature? Hunsaker and Johnson (1959) conclude that this is not the case in their studies of lizard and reptile pigments. Radiation damage results only when exposure intensities greater than those normally encountered in nature are experimentally supplied.

Thus, based upon existing evidence, I find no valid reason to conclude that normally encountered solar radiation intensities affect deep body tissues or that they are the adaptive basis of human skin pigmentation.

The Evolutionary Significance of Sunburn

The problems that have arisen with respect to the interpretation of sunburn focus attention on the problem of evolutionary adaptation relative to the historical environment of each animal species. Depigmented man's recent penetration of tropical environments from his ancestral temperate environments is an action completely out-side the evolutionary context. Accordingly, in the tropics the occur-rence of sunburn and the development of cancerous dermal lesions can also not be logically used as evidence to support the role of black pigment as radiation protection in indigenous tropical races. The same argument is applicable to albinos. That these mutants suffer distress is not surprising. They are evolutionary accidents, and acci-dents cannot be anticipated by evolutionary adaptations.

VITAMIN D HYPOTHESIS

This widely accepted hypothesis suggests that racial differences in skin pigmentation of man are related to adaptations optimizing vita-min D synthesis. Evidence favoring this hypothesis has been sum-marized by a biochemist, W. F. Loomis (1967). The following discus-sion emphasizes his arguments. In fairness to other advocates of this hypothesis, however, it should be emphasized that Loomis's treatment suggests a broader applicability than was intended by the originators and early advocates of this hypothesis. Rejection of some of Loomis's evidence does not necessarily imply rejection of a more limited hypothesis, as stated by these earlier and more conservative investigators.

Vitamin D Synthesis and Vitamin Disease

Vitamin D is synthesized in man by the action of ultraviolet light (290 to 320 millimicrons) upon a precursor steroid located through-out the epidermis. Vitamin D also occurs naturally in fish liver oils and a few other natural foods (Table 10–1). Failure to ingest or syn-thesize enough vitamin D results in serious bone and tooth problems in man. The minimum dose required to avoid these difficulties is about 400 international units (I.U.) per day. More vitamin D than this minimum seems to be harmless unless massive amounts of the

Table 10 –1.   The vitamin D content of some natural foods. (After Coward, 1938.)

Item	Vitamin D, I.U./gm
Halibut liver oil	2,000 – 4,000
Cod liver oil	60 – 300
Egg yolk	1.5 – 5.0
Butter	0.0 – 4.0
Cream	0.5
Milk (nonirradiated)	0.1
Calves' liver	0.0

synthetic form of this vitamin are ingested. Ingestion of 100,000 international units per day results in elevated blood calcium and phosphorous levels and calcification of soft tissues. Kidney stones form, the kidneys become diseased, and death may follow. This level, then, is clearly an insult dosage, and lower doses can be expected to have deleterious effects. If such concentrations of vitamin D accumulate as a result of overingestion of vitamin D or by excessive dermal synthesis, serious consequences can be anticipated.

Skin pigmentation influences the amount of UV radiation absorbed and thus influences vitamin D synthesis rates. For example, the average transmittance of ultraviolet light (300 to 400 millimicrons) through the stratum corneum of Europeans is 64 percent, compared with 18 percent for black Africans (Thompson, 1955). For practical purposes this difference, a factor of 3.5, can be taken as the potential range of control of dermal vitamin D synthesis by the races of man. This range can, of course, be expanded relative to incident sunlight by behavioral and cultural manipulations such as time of exposure and use of clothing.

Can the Vitamin D Hypothesis Explain the Colors of Man?
From these facts, Loomis interprets man's adaptation to the control of vitamin D synthesis. His hypothesis is that the degree of pigmentation of the races of man is an adaptation to optimizing dermal vitamin D synthesis. According to this hypothesis, there is too little UV radiation at northern latitudes relative to the vitamin D requirements of man, especially in the winter when clothing must cover most of the body surface where vitamin D synthesis might take place and when the amount of radiant energy is drastically reduced. Hence, he reasoned, northern man has reduced his pigmentation to permit maximum light penetration. This explanation would agree with the latitudinal gradient in skin coloration, from dark in the tropics to pale at the poles and seems to be a particularly convincing explanation of the skin color of depigmented man, although there are some alternatives (pages 183-187). This hypothesis is not original to Loomis. It is probably the most widely held explanation of depigmented man's coloration.

The unique part of Loomis's hypothesis (1967) concerns his explanation of the evolution of the dark races of man. Loomis reasoned that, if depigmented man had a problem getting enough ultraviolet light, the tropical races might get too much. Thus, heavy pigmentation of the dark races might be an adaptation to prevent excessive vitamin D synthesis where potentially hazardous UV light intensities prevail.

This hypothesis has one outstanding merit; it can explain the colors of not only black man and depigmented man, but the intermediate races of mankind as well:

> The known correlation between the color of human skin and latitude (Figure 10-2) is explainable in terms of two opposing positive adaptations to solar ultraviolet radiation, weak in northern latitudes in winter yet powerful the year around near the equator. In northern latitudes there is selection for white skins that allow maximum photoactivation of 7-dehydrocholesterol into vitamin D at low intensities of ultraviolet radiation. In southern latitudes, on the other hand, there is selection for black skins able to prevent up to 95 percent of the incident ultraviolet from reaching the deeper layers of the skin where vitamin D is synthesized. Selection against the twin dangers of rickets on the one hand and toxic doses of vitamin D on the other would thus explain the world-wide correlation observed between skin pigmentation and nearness to the equator.
>
> Since intermediate degrees of pigmentation occur at intermediate latitudes, as well as seasonal fluctuation in pigmentation (through reversible suntanning), it appears that different skin colors in man are adaptations of the stratum corneum which regulate the transmission of solar ultraviolet to the underlying stratum granulosum, so that vitamin-D photosynthesis is maintained within physiological limits throughout the year at all latitudes (Loomis, 1967, p. 506).

To this point the discussion of the vitamin D hypothesis has concentrated on the strengths of the argument. It is for this reason that several of the points elaborated by Loomis have not been included. This additional evidence will now be included in my evaluation of the validity of this hypothesis.

Objections to the Vitamin D Hypothesis
As a first approach, let us consider some quantitative aspects of the problem. First inspection suggests that such aspects are most likely to offer finite solutions. The hypothesis suggests that overproduction of vitamin D (hypervitaminosis) is a tropical problem. Assuming 22,500 cm^2 on the surface of the body and a vitamin D synthesis rate for depigmented man of 6 I.U. cm^2/hr (Beckemeier, 1958), Loomis determined a potential daily synthesis rate of vitamin D of 800,000 I.U./day, far in excess of toxic levels *as determined for ingested synthetic vitamin D*. This calculation apparently is based upon the 12-hour tropical day and upon the impossibility of sunning more than half the body at any one time:

$$\frac{\text{Area (22,500 } cm^2)}{2} \times \text{rate/day (6 I.U.)} \times \text{hr/day (12)} = 810,000 \text{ I.U./day}$$

The exposure of a black African would be less than this because (1) he spends part of the day in the shade, (2) during parts of some days the sun is obscured by cloud cover, (3) during part of the day the sun is low in the sky and the ultraviolet rays are being filtered out before they reach the body, (4) a portion of the body may be covered by clothing, (5) postural attitudes may reduce the exposure, and (6) his pigmentation reduces exposure 3.5 times. Unfortunately, we have only one quantitative figure to supply, the 3.5 value for color, which reduces maximum potential exposure to 225,000 I.U. From here the quantitative aspects of the argument degenerate to guess-work, and the guesses about these additional values cannot be restricted beyond broad limits. Suppose that only one-half the day is spent in full sunlight and that one-third of the body is covered with clothing. This would already push the value well below 100,000 I.U./day. Another estimate might place these figures considerably higher or much lower. In any case, Loomis (1968) has pointed out that 100,000 I.U. is an estimate which might be high by as much as a factor of 10. We are in a swamp of estimates, and the limited quantitative data are hopelessly inadequate to evaluate the hypothesis.

The remaining evidence favoring the hypothesis is primarily concerned with clinical vitamin D deficiency problems of black man in temperate cities, or of tropical lions in northern zoos. The inadequacy of this line of reasoning in an evolutionary argument is apparent (see page 198).

Depigmented Man and Vitamin D

The argument that the depigmentation of man is an adaptation to avoiding vitamin D deficiency is more plausible. Blois (1968) has already pointed out that if Loomis's data can be relied upon, we are at best forced to one side or the other of the argument. The reason is that control of synthesis by pigmentation varies by a factor of 3.5, while the tolerable limits range from 400 to 100,000 I.U. or a factor of 250×, or 25× if the 100,000 I.U. figure is assumed to be high by a factor of 10. Thus, for control by pigmentation to be effective, it can operate at one end of the range or the other, but not at both.

Whether or not we reject the vitamin D hypothesis makes little difference to our interpretation of the evidence. Black man was probably so adapted to vitamin D synthesis that under normal conditions he synthesized the appropriate amounts of vitamin D. The time scale for appropriate adaptation would have been no problem. Black man has probably been hairless for millions of years, and in any case, his loss of hair would not have proceeded more rapidly than his ability to withstand the problems provided by radiation. That is to say, his evolution would not have been degenerative.

According to all evidence, man's departure from the tropics was quite sudden. He took his culture and his clothes with him. Clothing and a knowledge of shelters made otherwise unsuitable environments habitable, and the archaeological evidence shows that man spread quite rapidly indeed, perhaps considerably faster than his ability to adjust his rate of vitamin D synthesis. The problem could be quickly balanced by reducing his skin pigmentation, since pigmentation is a relatively uncomplicated evolutionary change and one that we know can take place relatively rapidly from comparisons of the New World tribes of man.

The argument takes on quite a different complexion if one assumes that depigmented man was the original hairless man (page 184). If this were the case, the entire argument could be reversed. Depigmented man would now balance vitamin synthesis rates to rates of hair loss, and reinvasion of the tropics would be accomplished largely by cultural adaptation. If this line of reasoning is accepted, dark pigmentation becomes the more probable adaptation to regulation of vitamin D synthesis. However, since another functional basis for black coloration has already been established, the need for the hypothesis is reduced and its probable validity is minimal.

Future Evaluations of the Hypothesis
The respective disciplinary perspective of each investigator has, to a considerable extent, influenced his choice of hypothesis to explain human skin coloration. The vitamin D hypothesis has been the pet of biochemists, physiologists, and medical men. Much of the evidence relative to this hypothesis and its ramifications certainly falls within the domain of these specialties, but the problem of adaptation is basically one of evolution, and evaluation and synthesis require an evolutionary perspective regardless of one's discipline. Analysis from this perspective remains deficient because the right sorts of data are unavailable, are not being gathered, and thus cannot be applied to the problem.

Based upon all the discussions of this hypothesis that I know of, I would like to suggest the kinds of evidence, largely unavailable, which might be the basis of further evaluations of this hypothesis:

1 The average pigmentation of undiluted human populations where they evolved should be measured.
2 The general radiation characteristics of the environment of these populations should be determined.

3   The amount of radiation actually absorbed by individuals in the population during normal activities should be determined. Today there are no techniques available for making such determinations. One way to start would be by making a time-motion analysis of individuals during normal activities. At a minimum these should be correlated with standard meteorological records of temperature, connection, and net radiation.
4   Measurements should include and emphasize individuals active at evolutionarily relevant trades and activities.
5   Measurements should be made for the entire annual cycle.

This is a demanding set of requirements, especially since to be relevant it needs to be applied to a large number of individuals making up several populations. The problem of finding relevant populations satisfying requirements 1 and 4 is a difficult one, because they are vanishing rapidly. This is all the more reason why it is urgent that measurements be secured while it is still possible.

BACKGROUND MATCHING MAN

It has been suggested that the adaptive significance of the black man's skin coloration is its role in camouflage (Cowles, 1959). It may interest the reader at this point to see how convinced another author is of the validity of his own favorite hypothesis—in this case, in response to the original publication (Hamilton and Heppner, 1967) of the sunlight-absorption hypothesis for human skin coloration:

> Other arguments in favor of the theory of concealment rather than for any definitive physiological advantages (these doubtless occur but are less important) have been proposed (Cowles, 1959), but it seems probable that need for concealment almost invariably takes precedence over any attendant metabolic benefits or dangers and that this may have been true for the evolution of some prototypal human skin color (Cowles, 1967, p. 1341).

Evidence Supporting the Camouflage Hypothesis
Cowles' argument (1959), in summary, is that:

1   Early men commonly engaged in tribal warfare, hunted, or did both. The same is true of many tribes today.
2   Adaptations to tribal warfare and hunting efficiency were and are, therefore, significant survival factors.
3   In the forest environments where these conflicts take place, dark skin is better camouflage than depigmented skin.

4   Therefore, tribal warfare and hunting effectiveness have, in combination, led to the evolution of man's dark skin coloration.

Cowles cites as additional evidence the effectiveness of black men as jungle fighters during the Second World War. Evolutionarily, Cowles suggests, dark skin coloration might suit jungle man to an effective hunting life. In addition, Cowles suggests that effective camouflage would also protect women and children from large predators, such as leopards.

Evidence Contrary to the Camouflage Hypothesis

There is little doubt that the darker-skinned races of man are, in most circumstances, better camouflaged than depigmented man in forest environments. But black coloration is *intermediate* in its conspicuousness in all but a few exceptional (lava black) environments (Chapter 9), and thus man is less effectively camouflaged than he would be if he were to match local backgrounds precisely. Forest animals such as antelopes, monkeys, or grasshoppers, many of which are camouflaged, are generally brown or grey, not black, and much paler than the brown-black of most forest-dwelling Africans, the pygmies excepted. The brownish color of pygmies is close to that of the forest antelope and the other camouflaged animals they hunt. Modern jungle guerilla fighters do not don black garb; the optimum garment is a *patterned* green and brown, which agree with the colors of backgrounds and of predatory and prey forest animals. Man also lacks the discontinuities which might also suit him well to camouflage. Black coloration certainly camouflages better than brighter colors or than depigmentation. But if dark human skin coloration were basically an adaptation to background matching, a color more closely resembling the browns of background-matching birds and mammals would be required. Also, being a relatively large animal, man should not be homogeneously colored if he were to depend upon his natural camouflage. Alternative explanations of black man's skin coloration are called for.

There is another line of evidence applicable to the matter of camouflage and human skin coloration. In the arguments already presented concerning the sequence of adaptations leading to man's hairlessness (page 173), it was concluded that human hairlessness could not have developed without the invention of clothing. If so, clothing would have been an available form of camouflage, leaving the skin surface free to adopt (or retain) coloration based upon other advantages. This argument is only partially relevant because it is possible that man was hunting at times when, say during the heat of day, or in places where clothing would impose a thermal burden and thus be disadvantageous. However, these may not have been the times or places of man's concentrated hunting activities.

If, in spite of this evidence, one agreed with Cowles (1959, 1967) that human skin coloration were camouflage, the place where man's color would be most relevant to camouflage would be the forest. There, in shadows, black man is relatively well hidden. In the discussion below of the place of man's origin, some reasons are advanced why the forest is not a likely candidate. The thrust of this argument is that man shares a constellation of traits with a group of rather unusual mammals: (1) They fail to match their backgrounds precisely. (2) They have a broad ecological distribution and broadly defined ecological requirements. (3) They practice a refuging social organization. (4) They are hairless. (5) And they have potent defense mechanisms, weak powers of locomotion, and exceptional longevity (Chapter 6). These animals make little behavioral concession to camouflage, and it seems unimportant to them.

BLACK COLORATION AS A SOCIAL SIGNAL

Recently Guthrie (1970) advanced the hypothesis that dark coloration in man is a social signal—the degree of pigmentation indicating the level of threat. The observation that apparently led Guthrie to this conclusion is that in many populations of man and certain other animals the male tends to be darker (Hulse, 1968) and more aggressive. From this hypothesis Guthrie developed several additional conclusions concerning man's coloration. One is that depigmentation is an adaptation to the minimization of threat, and that "depigmentation, like nakedness and smooth, soft skin, seems to be a part of the general deemphasis of the ancestral threat devices resulting from a more complex social level of interaction and interdependence" (Guthrie, 1970, p. 280).

This argument assumes that black men were, during the period of man's skin-color evolution, in a relatively low state of social organization. The logic of this line of reasoning is reminiscent of Wallace's early attempts (1878) (see page 186) to explain man's coloration. A consideration of the high level of social integration and organization known to have existed in the tropical regions where the aboriginal inhabitants were relatively dark (see Figure 10-2) should dispel any notion that comparative evidence supports this claim.

The main problem with Guthrie's argument is that it fails to distinguish between evolution acting within a population of an animal species and selection adapting local populations to their environment.   An observation nuclear to his conclusions is that males of many species are darker than females. Comparative (Hershkovitz, 1968; and Guthrie, 1970) and experimental (Marler, 1955) evidence do indeed suggest that signals may reinforce the dominance of males in the sexual hierarchy. But why should conclusions derived from these observations be extended to interpretations of sexual dimorphism? We know in other instances that the selective pressures resulting in differentiation between populations, whether they be men or animals, are usually based upon environmental nature than social characteristics. Thus, there does not seem to be any substantive evidence in support of the conclusion that social phenomena have played a role in shaping the coloration of the numerous populations of mankind.

MAN'S PLACE OF ORIGIN

The preceding discussion of man's coloration includes the tacit assumption that he was originally a tropical plains animal and that his utilization of other environments is a derived condition. Is the evidence for this conclusion, now widely held by anthropologists, correct? The answer has particular relevance to an understanding of black man's coloration. It may seem superfluous to question the matter of tropical origin since man is a primate, and primates are tropical animals. However, there are modern primates well adapted to temperate regions in Japan and other cool parts of Asia and Africa. These species establish that the potential range of physiological primate adaptations includes regions of regular snowfall. Man *is* an unusual species, and he could have been derived from an unusual ancestry. Three lines of evidence from modern man are helpful in establishing his place of origin: hairlessness and black skin, social organization, and posture.

Hairlessness and Black Skin

The correlation of hairlessness with black coloration among mammals and the predominance of such adaptations among tropical animals (Figure 10-2) suggest that man's hairless black skin is indeed an attribute adapted to tropical conditions. There is more to this judgment than the simple correlation of these traits with the tropics in other species and groups. Uninsulated black surface is an adaptation dependent upon relatively even, persistently sunny conditions and a relatively moderate climate, to be utilized effectively by a large homeotherm.

Refuging and Man's Original Environment

Although man may have originated in the tropical forests, his uniquely human characteristics did not. Man's culture was probably developed in the context of a refuging social organization and it is unlikely that refuging developed in the forests. In forests potential resting places or dispersal centers are available more or less throughout the habitable and exploitable environment. Chimpanzees fabricate crude nests in the jungle understory, or they may seek shelter under the mammoth buttressed trunks of forest trees, although this appears to be an uncommon occurrence (Jones and Pi, 1971). Their nests are seldom, if ever, used more than once, and can be produced at nightfall regardless of where the ape is. The same applies to lowland gorillas, which may rest on a crude mat of vegetation on the forest floor (Jones and Pi) or form an equally crude arboreal nest (Schaller, 1963). These nests provide no overhead protection, and in the case of ground nests they seem adapted to providing protection from the cold damp of the earth more than anything else. All these structures can be and are produced almost anywhere within the home range of the troop. Thus, to a forest primate there is no particular advantage of refuging. A refuging pattern is less economical under such conditions than a system distributing the population more evenly within this space.

On the plains, conditions are in striking contrast. Plains are not the ordinary range of the primate, and primates have not undergone the adaptive radiation there that typifies forest environments. Yet antelopes, for example, are proof that plains are not unsuitable for diurnal mammals, but merely for primates. What would have influenced primates to live there, however, is a shift to a resource-acquisition system allowing them to exploit the resource reserves of the plains. Refuging was an adaptation that would have occurred as a result. The social organization of preman seems to have been adapted to a plains environment by such means.

Posture

Man's upright posture also seems to be an adaptation to savannah or plains conditions. The upright attitude of man, unlike the gibbon, is unrelated to a recent arboreal existence, and he is unique among primates in maintaining this posture. It has advantages:

1 The eyes are elevated, extending the range of visual perception, a matter of special significance to a ground-dwelling animal. It is also a special benefit in a plains environment where visibility may be restricted by terrain contour and short vegetation.

2   The hands are freed for manipulative tasks, and the opposable thumb becomes preadapted to tool use.

But the upright position also has disadvantages:

1   It is relatively unsatisfactory in the forest because of the large surface area exposed to vegetation such as vines and small trees which may interfere with lateral movement. Anyone who tries to push through jungle undergrowth without a cutting tool will appreciate the advantages of proceeding on all fours and may actually be forced to that stance.

2   Locomotion speed is reduced. As a result, even the most highly trained human runner is incredibly slow for a mammal or primate of his size (Table 6–4). This slowness is partly attributable to the erect posture, which has halved the number of locomotion members, has reduced streamlining and balance, and has eliminated the effectiveness of the spine in locomotion. Speedy locomotion is potentially advantageous to most animals regardless of their environment. A band of gorillas or forest antelope flees at remarkable speeds, and a running forest leopard is not much slower than his plains counterpart. (I have been unable to find determinations of the actual speed of these animals, which is not surprising. Even a fast man cannot keep up with them, and they do not accommodate by running alongside forest roads or trails. Anyone who has the opportunity to make such a measurement, however fragmentary, should report his observations in detail.) The advantage of great locomotion speed has been sacrificed for an increased visual field and forelimb freedom. Therefore, there are several compelling reasons to argue for a tropical plains ancestry for man. The advantage of an enhanced perceptual field would be relevant mainly in a plains environment. Problems with an upright stance relative to brush would be minimal. A refuging social organization is well suited to such an environment, and its value is increased by an enhanced perceptual field and freedom of the hands to transport tools and food to and from the cove.

Coloration and Man's Place of Origin

Obviously, the adaptive significance of man's coloration is subject to a number of alternate explanations. If man's coloration and his hairlessness are adaptations to heat exchange, evidence concerning the region of the earth where he emerged can be developed. It is particularly important because paleontologists have been mainly concerned with two regions, Africa and Asia. The almost monthly discoveries emerging from Africa at this time emphasize this area, but it is a region where a massive search effort is under way. China and most of Asia are much less accessible, and one might legitimately argue that a lesser effort is the cause of the considerably smaller number and less ancient finds of preman there.

Here the coloration of man is most helpful. From the evidence presented in Chapters 9 and 10, I concluded that man probably emerged hairless and black. Today the blackest men and the most widely distributed black men are African. In the Orient, particularly north of the Himalayas, paler skin colors predominate (Figure 10-2). Until recent centuries, human populations have been relatively immobile, and the colors of pre-Roman Old World man were probably closely adapted to the region they inhabited. If so, and if we accept black man as the original man, we are returned to an African origin of man. Elsewhere I concluded that plains or savannahs were the relevant habitat. We can probably come no closer than this, but the comparative evidence supports those who search the ravines and caves of the high, arid African plains for clues to their beginnings.

Ample evidence confirms the fact that arid plains conditions accompanied human development in eastern and southern Africa. In the same deposits where the earliest hominid bones and artifacts are excavated, there are remains of mammals similar to the animals which roam the plains above the gorges where these excavations are taking place today. There are buffalo, considerably different in detail but so sufficiently similar that even an untrained observer would recognize them. There are wildebeest by the score, rhinoceroses, giraffes, antelope, etc. At least in this part of the world emerging man had company that would have seemed familiar to modern man. And thus he must also have had a similar environment. The environmental relationships of these large mammals were much the same 20 million years ago as they are today.

In the course of this chapter, a number of hypotheses have been reviewed and evaluated. This evaluation is typical of the kinds of discussions in the scientific literature concerned with the "why" questions of life. It is this sort of discussion that has given evolutionary ecology a rather bad name. The difficulty is this: To each argument there is a counterargument, and the most recent "authority" to pronounce on each subject seems to hold the day until the next brainstorm emerges. Has anything been established? What can be relied upon? What steppingstones are there to further hypothetical constructs? If the next authority will inevitably overthrow the hypothesis that stands today, is the system making any progress? In fact, is it not true that this sort of biology is a soft science, not far removed from philosophy?

These questions are indeed relevant, but only at the level of inter-pretation. Experimentation and measurement are being taken to a high degree of sophistication in biology. It is perhaps for this reason that so many biologists, physiologists in particular, refuse to deal with the "why" questions, an approach which certainly solves the problem. Speaking of the problem at hand, human skin coloration, Blum (1968) concluded: "All such speculation seems to little purpose . . . in light of the complexity of the problem and our lack of knowl-edge" (p. 652). But to disallow the "why" questions would also re-move for many of us the reason for studying biology in the first place.

Furthermore, there is a way to evaluate "why" hypotheses in a rigorous scientific manner. The way is to develop each hypothesis until it is so weakened by conflicting evidence that it or a part of it is inadequate to be continued as an explanation of observations and experiments. At the same time, progressive elimination of alterna-tives may fortify some hypothesis which continues to be confirmed by each new comparison and each new bit of quantitative evidence. The evidence must eventually interrelate perfectly before an explana-tion can be considered convincing. The arguments for every hypoth-esis considered here are based upon imperfect evidence, and in most cases the imperfections are apparent. What needs to be done to evaluate the ideas is generally equally obvious. Massive amounts of experimentation and observation lie ahead before a body of in-formation may become available and more convincing answers to the "why" questions may be found. But the magnitude of the task is no excuse for not asking the questions and trying to find answers to them.

CONCLUSIONS

1 Man may undergo a daily temperature cycle amounting in some cases to over 1,000 calories.
2 This caloric expenditure and the cost of maintaining a homeo-thermic body temperature can be paid for with metabolic or ambient heat.
3 In tropical man it is cheaper to supply the costs of homeothermy from environmental heat. Dark human skin may be an adaptation to optimizing the process because it maximizes the absorption of radiant solar energy.
4 The evidence that dark human skin is an adaptation to preventing solar radiation damage is unconvincing, because all such evi-dence concerns the problems of human populations and individ-uals outside their long-term evolutionary context.

5   Human skin pigmentation or lack of it may be adapted to optimizing vitamin D synthesis. However, this hypothesis is inadequate to explain the full spectrum of human skin colors. The hypothesis seems most plausible as an explanation of depigmented man.

6   It has been suggested that black man's coloration is an adaptation to camouflage.   This hypothesis is rejected on comparative grounds.

REFERENCES

Adams, P. A., and J. E. Heath: "Temperature Regulation in the Sphinx Moth, *Celerio leneata*," *Nature*, 201:20–22, London, 1964.

Altmann, M.: "Patterns of Herd Behavior in Free-ranging Elk of Wyoming, *Cervus canadensis nelsoni*," *Zoologica*, 41:65–71, 1956.

Ardrey, R.: *African Genesis*, Dell Publishing Co., Inc., New York, 1963.

Aubertin, D., A. E. Ellis, and G. C. Robson: "The Natural History and Variation of the Pointed Snail *Cochlicella acuta* (Müll)," *Proceedings of the Zoological Society of London*, pp. 1027–1055, 1930.

Axtell, R. W.: "Orientation by *Holbrookia maculata* (Lacertilia, Iguanidae) to Solar and Reflected Heat," *Southwestern Naturalist*, 5:45–47, 1960.

Baker, J. J. W.: letter in *Science*, 151:935, 1966.

Baker, P. T.: "The Biological Adaptation of Man to Hot Deserts," *American Naturalist*, 92:337–357, 1958a.

————: "Racial Differences in Heat Tolerance," *American Journal of Physical Anthropology*, 16:287–305, 1958b.

Barnes, R. B.: "Thermography of the Human Body," *Science*, 140:870–877, 1963.

Bartholomew, G. A., and T. J. Cade: "The Body Temperature of the American Kestrel, *Falco sparverius*," *Wilson Bulletin*, 69:149–154, 1957.

———— and W. R. Dawson: "Body Temperature and Water Requirements in the Mourning Dove, *Zenaidura macroura marginella*," *Ecology*, 35:181–187, 1954.

Bates, M.: "Black, White, Colored," *Natural History*, pp. 22–23B, March, 1968.

Beckemeier, H.: "Versuche zur maximalen antirachitischen UV-Aktivierung isolierter menschlicher Haut," *Acta Biologica et Medica Germanica*, 1:756, 1958.

Beebe, W.: "*Pheasants, Their Lives and Homes*," vols. 1 and 2, Doubleday Page & Co., Garden City, N.Y., 1926.

Benedict, F. G.: "*The Physiology of Large Reptiles with Special Reference to the Heat Production of Snakes, Tortoises, Lizards, and Alligators*," publication no. 425, Carnegie Institution, Washington, 1932.

Blois, M. F.: "Vitamin D, Sunlight, and Natural Selection," letter in *Science*, 159:652, 1968.

Blum, H. F.: "The Physiological Effects of Sunlight on Man," *Physiological Reviews*, 25:483–530, 1945.

————: "Does the Melanin Pigment of Human Skin Have Adaptive Value?" *Quarterly Review of Biology*, 36:50–63, 1961.

————: "Vitamin D, Sunlight, and Natural Selection," letter in *Science*, 159:652, 1968.

Bodenheimer, F. S.: "Problems of Physiology and Ecology of Desert Animals," in J. L. Cloudsley-Thompson (ed.), *Biology of Deserts*, Institute of Biology, London, 1954, pp. 162–167.

Bogoras, W.: "The Chukchee," Publications of the Jesup North Pacific Expedition, in Franz Boas (ed.), *Memoirs of the American Museum of Natural History*, vol. 11, 1904–1909.

Bolwig, N.: "Experiments on the Regulation of Body Temperature of Certain Tenebrionid Beetles," *Journal of the Entomological Society of South Africa*, 20:454–458, 1957.

Boycott, B. B.: "Learning in *Octopus vulgaris* and Other Cephalopods," *Pubblicazioni della Stazione Zoologica di Napoli*, 25:67–93, 1954.

Brace, C. L.: letter in *Science*, 153:362, 1966.

—— and M. F. A. Montagu: *Man's Evolution*, The Macmillan Company, New York, 1965.

Brain, C. K.: "Observations on the Temperature Tolerance of Lizards in the Central Namib Desert, South West Africa," *Cimbebasia*, 4:1–5, 1962.

—— and O. P. M. Prozesky: "On the Body Temperatures of Birds Collected on the Carp-Transvaal Museum Namib Desert Expedition," *Cimbebasia*, 5:13–20, 1962.

Broekhuysen, G. J.: "A preliminary Investigation of the Importance of Desiccation, Temperature, and Salinity as Factors Controlling the Vertical Distribution of Certain Intertidal Marine Gastropods in False Bay, South Africa," *Transactions of the Royal Society of South Africa*, 28:255–292, 1940.

Bryant, W. E.: "Preliminary Description of a New Species of the Genus *Lepus* from Mexico," *Proceedings of the California Academy of Science* (2d ser.), 3:92, 1891.

Burton, A. C., and O. G. Edholm: *Man in a Cold Environment*, Edward Arnold (Publishers) Ltd., London, 1954.

Buskirk, E. R., and D. E. Bass: "Climate and Exercise," in W. R. Johnson (ed.), *Science and Medicine of Exercise and Sports*, Harper and Row, New York, 1960, pp. 311–338.

Buxton, P. A.: *Animal Life in Deserts*, Edward Arnold and Co., London, 1923.

——: "Heat, Moisture, and Animal Life in Deserts," *Proceedings of the Royal Society (London), Series B*, 96:123–131, 1924.

Carlisle, D. B.: "Colour Change in Animals," in *Colour and Life*, symposium no. 12, Institute of Biology, London, 1964, pp. 61–67.

Carpenter, C. R.: *Naturalistic Behavior of Nonhuman Primates*, The Pennsylvania State University Press, University Park, 1964.

Clark, L. R.: "An Ecological Study of the Australian Plague Locust (*Chortoicetes terminifera* Walk.) in the Bogan-Macquarie Outbreak Area, N.S.W." *Bulletin. Commonwealth Scientific and Industrial Research Organization, Melbourne*, no. 226, 1947.

Clarke, R. F.: "An Ecological Study of Reptiles in Osage County, Kansas," *Emporia State Research Studies*, 7:1–52, 1958.

Clench, H. K.: "Behavioral Thermoregulation in Butterflies," *Ecology*, 47:1021–1034, 1966.

Cole, L. C.: "Experiments on Toleration of High Temperature in Lizards with Reference to Adaptive Coloration," *Ecology*, 24:94–108, 1943.

Collette, B. B.: "Correlations between Ecology and Morphology in Anoline Lizards from Havana, Cuba and Southern Florida," *Bulletin of the Museum of Comparative Zoology at Harvard College*, 125:135–162, 1961.

Coon, C. S.: *The Living Races of Man*, Alfred A. Knopf, Inc., New York, 1965.

——, S. M. Garn, and J. B. Birdsell: *Races. A Study of the Problems of Race Formation in Man*, Charles C Thomas, Publisher, Springfield, Ill., 1950.

Costill, D. L.: *What Research Tells the Coach about Distance Running*, American Association for Health, Physical Education, and Recreation, Washington, 1968.

Cott, H. B.: *Adaptive Coloration in Animals*, Methuen & Co., Ltd., London, 1940.

Coward, K. H.: *The Biological Standardisation of the Vitamins*, William Wood & Company, Baltimore, 1938.

Cowles, R. B.: "Fur and Feathers, a Result of High Temperatures?" *Science*, 103:74–75, 1946.

————: "Possible Origin of Dermal Temperature Regulation," *Evolution*, 12:347–357, 1958.

————: "Some Ecological Factors Bearing on the Origin and Evolution of Pigment in the Human Skin," *American Naturalist*, 93:283–293, 1959.

————: "Hyperthermia, Aspermia, Mutation Rates and Evolution," *Quarterly Review of Biology*, 40:341–367, 1965.

————: "Black Pigmentation: Adaptation for Concealment or Heat Conservation?" *Science*, 158:1340–1341, 1967.

————, and C. M. Bogert: "A Preliminary Study of the Thermal Requirements of Desert Reptiles," *Bulletin of the American Museum of Natural History*, vol. 83, New York, 1944.

Darby, H. H., and E. M. Kapp: "Observations on the Thermal Death Points of *Anastrepha ludens* (Loew.)," U.S. Department of Agriculture Technological Bulletin no. 400, 1933.

Darlington, C. D.: *The Evolution of Man and Society*, Simon and Schuster, New York, 1969.

Dart, R. A.: "The Ecology of the South African Man-Apes," in D. H. S. Davis (ed.), *Ecological Studies in Southern Africa*, (Monographiae Biologicae, 14):49–52, Junk Publishers, The Hague, 1964.

Dawson, W. R.: "Temperature Regulation and Water Requirements of the Brown and Albert towhees, *Pipilo fuscus* and *Pipilo alberti*," *University of California (Berkeley) Publications in Zoology*, 59:81–124, 1954.

Denton, E. J., and J. A. C. Nicol: "Direct Measurements on the Orientation of the Reflecting Surfaces in the Tapetum of *Squalus acanthias*, and Some Observations on the Tapetum of *Acipenser sturio*," *Journal of the Marine Biological Association of the United Kingdom*, 45:739–742, 1965.

DeWitt, C. B.: "Behavioral Thermoregulation in the Iguanid Lizard, *Dipsosaurus dorsalis*," Ph.D. dissertation, University of Michigan, Ann Arbor, 1963.

————: "Precision of Thermoregulation and its Relation to Environmental Factors in the Desert Iguana *Dipsosaurus dorsalis*," *Physiological Zoology*, 40:49–66, 1967.

Dice, L. R.: "Minimum Intensities of Illumination Under Which Owls Can Find Dead Prey by Sight," *American Naturalist*, 79:385–416, 1945.

————: "Effectiveness of Selection by Owls of Deermice (*Peromyscus maniculatus*) which Contrast in Color with their Background," *Contributions to the Laboratory of Vertebrate Biology, University of Michigan*, (34):1–20, 1947.

Digby, P. S. B.: "Factors Affecting the Temperature Excess of Insects in Sunshine," *Journal of Experimental Biology*, 32:279–298, 1955.

Dingle, H., and J. B. Haskell: "Phase Polymorphism in the Grasshopper *Melanoplus differentialis*," *Science*, 155:590–592, 1967.

Dubois, E. F.: "Why Are Fever Temperatures over 106°F Rare?" *American Journal of the Medical Sciences*, 217:361–368, 1949.

Dudley, B.: "The Effects of Temperature and Humidity upon Certain Morphometric and Colour Characters of the Desert Locust (*Schistocerca gregaria* Forskål) Reared under Controlled Conditions," *Transactions of the Royal Entomological Society (London)*, 116:115–129, 1964.

Edney, E. B.: "The Water and Heat Relationships of Fiddler Crabs (*Uca* spp.)," *Transactions of the Royal Society of South Africa*, 36:71–91, 1961.

——: "Water Balance in Desert Arthropods," *Science*, 156:1059–1066, 1967.

Edwards, W. F.: *De l'influence des agens physique sur la vie*, Crochard, Paris, 1824.

Ehrlich, P. R., and R. W. Holm: "Patterns and Populations," *Science*, 137: 652–657, 1962.

——, and P. Raven, "Differentiation of Populations," *Science*, 165:1228–1232, 1969.

Einarsen, A. S.: *The Pronghorn Antelope and Its Management*, Wildlife Management Institute, Washington, D.C., 1948, p. 238.

Eisner, T., and J. Meinwald: "Defensive Secretions of Arthropods," *Science* 153:1341–1350, 1966.

Ellis, P. E.: "Changes in the Social Aggregation of Locust Hoppers with Changes in Rearing Conditions," *Animal Behaviour*, 11:142–151, 152–160, 1963.

——, and D. B. Carlisle: "The Prothoracic Gland and Color Change in Locusts," *Nature*, 190:368–369, 1961.

Enger, P. S.: "Heat Regulation and Metabolism in Some Tropical Mammals and Birds," *Acta Physiologica Scandinavica*, 40:161–166, 1957.

Etchecopar, R. D., and F. Hüe: "Données Écologiques sur l'avifaune de la zone Désertique Arabo-Saharienne," in *Arid Zone Research*, 8 (Human and Animal Ecology, Reviews of Research):138–163, UNESCO, 1957.

Evans, R. G.: "The Lethal Temperatures of Some Common British Littoral Molluscs, *Journal of Animal Ecology*, 17:165–173, 1948.

Fentress, J. C.: letter in *Science*, 151:935–936, 1966.

Fink, B. D.: "Observation of Porpoise Predation on a School of Pacific Sardines," *California Fish and Game*, 45:216–217, 1959.

Fisher, E. M.: "Habits of the Southern Sea Otter," *Journal of Mammalogy*, 20:21–36, 1939.

Fisher, R. A.: *The Genetical Theory of Natural Selection*, The Clarendon Press, Oxford, 1930.

Fitzpatrick, T. B.: introductory lecture in E. J. Bowen (ed.), *Recent Progress in Photobiology*, Academic Press, New York, 1965, pp. 365–373.

——, M. Seiji, and A. P. McGugan: "Medical progress, Melanin pigmentation," *New England Journal of Medicine*, 265:328, 374, 430, 1961.

Fraenkel, G.: "Resistance to High Temperatures in a Mediterranean Snail, *Littorina neritoides*," *Ecology*, 42:604–606, 1961.

Fuzeau-Braesch, S.: "Étude biologique et biochimique de la pigmentation d'un insecte, *Gryllus bimaculatus* de Geer (Gryllide, orthopetere)," *Bulletin biologique de la France et de la Belgique*, 94:527–627, 1960.

Garn, S. M.: *Human Races*, Charles C Thomas, Publisher, Springfield, Ill., 1961.

Gates, D. M.: "Spectral properties of plants," *Applied Optics*, 4:11–20, 1965.

Gause, G. F., N. P. Smaragdova, and A. A. Witt: "Further Studies of Interactions between Predators and Prey," *Journal of Animal Ecology*, 5:1–18, 1936.

Geist, V.: "The Evolution of Horn-like Organs," *Behavior*, 27:12–214, 1966.

Gilliard, E. T.: "A Comparative Analysis of Courtship Movements in Closely

Allied Bowerbirds of the Genus *Chlamydera,*" *American Museum Novitates,* no. 1936, 1959.

————: "The Evolution of Bowerbirds," *Scientific American,* 209:38–46, 1963.

Glass, B.: "Evolution of Hairlessness in Man," letter in *Science,* 152:294, 1966.

Glass, N. R.: "A Technique for Fitting Models with Nonlinear Parameters to Biological Data, *Ecology,* 48:1010–1013, 1967.

Goodwin, T. W.: "The Biochemistry of Locust Pigmentation," *Biological Reviews,* 27:439–460, 1952.

Grange, W. B.: "Observations on the Snowshoe Hare, *Lepus americanus phaeonotus* Allen," *Journal of Mammalogy,* 13:1–19, 1932.

Grant, P. R.: "Plumage and the Evolution of Birds on Islands," *Systematic Zoology,* 14:47–52, 1965.

Greenewalt, C. H.: *Hummingbirds,* Doubleday & Company, Inc., Garden City, N.Y., 1960.

Guthrie, R. D.: "Evolution of Human Threat Display Organs," *Evolutionary Biology,* 4:257–302, 1970.

Hailman, J. P.: letter in *Science,* 153:362–364, 1966.

Hall, K. R. L.: "Tool-using Performances as Indicators of Behavioural Adaptability," *Current Anthropology,* 4:479–494, 1963.

————, and G. B. Schaller: "Tool-using Behavior of the California Sea-otter, *Journal of Mammalogy,* 45:287–298, 1964.

Hamilton, W. J., Jr.: *American Mammals,* McGraw-Hill Book Company, New York, 1939.

Hamilton, W. J., III: 1965. "Sun-oriented Display of the Anna's Hummingbird," *Wilson Bulletin,* 77:38–44, 1965.

————, and C. G. Coetzee: "Thermoregulatory Behavior of the Vegetarian Lizard *Anglosaurus Skoogi* on the Vegetationless Northern Namib Desert Dunes," *Scientific Papers of the Namib Desert Research Station,* 47:95–103, 1969.

————, W. M. Gilbert, F. H. Heppner, and R. Planck: "Starling Roost Dispersal and a Hypothetical Mechanism Regulating Rhythmical and Animal Movement to and from Dispersal Centers, *Ecology,* 48:825–833, 1967.

————, and M. E. Hamilton: "Breeding Characteristics of Yellow-billed Cuckoos in Arizona, *Proceedings of the California Academy of Science,* 32:405–432, 1965.

———— and F. Heppner: "Radiant Solar Energy and the Function of Black Homeotherm Pigmentation: An Hypothesis," *Science,* 155:196–197, 1967.

———— and R. M. Peterman: "Countershading in the Colourful Reef Fish *Chaetodon lunula*: Concealment, Communication or Both," *Animal Behavior,* 19:353–360, 1971.

———— and K. E. F. Watt: "Refuging," *Annual Review of Ecology and Systematics,* 1:263–286, 1970.

Hammel, H. T.: "Terrestrial Animals in Cold: Recent Studies of Primitive Man," in *Handbook of Physiology,* sec. 4, Adaptation to the Environment, 1964, pp. 413–434.

————, R. W. Elsner, K. L. Andersen, P. F. Scholander, C. S. Coon, A. Medina, L. Strozzi, F. A. Milan, and R. J. Hock: "Thermal and Metabolic Responses of Australian Aborigine to Moderate Cold in Summer," *Journal of Applied Physiology,* 14:605–615, 1959.

Hardy, J. D.: "The Radiation of Heat from the Human Body. I. An Instrument for Measuring the Radiation and Surface Temperature of the Skin," *Journal of Clinical Investigations*, 13:593–604, 1934a.

———: "The Radiation of Heat from the Human Body. III. The Human Skin as a Black Radiator," *Journal of Clinical Investigations*, 13:615–620, 1934b.

Harker, J. E.: "The Effect of Temperature on the Final Instar Nymphs of Three Species of Australian Ephemeroptera," *Proceedings of the Royal Entomological Society (London), Series A*, 25:111–114, 1950.

Hart, J. S.: "Geographic Variation of Some Physiological and Morphological Characters in Certain Freshwater Fish," *University of Toronto Biological Service 60*; *Publications of the Ontario Fisheries Research Laboratory*, 62:1–79, 1952.

Heim de Balzac, H.: "Biogeographie des mammiferes et des oiseaux de l'Afrique du Nord," *Bulletin biologique supplement*, 21:1–477, 1936.

Hellmich, W.: "Die biogeographischen Grundlagen Chiles," *Zoologische Jahrbücher, Abteilung für Systematik*, 64:165–226, 1933.

Henderson, J. T.: "Lethal Temperatures of Lamellibranchiata," *Contributions to Canadian Biology and Fisheries, New Series*, 4:399–411, 1929.

Hershkovitz, P.: letter in *Science*, 153:362, 1966.

———: "Metachromism or the Principle of Evolutionary Change in Mammalian Tegumentary Colors, *Evolution*, 22:556–575, 1968.

———: "Metachromism Like It Is," *Evolution*, 24:644–648, 1970.

Hess, S. L.: *Introduction to Theoretical Meteorology*, Holt, Rinehart and Winston, Inc., New York, 1959.

Hesse, R., W. C. Allee, and K. P. Schmidt: *Ecological Animal Geography*, John Wiley & Sons, Inc., New York, 1937.

Hildebrand, M.: "How Animals Run," *Scientific American*, 202:148–157, 1960.

Hill, A. V.: "The Dimensions of Mammals and Their Muscular Dynamics," *Science Progress*, 38:209–230, 1950.

Hill, L., and H. J. Taylor: "Locusts in Sunlight," *Nature*, 132:276, 1933.

Hingston, R. W. G.: *Animal Colour and Adornment*, Arnold and Co., London, 1933.

Howell, A. B.: *Speed in Animals: Their Specialization for Running and Leaping*, The University of Chicago Press, Chicago, 1944.

Huddleston, J. A.: "Some Notes on the Effects of Bird Predators on Hopper Bands of the Desert Locust (*Schistocerca gregaria* Forskal)," *Entomologist's Monthly Magazine*, 942:210–214, 1958.

Huffaker, C. B., "Experimental Studies on Predation: Dispersion Factors and Predator-Prey Oscillations," *Hilgardia*, 27:343–383, 1958.

Hulse, F. S.: "Selection for Skin Color among the Japanese," *American Journal of Physical Anthropology*, 27:143–156, 1968.

Hunsaker, D., II, and C. Johnson: "Internal Pigmentation and Ultraviolet Transmission of the Integument in Amphibians and Reptiles," *Copeia*, 4:311–315, 1959.

Hunter-Jones, P.: "The Effect of Constant Temperature on Egg Development in the Desert Locust, *Schistocerca gregaria* (Forsk.)," *Bulletin of Entomological Research*, 59:707–718, 1968.

Huntsman, A. G., and M. I. Sparks: "Limiting Factors for Marine Animals Relative Resistance to High Temperatures," *Contributions to Canadian Biology*, Biological Board of Canada, New Series, 2(6):97–144, 1924.

Huxley, J. S.: "The Courtship Habits of the Great Crested Grebe (*Podiceps cristatus*); With an Addition to the Theory of Sexual Selection," *Proceedings of the Zoological Society of London*, pp. 491–562, 1914.

Irving, L.: "Terrestrial Animals in Cold: Birds and Mammals," in *Handbook of Physiology*, sec. 4: Adaptation to the Environment, American Physiological Society, Washington, 1964.

Ivlev, V. S.: *Experimental Ecology of the Feeding of Fishes*, Yale University Press, New Haven, Conn., 1961.

Iwao, Syun'iti: "Studies on the Phase Variation and Related Phenomena in Some Lepidopterous Insects, *Memoirs of the Kyoto University Agriculture*, Entomology Series 12, no. 84, 1962.

———: "Some Behavioural Changes Associated with Phase Variation in the Armyworm, *Leucania separata* Walker. I. Reaction of larvae to mechanical stimuli," *Japanese Journal of Applied Entomology and Zoology*, 7:125–131, 1963.

———: "Some Effects of Grouping in Lepidopterous Insects," English translation in "L'effet de groupe chez les animaux," *Colloques Internationaux du Centre National de la Recherche Scientifique (Paris)*, 173:185–212, 1968.

Jackson, F. J.: *The Birds of Kenya Colony and the Uganda Protectorate*, vol. 1, Gurney & Jackson, London, 1938.

Jones, C., and S. Pi: "Sticks used by Chimpanzees in Rio Muni, West Africa," *Nature*, 223:100–101, 1969.

——— and ———: "Comparative Ecology of *Gorilla gorilla* (Savage and Wyman) and *Pan troglodyte* (Blumenbach) in Rio Muni, West Africa," *Bibliotheca Primatologica*, vol. 13, 1971.

Jones, F. M.: "Insect Coloration and the Relative Acceptability of Insects to Birds," *Transactions of the Royal Entomological Society of London*, 80: 345–386, 1932.

———: "Further Experiments on Coloration and Relative Acceptability of Insects to Birds," *Transactions of the Royal Entomological Society of London*, 82:443–453, 1934.

Kalmus, H.: "Physiology and Ecology of Cuticle Colour in Insects," *Nature*, 148:428–431, 1941a.

———: "The Resistance to Desiccation of *Drosophila* Mutants Affecting Body Colour," *Proceedings of the Royal Society of London, Series B*, 130: 185–201, 1941b.

Kashkarov, D., and V. Kurbatov: "Preliminary Ecological Survey of the Vertebrate Fauna of the Central Kara-Kum Desert in West Turkestan," *Ecology*, 11:35–60, 1930.

Kennedy, J. S.: "Continuous Polymorphism in Locusts," in J. S. Kennedy (ed.), "Insect Polymorphism," Symposium no. 1, *Proceedings of the Royal Entomological Society of London*, pp. 80–90, 1961.

Kennington, G. S.: letter in *Science*, 153:364, 1966.

Key, K. H. L.: "Kentromorphic Phases in Three Species of Phasmatodea," *Australian Journal of Zoology*, 5:247–284, 1957.

——— and M. F. Day: "A Temperature-controlled Physiological Colour Response in the Grasshopper *Kosciuscola tristis* Sjöst (Orthopetera:Acrididae)," *Australian Journal of Zoology*, 2:309–339, 1954a.

——— and ———: "The Physiological Mechanism of Colour Change in the Grasshopper *Kosciuscola tristis* Sjöst (Orthoptera, Acrididae)," *Australian Journal of Zoology*, 2:340–363, 1954b.

Klauber, L. M.: "Studies of Reptile Life in the Arid Southwest. Pt. II, Speculations on Protective Coloration and Protective Reflectivity," *Bulletin of the Zoological Society*, 14:65–79, San Diego, Calif., 1939.

Kleiber, M.: *The Fire of Life*, John Wiley & Sons, Inc., New York, 1961.

Koch, C.: "Some Aspects of Abundant Life in the Vegetationless Sand of the Namib Desert Dunes," *Journal of the Southwest Africa Scientific Society*, 15:8–34, 77–92, 1961.

————: "The Tenebrionidae of Southern Africa. XXXI. Comprehensive notes on the Tenebrionid fauna of the Namib Desert," *Annals of the Transvaal Museum*, Pretoria, 24:61–106, 1962a.

————: "The Tenebrionidae of Southern Africa. XXXII. New psammophilous species from the Namib Desert," *Annals Transvaal Museum*, Pretoria, 24:107–159, 1962b.

Koford, C. B.: *The California Condor*, research report no. 4, National Audubon Society, New York, 1953.

Kortlandt, A.: "How Do Chimpanzees Use Weapons when Fighting Leopards?" *Yearbook of the American Philosophical Society*, pp. 327–332, 1965.

Kraft, R. W.: letter in *Science*, 151:935, 1966.

Kramer, G.: "Veränderungen von Nachkommenziffer und Nachkommengröss sowie der Altersverteilung von Inseleidechsen," *Zeitschrift fur Naturforschung*, 1:700–710, 1946.

————: "Über Inselmelanismus bei Eidechsen," *Zeitschrift induktive Abstammungsund Vererbungs-lehre*, 83:157–164, 1949.

————: "Body Proportions of Mainland and Island Lizards, *Evolution*, 5:193–206, 1951.

———— and R. Mertens: "Rassenbildung bei westistrianischen Inseleidechsen in Abhängigkeit von Isolierungsalter und Arealgrösse," *Archiv für Naturgeschichte*, 7(neue Folge):189–234, 1938.

Krehl, L., and F. Soetbeer: "Untersuchungen über die Wärmeokönomie der poikilothermen Wirbeltiere," *Archiv fuer die Gesamte Physiologie des Menschen und der Tiere, Pflugers*, 77:611–638, 1899.

Kubitschek, H. E.: "Mutagenesis by Near Visible Light," *Science*, 155:1545–1546, 1967.

Lack, D.: *The Natural Regulation of Animal Numbers*, Oxford University Press, London, 1954.

————: *Biological Adaptations for Breeding in Birds*, Methuen & Co., Ltd., London, 1968.

Laue, E. G., and A. J. Drummond: "Solar Constant: First Direct Measurement," *Science*, 161:888–891, 1968.

Laughlin, W. S.: "Hunting: An Integrating Biobehavior System and its Evolutionary Importance," in R. B. Lee and I. De Voe (eds.), *Man the Hunter*, Aldine Publishing Company, Chicago, pp. 304–320, 1968.

Lawick-Goodall, J. van: The Behaviour of Free-living Chimpanzees in the Gombe Stream Reserve," *Animal Behaviour Monographs*, 1(3):161–311, 1968.

Lawlor, T. E.: "The Principle of Metachromism: A Critique," *Evolution*, 23:509–512, 1969.

Licht, P., W. R. Dawson, V. H. Shoemaker, and A. R. Main: "Observations on the Thermal Relations of Western Australian Lizards," *Copeia*, 97–110, 1966.

Lindauer, M.: "The Water Economy and Temperature Regulation of the Honeybee Colony," *Bee World*, 36:62–72, 81–92, 105–111, 1955.

Lloyd, B. B.: "World Running Records as Maximal Performances," in *Physiology of Muscular Exercise*, American Heart Association, Monograph 15, 1967.

Longley, W. H.: "Studies upon the Biological Significance of Animal Coloration. 1. The Colors and Color Changes of West Indian Reef-fishes," *Journal of Experimental Zoology*, 22:553–601, 1917.

Loomis, W. F.: "Skin-pigment Regulation of Vitamin-D Biosynthesis in Man," *Science*, 157:501–506, 1967.

————: "Vitamin D, Sunlight, and Natural Selection," rebuttal letter to M. F. Blois and H. F. Blum, *Science*, 159:652, 1968.

Lorenz, K.: *On Aggression*, Harcourt Brace Jovanovich, Inc., New York, 1966.

Lowe, C. H., and D. S. Hinds: "Thermoregulation in Desert Populations of Roadrunners and Doves," in C. C. Hoff and M. L. Riedesel (ed.), *Physiological Systems in Arid and Semiarid Environments*, 1969, p. 113.

Marler, P.: "Studies of Fighting in Chaffinches. (2). The Effect on Dominance Relations of Disguising Females as Males," *British Journal of Animal Behaviour*, 3:137–146, 1955.

————, and W. J. Hamilton III: *Mechanisms of Animal Behavior*, John Wiley & Sons, Inc., New York, 1966.

Marsh, F.: "Reactions to Great Environmental Heat Animals," in J. L. Cloudsley-Thompson (ed.), *Biology of Deserts*, Institute of Biology, London, 1954, pp. 188–192.

Masters, W. H., and V. E. Johnson: *Human Sexual Response*, Churchill, London, 1966.

Mayr, E.: *Systematics and the Origin of Species*, Columbia University Press, New York, 1942.

————: *Animal Species and Evolution*, Harvard University Press, Cambridge, Mass., 1963.

McGinnis, S. M., and C. W. Brown: "Thermal Behavior of the Green Iguana, *Iguana iguana*," *Herpetologica*, 22:189–199, 1966.

McWhirter, R.: *Guinness Book of World Records*, Sterling Publishing Co., Inc., New York, 1968.

Mech, L. D.: *The Wolves of Isle Royale*, U.S. Department of the Interior, National Park Service, fauna ser. 7, 1966.

Meinertzhagen, R.: *Birds of Arabia*, Oliver and Boyd, Edinburg, 1954.

Miller, R. R.: "Hot Springs and Fish Life," *Aquarium Journal*, 20:286–288, 1949.

Millikan, G. C., and R. I. Bowman: "Observations on Galapagos Tool-using Finches in Captivity," *Living Bird*, 6:23–41. 1967.

Milum, V. G.: "Temperature Relations of Honeybees in Winter," *Annual Report, Illinois State Beekeepers' Association*, 28:98–130, 1928.

Morris, Desmond: *The Naked Ape; A Zoologist's Study of the Human Animal*, McGraw-Hill Book Company, New York, 1969.

————: *Patterns of Reproductive Behavior*, McGraw-Hill Book Company, New York, 1971.

Morse, D. H.: "The Use of Tools by Brown-headed Nuthatches," *Wilson Bulletin*, 80:220–224, 1968.

Moynihan, M.: "Some Adaptations which Help to Promote Gregariousness," *Proceedings of the Twelfth International Ornithological Congress*, (2) 1958:523–541, Helsinki, 1960.

————: "The Organization and Probable Evolution of Some Mixed Species Flocks of Neotropical Birds," *Smithsonian Institution Publications. Miscellaneous Collections*, 143 (7):1–140, 1962.

————: "Social Mimicry; Character Convergence versus Character Displacement," *Evolution*, 22:315–331, 1968.

Narayanan, E. S., G. W. Angalet, B. R. Subba Rao, and G. I. D'Souza: "Effect of the Refrigeration of the Pupae of *Microbracon brevicornis* Wesm. on the Pigmentation of the Adult," *Nature*, 173:503–504, 1954.

Norris, K. S.: "The Ecology of the Desert Iguana *Dipsosaurus dorsalis*," *Ecology*, 34:265–287, 1953.

————: "Color Adaptation in Desert Reptiles and its Thermal Relationships," in W. W. Milstead (ed.), *Lizard Ecology: A Symposium*, University of Missouri Press, Columbia, 1967.

———— and C. H. Lowe: "An Analysis of Background Color-matching in Amphibians and Reptiles," *Ecology*, 45:565–580, 1964.

Norris, M. J.: "Accelerating and Inhibiting Effects of Crowding on Sexual Maturation in Two Species of Locusts," *Nature*, London, 203:784–5 (298,352), 1964.

Ohmart, R. D., and R. C. Lasiewski: "Roadrunners: Energy Conservation by Hypothermia and Absorption of Sunlight," *Science*, 172:67–69, 1970.

Olson, W. S.: letter in *Science*, 153:364, 1966.

Pearson, O. P.: "Habits of the Lizard *Liolaemus multiformis multiformis* at High Altitudes in Southern Peru," *Copeia*, 2:111–116, 1954.

Pedersen, A.: *Polar Animals*, Taplinger Publishing Co., Inc., New York, 1966.

Platt, J. R.: *The Step to Man*, John Wiley & Sons, Inc., New York, 1966.

Porter, W. P.: "Solar Radiation through the Living Body Walls of Vertebrates with Emphasis on Desert Reptiles," *Ecological Monographs*, 37:273–296, 1967.

Poulton, E. B.: *The Colours of Animals*, D. Appleton & Company, Inc., New York, 1890.

Pradhan, S.: "The Ecology of Arid Zone Insects (Excluding Locusts and Grasshoppers)," in *Arid Zone Research*, 8 (Human and Animal Ecology, Reviews of Research):199–240, UNESCO, 1957.

Prop, N.: "Protection against Birds and Parasites in Some Species of Tenthredinid Larvae," *Archives Neerlandaises de Zoologie*, 13:380–447, 1960.

Pugh, L. G. C. E., J. L. Corbett, and R. H. Johnson: "Rectal Temperatures, Weight Losses, and Sweat Rates in Marathon Running," *Journal of Applied Physiology*, 23:347–352, 1967.

Rasmussen, K.: *Across Arctic America*, G. P. Putnam's Sons, New York, 1927.

Reynolds, V., and F. Reynolds: "Chimpanzees of the Budongo Forest," in I. Devore (ed.), *Primate Behaviour*, Holt, Rinehart and Winston, Inc., New York, 1965, pp. 368–424.

Ripley, S. D.: *The Land and Wildlife of Tropical Asia*, Time-Life Books, New York, 1964.

Robinson, S.: "Temperature Regulation in Exercise," *Pediatrics*, 32:691–702, 1963.

Robinson, K. W., and D. H. K. Lee: "Animal Behaviour and Heat Regulation in Hot Atmospheres," *Papers from the Department of Physiology, University of Queensland*, 1:1–8, Brisbane, 1946.

Rupert, C. S., and W. Harm: "Reactivation after Photobiological Damage," *Advances in Radiation Biology*, 2:1–81, 1966.

Salt, G. W.: "Predation in an Experimental Protozoan Population (*Woodruffia-Paramecium*)," *Ecological Monographs*, 37:113–144, 1967.

Schaller, G. B.: *The Mountain Gorilla, Ecology and Behavior*, The University of Chicago Press, Chicago, 1963.

Schlottke, E.: "Über die Variabilität der schwarzen Pigmentierung und ihre Beeinflußbarkeit durch Temperaturen bei *Habrobracon juglandis* Ashmead," *Zeitschrift fuer Vergleichende Physiologie*, 3:692–736, 1926.

Schmid, W. D.: "High Temperature Tolerance of *Bufo hemiophrys* and *Bufo cognatus*," *Ecology*, 46:559–560, 1965.

Schmidt-Nielsen, K.: *Desert Animals*, Oxford University Press, London, 1964.

———, B. Schmidt-Nielsen, S. A. Jarnum, and O. U. Houpt: "Body Temperature of the Camel and its Relation to Water Economy," *American Journal of Physiology*, 188:103–112, 1957.

Scholander, P. F., H. T. Hammel, J. S. Hart, D. H. Le Messurier, and J. Steen: "Cold Adaptation in Australian Aborigines," *Journal of Applied Physiology*, 13:211–218, 1958.

———R. Hock, V. Walters, L. Irving, and F. Johnson: "Body Insulation of Some Arctic and Tropical Mammals and Birds, *Biological Bulletin*, 99: 225–236, 1950a.

———: "Heat Regulation in Some Arctic and Tropical Mammals and Birds," *Biological Bulletin*, 99:237–258, 1950b.

———: "Adaptation to Cold in Arctic and Tropical Mammals and Birds in Relation to Body Temperature, Insulation, and Basal Metabolic Rate," *Biological Bulletin*, 99:259–271, 1950c.

Smith, N. G.: "Evolution of Some Arctic Gulls (*Larus*): An Experimental Study of Isolating Mechanisms," *Ornithological Monographs of the American Ornothologists' Union*, no. 4, 99 pp., 1966.

Somero, G. N., and A. L. De Vries: "Temperature Tolerance of Some Antarctic Fishes," *Science*, 156:257–258, 1967.

Stark, A. C.: *The Birds of South Africa*, vol. 1, R. H. Porter, London, 1900.

Stebbins, R. C.: "Body Temperature Studies in South African Lizards," *Koedoe*, 4:54–67, 1961.

———, and H. B. Robinson: "Further Analysis of a Population of the Lizard *Sceloporus graciousus gracilis*," *University of California* (*Berkeley*) *Publications in Zoology*, 48:149–168, 1946.

Stoddard, R. L.: *The Bobwhite Quail*, Charles Scribner's Sons, New York, 1936.

Strelnikov, I. D.: "Effect of Solar Radiation and the Microclimate upon the Body Temperature and the Behaviour of the Larvae of *Locusta migratoria* L." (in Russian, English summary), *Akademiya nauk, SSSR, Zoologicheskii Institut Trudy* 2 (1935):637–733, Travaux Institute of Zoology, Academy of Sciences, U.S.S.R., 1936.

Stullken, D. A., and W. A. Heistand: "An Experimental Study of the Influence of Pelage Pigmentation on Metabolic Rate and its Possible Relationships to Body Temperature Control and Ecological Distribution," *Ecology*, 34: 610–613, 1953.

Svihla, A.: "The Relation of Coloration in Mammals to Low Temperature," *Journal of Mammalogy*, 37:378–381, 1956.

Tappen, N. C.: "Problems of Distribution and Adaptation of the African Monkeys," *Current Anthropology*, 1(2):91–120, 1960.

Thayer, G. H.: *Concealing-Coloration in the Animal Kingdom*, The Macmillan Company, New York, 1918.

Thomson, M. L.: "The Relative Efficiency of Pigment and Horny Layer Thickness in Protecting the Skin of Europeans and Africans against Solar Ultraviolet Radiation," *Journal of Physiology (London)*, 127:236, 1955.

Tinbergen, N.: *The Study of Instinct*, Oxford University Press, London, 1951.

————: *The Herring Gull's World*, Basic Books, Inc., Publishers, New York, 1960.

Tobias, P. V.: "Bushmen Hunter-Gatherers: A Study in Human Ecology," in D. H. S. Davis (ed.), *Ecological Studies in Southern Africa* (vol. 14 in *Monographiae Biologicae*), Junk Publishers, The Hague, 1964, pp. 67–86.

Tucker, V. A.: "Diurnal Torpor and its Relation to Food Consumption and Weight Changes in the California Pocket Mouse *Perognathus Californicus*," *Ecology*, 47:245–252, 1966.

Tyndall, J.: *Fragments of Science*, vol. 1, D. Appleton & Company, Inc., New York, 1897.

Uvarov, B. P.: *Anatomy, Physiology, Development, Phase Polymorphism, Introduction to Taxonomy*, vol. 1 in *Grasshoppers and Locusts*, Cambridge University Press, London, 1966.

Wallace, Alfred R.: *Tropical Nature and Other Essays*, Macmillan and Co., London, 1870.

Walter, H.: "Der Zussamenhang von Hautfarbenverteilung und Intensität der ultravioletten Strahlung," *Homo*, 9:1–13, 1958.

Wickler, W.: "Socio-sexual Signals and Their Intraspecific Imitation among Primates," in D. Morris (ed.), *Primate Ethology*, Aldine Publishing Company, Chicago, 1967.

————: *Mimicry in Plants and Animals*, World University Library, London, 1968.

Williams, G. C.: *Adaptation and Natural Selection*, Princeton University Press, Princeton, N.J., 1966.

Young, J.: "Learning and Discrimination in the Octopus," *Biological Reviews*, 36:32–96, 1961.

INDEX